LOCAL AUTHORITY PROPERTY MANAGEMENT

Local Authority Property Management

Initiatives, strategies, re-organisation and reform

Edited by
MARK DEAKIN
Napier University

Routledge
Taylor & Francis Group
LONDON AND NEW YORK

First published 1999 by Ashgate Publishing

Reissued 2018 by Routledge
2 Park Square, Milton Park, Abingdon, Oxon, OX14 4RN
52 Vanderbilt Avenue, New York, NY 10017

Routledge is an imprint of the Taylor & Francis Group, an informa business

Publisher's Note
The publisher has gone to great lengths to ensure the quality of this reprint but points out that some imperfections in the original copies may be apparent.

A Library of Congress record exists under LC control number:

ISBN 13: 978-1-138-36083-9 (hbk)
ISBN 13: 978-0-429-43287-3 (ebk)

Contents

PART 4 THE WAY AHEAD

List of Figures

List of Tables

List of Contributors

Alastair Adair is Professor of Real Estate at Ulster University.

Peter Bower is Head of Property and Construction at the Business School, Staffordshire University.

Elizabeth Carter is a Senior Lecturer in the Department of Land Management, School for the Built Environment, De Monfort University.

Owen Connellan is a Visiting Research Fellow in the School of Built Environment, Glamorgan University.

Mark Deakin is a Senior Lecturer and Teaching Fellow in the Department of Building and Surveying, Napier University.

Peter Dent is a Principal Lecturer in the School of Real Estate Management, Oxford Brooks University.

Nick French is Acacia Lecturer and Laing Research Fellow in the Department of Land Management and Development at Reading University.

Louise Hague is an Estates Surveyor in Hampshire County Council.

Ewan Hall is Head of Property at Scottish Enterprise.

Geoffrey Heath is a Senior Lecturer in Accounting and Finance at the Business School, Staffordshire University.

Alex Linkston is Chief Executive of West Lothian Council.

Neil Martindale is Principal Valuer in the Department of Property at the London Borough of Waltham Forest.

Jean Morgan is Head of Economic Studies at the Business School, Staffordshire University.

Michael Nevin is Advisor to the Scottish Office Private Finance Unit.

Gaye Pottinger is a Research Assistant at the College of Estate Management.

Martin Ralphs is a Senior Lecturer in the School of Surveying, University of East London.

Peter Reynolds is Head of the Economics Division at the Business School, Staffordshire University.

Marion Weatherhead is a Principal Consultant in Gardiner and Theobald Management.

Beverley Wilson is an Economic Research Officer at Crewe and Nantwich Borough Council.

Peter Wyatt is a Lecturer in the School of Valuation and Estate Management at the University of the West of England.

Joan Wyld is a Senior Lecturer in Economics at the Business School, Staffordshire University.

Acknowledgement

Six of the chapters appearing in this book have previously appeared in two 'themed' issues of *Property Management.* The chapters in question are those provided by Martin Ralphs and Peter Wyatt, Peter Dent, Owen Connellan, Mark Deakin (chapter eight), Neil Martindale and Peter Bower, Geoffrey Heath, Jean Morgan, Peter Reynolds and Joan Wyld. The chapters first published in *Property Management*, vols. 15 (4), 16 (2) and (4) respectively, form part of two issues drawn from the Local Authority Property Management Conference, organised by the editor and held at the Edinburgh International Conference Centre in October, 1996. The remaining ten chapters forming the rest of the book are papers that were either presented at the conference and revised for publication, or commissioned especially for inclusion in this book.

The editor would like to thank the publishers of *Property Management*, MCB University Press, for agreeing to the transfer of copyright over the six chapters in question and allowing the said contributions to be included in this book.

Mark Deakin

Foreword

Until recently the management of local authority and corporate property portfolios was primarily a reactive process rather than a proactive activity. Across many estates the full extent of property holdings was sometimes unknown with uncertainty arising over the value of holdings and the actual extent of ownership within the portfolio. However since the 1980s there has been a substantial shift in the ethos of property management from a focus on individual buildings to a more strategic and quantitative approach. This exchange in emphasis reflects the influence of property investment management which sets real estate in the context of other assets and the wider economy.

It is only in the 1990s that the development of corporate strategy has witnessed a serious attempt by organisations to review their property holdings. Over the past decade many private and public sector organisations have set in place their own asset registers usually in conjunction with a full valuation of property holdings as a first step to a rational property audit. In this respect the fullest utilisation of property holdings is fundamental to meeting the value for money test and delivery of economic, efficient and effective services.

Local Authority Property Management: Initiatives, Strategies, Re-organisation and Reform, is an important breakthrough in facilitating the effective management of local authority property. The text provides a structured response to the criticisms of the 1980s reports by the Audit Commission and the Chartered Institute of Public Finance and Accountancy which suggested that significant improvements could be made to the way local authorities managed their property holdings.

One of the primary objectives of the book is to provide a signpost marking a significant development in the transition from estate to property management in local authorities. To this end the papers highlight a switch in attention away from the technical concerns over the informational basis of asset registers, property valuation, auditing, review and performance measurement initiatives and towards the development of communicative structures for the strategic (predominantly financial and commercial) management of assets currently held by local authorities. The significant contribution of this text is that it provides an authoritative overview of the theory, methodology and techniques of local authority property management. Its publication is opportune given the increasing international interest in the strategic management of property and quantification of costs associated with the use of assets. Most importantly the text illustrates that the concept of property as a resource is now an increasingly important part of the local authority business agenda and an issue which is seen as critical to the effective management of service delivery in the public sector.

The content of the book, linking theory, method and techniques with practice, makes it a vital source of information for those with an interest in obtaining the most effective management of property.

Alastair Adair
Professor of Real Estate
Ulster University

INTRODUCTION

1 The Underlying Issues, Aims, Model and Post-AC Studies

Mark Deakin, Department of Building and Surveying, Napier University

Introduction

This book examines the debate that has surfaced in the property profession since the Audit Commission's (AC 1988a, b) reports on *Local Authority Property Management* (LAPM). The text brings together sixteen studies from academics and practitioners with an interest in exchanging views, opinions and experiences on the development of LAPM.

The reason for bringing the post-AC studies together in the form of a book is simple. Ten years has now passed since the publication of the AC's reports and while it is evident the documents 'opened-up' a dialogue between the Royal Institution of Chartered Surveyors (RICS), Incorporated Society of Valuers and Auctioneers (ISVA), Chartered Institute of Public Finance and Accountancy (CIPFA) and Association of District Councils (ADC's), it is also clear that little additional information has surfaced over the last few years to publicise the growing number of studies which have been carried out to further the debate on LAPM. The book suggests the lack of information currently available about such studies is unfortunate and a situation which needs to be redressed because:

- the debate drew attention to the fact that the highly developed degree of professionalism in local authorities is based upon estate management and techniques surrounding the buying and selling of land, rather than the form of property management set out by the AC;
- it also drew attention to a number of additional weaknesses in the structure of LAPM - the need for a higher degree of corporatisation, with initiatives and strategies capable of bringing about an improvement in the standards of property management;
- the initiatives and strategies the AC proposed should be put in place are new, not traditionally found in local authorities and demand the development of additional skills;

- the development of such skills means that academics and practitioners in the profession face a steep learning curve and while the RICS, CIPFA and ADC have provided some assistance, it is evident the main responsibility for developing the required level of expertise rests with the property management divisions of local authorities;
- local authorities are relatively disadvantaged in developing such skills because most of the research into the corporatisation of service sector provision has focused upon the private, or newly privatised, as opposed to public sector;
- the information available on the public sector; for example: in the NHS and other sectors tends to be on service sectors functioning as authorities outside local government control;
- irrespective of this, the onset of local government re-organisation is set to bring a further set of reforms requiring a coherent response from the property management divisions of affected authorities.

The book suggests the lack of information currently available on the studies that have been undertaken to address such matters is unfortunate because it fails to recognise the considerable energies academics and practitioners have expended over the past few years to not only overcome the structural weaknesses of LAPM, but translate the debate about 'better standards' into a set of initiatives and strategies capable of bringing about an improvement in the management of property held by local authorities. The following will introduce the research that has been undertaken over the past decade as part of the search for better standards by examining the issues underlying the development of property management in local authorities. Having done this the discussion will go on to set out the aims of the examination, the model of LAPM it adopts and the post-AC studies the book brings together under the headings of initiatives, strategies re-organisation and reform.

Underlying issues

In many respects it might be argued that the term LAPM, referred to by the AC does not fully represent the relative under-development of the subject and gives the false impression of a well grounded, fully formed set of procedures for the management of property held by local authorities. As the aforementioned tends to indicate, this is anything but true and tends to under-estimate both the novelty and experimental nature of the issues the AC propose local authorities should address in the management of property. In view of this, it is perhaps best to see the development of LAPM as part of a transition from estate to property management and a process of change that takes place without any clear proto-type, model or trajectory. Looked at against the background of the publications currently available on the matter, it is a position perhaps best characterised by Stapleton's (1986, 1994) *Estate Management Practice* and the texts by Scarrett (1983, 1995) on *Property Management.* The former title, by definition, suggesting the subject is not sufficiently developed and is still 'stuck' in the traditions of the estate, the latter in contrast giving the impression the transition to property management is complete. The grey area in the middle is a matter that Britton, Connellan and Crofts (1989) have paid particular attention to. After much consideration of the AC reports and comments from the AC, RICS, CIPFA and ADC on the subject, it is a situation they characterise as a set of questions over the 'value for money test' (VFM) in the introduction of measures for the 'economic, efficient and effective management' (the 3 E's) of public sector landed estates.

Britton, Connellan and Crofts' (1989) report appears to be of the opinion the subject is stuck in the problems of the 'static estate' and 'running cost control' and as a consequence has not sufficiently developed to complete the transition. If we consider Lash and Urry's (1987, 1993) and Elcock's (1987, 1994) comments, the lack of progress might be put down to the tendency for academics and practitioners to over-professionalise the debate and search for a technical fix to the said problems. While subtle, the point of emphasis i.e. away from the legal and commercial transactions underlying VFM and the 3 E's and towards corporate and financial issues is an important one. This is because in shifting attention away from the 'transaction' based logic of what is now 'dubbed', the static estate, attention subsequently turns towards an examination of the values, economics and culture of the corporate and financial developments underlying the transition to a form of property management capable of resolving the problems of running cost control.

The shift of attention is also seen to be of significance for the following reasons:

- it highlights the transition is based upon a set of values whose logic is not transactional but process-orientated;

- this break with tradition represents a set of values and form of economics which transform the culture of property management;
- the transformation is one that forces a re-engineering, modelling and design of information systems capable of supporting the emerging structures of property management;
- the structures in question are more abstract in character, requiring a knowledge of the evaluative criteria, economics, culture, corporate and financial dimensions to the initiatives and strategies underlying the transition;
- the knowledge in question is technical, economic and cultural in character i.e. theoretical and methodological, informational and communicative, rather than self-evident, or practical in nature.

Looking at the research already undertaken on the transition, it is evident examples of initiatives in the 'building' of information systems and application of IT to produce communicative structures in the form of asset registers which assist the valuation of property, auditing, review and measurement of performance are plentiful. Indeed it appears as though it is not so much the initiatives that are in question - be they to do with the application of IT for asset registration, property valuation, audit, review or performance measurement, as the strategies underlying them which forms the main issue of concern. It is a point that has recently been made by Gibson and Carter (1996), who in drawing attention to the 'plethora' of initiatives on the application of IT, also refer to the 'enigma' of strategy and search for the strategic dimension to the management of property in local authorities.

Gibson's (1986, 1991, 1994) research (along with Avis, Gibson and Watts, 1989; Avis and Gibson, 1995) mirrors that currently taking place in the USA and represents an attempt to examine the relationship between the IT, corporate and financial dimensions to the management of property. In taking this form its influences include Veale (1988), Brown and Arnold (1993), Joroff, Lovargand, Lambert and Franklin (1993) - the latters' case-studies on, Hewlett Packard, Sun Microsystems, Kraft and Ford's management of the situation in particular. As such it attempts to redress the imbalance, or asymmetric relationship that has previously existed between initiatives and strategy. In doing so, it centres attention on the role of initiatives in the development of corporate strategy and the financial dimensions of property management. In taking this form there can be little doubt that the research undertaken by Avis, Gibson and

Watts, opens up a number of possibilities for those with a particular interest in the development of LAPM. It is valuable for the fact that the research introduces the technical and economic concerns over the informational basis of IT applications, the communicative structures of corporate strategy and the financial dimensions of property management in a form which addresses many of the issues raised by the AC, RICS, CIPFA and ADC. As such the programme of research can perhaps best be seen as a sign-post marking a significant development in the transition from estate to property management in local authorities. For what it does is switch attention away from the technical and economic concerns over the informational basis of IT applications for asset registers, property valuation, auditing, review and performance measurement (initiatives) and towards the culture of the communicative structures underlying the corporate strategy and financial instruments of property management in local authorities.

While significant and marking an important step forward, the research has to be put into context: firstly; there are some obvious difficulties over the 'Anglophonic' use of the terms real estate and property: secondly; the research tends to 'downplay' the technical and economic concerns about the informational basis of communicative structures in favour of the cultural question surrounding corporate strategy and the financial instruments: thirdly; as a consequence, the management thesis tends to 'blur' any distinction between values in terms of the technical, economic, and cultural composition of the informational basis and communicative structures in question: fourthly; all the publications from this school of thought illustrate an ambivalence towards the corporate strategy and financial dimensions of the public sector.

These four qualifications are important because in the first instance the question over property and real estate makes any cross-cultural comparisons of the development difficult - if not problematic. The second point is also significant because it is a development that tends to drive a wedge between the technical, economic and cultural dimensions of property management in local authorities. This having the effect of opening up the possibility for the more traditionally minded to search for a 'technical fix' to the problem of running cost control and becoming 'economistic' in their approach to property management. Economistic in the sense the brand of micro, or managerial economics adopted fails to give due consideration to the informational basis, culture, corporate strategy, or financial instruments underlying the communicative structures of property management in local authorities. The effect of this being seen in the tendency to reduce the significance of critical distinctions between the technical, economic, informational, cultural and communicative to little more than 'a play on words' and make any meaningful comparison of either the economic or cultural schools of property management difficult. It also has the effect of allowing the cultural school to distance itself from the technical and economic in the search for an informational basis providing an 'ideal form of communication'.

This is an important point because the 'wedge' in question has the effect of splitting the subject in two. Splitting it; in effect, into two schools of thought - the economic and cultural, each appearing alien to the other in their search for a 'technical fix' and 'ideal form of communication'. The effect of this being seen in the highly codified development of property management in local authorities. One that attempts to make sense of the division that exists between the technical/economic initiatives underlying the informational basis of LAPM and the cultural/communicative dimensions of the strategic response local authorities have made as part of the search for better standards of property management. It is a situation referred to as a 'plethora of initiatives and enigma and strategy'. The proposal here being that while a number of technical and economic based initiatives exist to support the development of property management in local authorities, they appear isolated running parallel to each other. The enigma lying in the knowledge that both the technical and economic issues surrounding the initiatives are linked in some way to the strategic dimension of property management. The question that arises being how to decode the technical, economic and cultural links between the various initiatives and solve the enigma of strategy?

In reference to the last point, it is perhaps Hambleton (1990) and Cochrane (1993) who best draw attention to the significance of the new managerialist thesis in the sense that in attempting to 'turn professionals into managers', it produces a set of technical experts who are unaware, insensitive and poorly educated as to the economics and culture of public service provision (also, see Lash and Urry, 1993; Urry, 1995). Unaware that structures of provision i.e. the combination of initiatives and strategy, forming the informational and communicative structures of LAPM, can be pro-private and public; central-administrative, bureaucratic, decentralist-market, consumer-orientated, based on uniform or plural values, with elitist or popularist sentiments. It is a set of possibilities Hambleton

(1990) characterises the technical, economic and cultural significance of as:

- the radical right strategy of cutting, reshaping public spending and promoting privatisation;
- the re-organisation of public services as the management of strategies for improving responsiveness and meeting consumer's needs;
- the reform of public services conceived of as a political strategy for empowering the consumer and citizen in order to strengthen democracy.

While Hambleton (1990) draws upon Hoggett's (1987, 1989) thesis on the crisis of the longstanding association between Taylor's 'scientific principles of management' and Fordist based mass production, the subsequent demise of a strong, centralist welfare-state and shift towards post-Fordism (see Stoker, 1990 and Cochrane, 1993), the degree to which all three forms of response to the new 'technical, economic cum cultural paradigm' focuses not on the technology or economics of initiatives but culture of strategy is noticeable. That is, not so much on the technology of the information systems i.e. informational basis, but the culture of the communicative structures underlying the strategies management adopt as a means to re-organise and reform local authorities by either; radically cutting and reshaping, improving responsiveness, or the strengthening of democratic values in the provision of public services (also, see Urry 1995; McGuigan, 1995 and Webster, 1996).

The influence of the first form - cutting and re-shaping, can be traced back to Peters and Waterman (1982) and Osbourne and Gaebler (1992) in terms of the USA, with Butt and Palmer (1985) providing the UK examples. The emphasis here being on the cultural dimension to the development and in that sense the use of language, theory and method by management in the design and modelling of the information systems as the technical and economic means to support the corporate strategy and financial instruments required to realise value from the transfer of structures across from the private sector. It is an issue Gibson (1990) reflects on in asking the question of who manages 'operational' property best? Interestingly, after noting the similarities between the two sectors, Gibson (1990) finds the culture of the corporate strategies and financial instruments make it difficult to establish whether one sector provides greater value than the other. It is a question Martindale (1995) has also asked in relation to 'investment' property.

The difficulty with this form of investigation lies in the fact it tends to focus on general trends in the development of the informational basis and communicative structures (in this case those underlying the development of the property management in local authorities) rather than particular experiences. As a result, the research into the privatisation of property management has no reference point from which to measure VFM or the 3E's that may materialise as a consequence of drawing upon either the technology or economics of the information systems, corporate strategy or financial instruments forming communicative structures in the independent sector.

To date it appears there is little research within the new managerialist thesis, as exemplified by Gibson, Avis, Gibson and Watt, which has attempted to look at the AC reports, RICS, CIPFA and ADC's proposals as a means to improve the responsiveness to consumer needs. While this ethic appears to be that 'embedded' in the earlier research of Britton, Connellan and Crofts (1989), the report in question only serves to document the early stages of the transition from estate to property management in local authorities (i.e. how to deal with the static estate) and is unable to establish the degree to which the 'strategic' response, corporatisation and development of financial instruments for such purposes have combined to improve the quality of services - be it measured in terms of VFM, the 3E's, or consumer satisfaction. It is a line of enquiry Deakin (1997 a,b) has sought to further by providing particular case-study examples of the response in question. By, in this instance, examining the development of a pro-quality, enterprise-minded, competitive, decentralised and accountable culture for LAPM and illustrating how this draws upon the technological and economic innovations of information systems in not only 'piecing together' the strategy required to corporatise property management, or produce the financial instruments local authorities need for such purposes, but in building a communicative structure commercial enough to tackle the problem of running cost control.

While it is noticeable the third issue Hambleton (1990) draws attention to is one that has attracted little, if any attention, it does go to highlight a further forgotten dimension of the new managerialist thesis. The fact the issues underlying the development of property management in local authorities do not only concern the informational basis of communicative structures - be they to do with the technology, economics, or culture of initiatives and strategies, but in representing the democratic rights of consumers in civil society are also about the politics of public sector service provision (see Hambleton, 1993). Given it is probably going to be this political dimension that will surface in the ongoing re-organisation and reform of local government along the lines of questions about 'civic responsibility' and the 'empowerment of citizens' as the consumers of public services, it is a matter the exponents of the thesis ought perhaps to 'build' more firmly into the corporate strategy and financial instruments drawn upon as communicative structures for the development of property management in local authorities.

As already pointed out, the transition from estate to property management also transforms the working practices of surveyors employed as professional officers in local authorities. To a large degree it is seen to mark the break-down of Taylorist style 'command and control' of managers in highly centralised bureaucracies, whose planned administration of 'landed estates' is organised through 'artificial structures' and departmental divisions. The structure of 'line management' that is hierarchical, concerned with the status of managers as professional officers and 'workers' as technicians providing 'back-up' support. Under the transition this type of command and control is transformed from a highly organised tight, rigid line management in estates departments, into a less protectionist, more open, flatter horizontal structure with group-based projects that take on an inter-departmental nature, becoming multi-disciplinary in form. In taking this form working practices are said to become pro-quality, enterprise-minded, and competitive, in the sense the development of property management leads to a greater degree of 'marketisation'. Here government bodies, such as the AC and the professions - RICS, ISVA and CIPFA - are seen to provide the guidelines for such developments - assisted by the ADC - while the officers are expected to provide the skills and expertise required to piece together initiatives in the technology and economics of information systems, modelling of data-bases to do with the registration of assets and testing of programmes for the valuation of property, audit, review and measurement of performance. In other words, provide the skills and expertise required for the development of the strategy whose accountable, decentred, competitive and enterprising qualities are cultural in the way they lead to a process of corporatisation (links with accountants and further horizontal connections with architects and planners) and set of financial instruments geared towards the commercialisation of property management in local authorities.

Although the task of giving due consideration to this much neglected question of property management in local authorities is not an easy one, a number of points can be drawn from the foregoing discussions:

- put into context, the AC reports represent a major challenge to the property profession and one that is particularly difficult for them to meet due to the fact the Taylorist form of organisation and bureaucratic management of technology, has (during the post-war development of the public sector in particular), tended to be routine, habit forming and centre upon the economics of commercial transactions underlying the buying and selling of estates;
- the shift towards the development of initiatives and strategies to strengthen the management of property in local authorities places new demands on the profession as members negotiate the transition from estate to property management in accordance with the standards set out by the AC, RICS, CIPFA and ADC for local authorities;
- over the past eight years or so, most headway has been made in the development of initiatives to introduce IT in the registration of assets, valuation of property, audit, review and measurement of performance to meet the VFM test and establish the 3 E's;
- in contrast, there has been a noticeable absence of expertise available to assist in the cultural development of both the corporate strategy and financial instruments required to form the framework for such initiatives, tests and criteria;
- such an integrated development requires careful consideration of the new managerialist thesis, its privileging of both the corporate strategy and financial instruments of communicative structures over the technology and economics of information systems vis-a-vis, application of IT in the drive towards VFM and the 3E's;
- the developments in question mark a major shift towards theoretical knowledge, systems design, modelling and testing (the building of meta-information data-bases and communication structures as expert systems). It also breaks with the hierarchically divided bureaucracy of standardised public service provision in the post-war welfare state (dominated by planners, rather than surveyors) and introduces what are termed 'post-Fordist structures', with flatter, more horizontal

arrangements addressing the risk and uncertainties of an enterprising, more competitive, decentred-market regime, accountable and corporatist perspective towards the management of property held by local authorities;

- while the developments can be seen as a response to the crisis of Fordism in the welfare state - in the form of the fiscal tightening, cut-back in public expenditure, search for VFM and 3 E's under 'zero-sum' budgets, the lack of data currently available on the transition makes it difficult to establish whether the initiatives and strategies underlying the emerging form of property management in local authorities represents a drive towards privatisation, improvement in responsiveness, or movement towards a greater degree of democratisation.

This goes some way to set out the significance of such developments and the importance of seeing LAPM as a combination of initiatives and strategies. The issue is also significant for a further reason: for the fact that in dealing with the organisation of resources, they - the initiatives and strategies in question - have become an even more salient aspect of LAPM due in part to the environment of zero sum budgets, funding shortages, capital spending restrictions, standard spending assessments and service cut backs which accompany the re-organisation and reform of public sector service provision by local government. The emphasis here being not on the development of additional initiatives, but of strategies for radical cutbacks, improving responsiveness and the democratisation of public sector service provision in the search for value for money under tighter economic circumstances, efficiency drives and effectiveness tests. In contrast to the technical, economic and cultural developments in the initiatives and strategies already referred to, this has to be seen as a matter that is of particular significance for the question of re-organisation and reform and represents a terrain which has not yet been mapped out.

It is for this combination of reasons that the book on post-AC studies in *Local Authority Property Management* is qualified in terms of initiatives, strategies, re-organisation and reform. In qualifying the text in this manner, the book sets out to provide a review of past initiatives, monitor what headway has been made in understanding the contribution strategies make to LAPM and focus on what can be applied in the context of local government re-organisation and reform.

Aims

Under the theme of 'surveying the initiatives, planning the strategies, re-organisation and reform', the book brings together a number of post-AC studies in LAPM with the aim of:

- reviewing the institutional framework for the development of LAPM and examing the initiatives taken by local authorities to ground property management in examples of best practice;
- identifying the strategies local authorities have designed and sought to operate to support the development of LAPM;
- focusing attention on the structure of LAPM developing under such initiatives and strategies and assessing the demands the re-organisation of local government will place on authorities to reform the management of property in local authorities.

The review aims to document the initiatives and bring forward the much needed material on the experiences of attempts made by local authorities to introduce the technologies and economics of information systems (IT) in the form of asset registers, Red/White Book - now the *Appraisal and Valuation Manual*, - standards of property valuation, auditing, review and performance measurement in the management of holdings. The subsequent aim seeks to bring case-study material forward which also highlights attempts made by members of the profession to augment the development of such initiatives in the informational basis of property management with strategies towards the communicative and allocative dimensions of resource management in local authorities. It is anticipated that when placed side-by-side, the initiatives and strategies should illustrate the structure of LAPM and provide a point of reference to establish what effect the re-organisation of local government is having on the management of property in local authorities. Whether, that is, it means just more for the same, or if the re-organisation is of a nature which demands further reforms of property management in local authorities.

Modelling LAPM

In the interests of helping to focus attention on the underlying issues and sharpen debate, a model of LAPM is provided to characterise the development in question. As can be seen, it outlines the development in terms of the initiatives and strategies underlying the informational and communicative structure of property management for local government re-organisation and reform (see Figure 1.1). In this capacity, the model has the role of focusing attention on the issues surrounding LAPM. Acting in this capacity, the model should be seen as a pedagogical tool: a learning device, useful in the sense it captures the present state of affairs in the development of property management and highlights matters of particular concern to local authorities. As such the model ought to be seen as providing a rather formal representation of LAPM. One that seeks to do little more than pre-figure the issues referred to in the studies and set the examinations of LAPM into context. As can be seen, it follows the logic of the discussions which have taken place so far, with the contribution the property profession and supporting institutes have made to the development of LAPM forming the focus of attention. It identifies the form and content of the initiatives in question and draws attention to the strategies that underpin these particular developments.

The post-AC studies

The first contribution by Mark Deakin aims to 'map out' and review the institutional framework in which the development of LAPM takes place. It also draws attention to the magnitude of the changes that have taken place in response to the call by the AC for better standards of property management in local authorities.

The chapter by Nick French and Louise Hague, sub-divides into three sections. In the post-AC search for VFM and the 3 E's (the components making up 'good, high quality property management'), the paper identifies two major initiatives : the development of asset registers and property valuation. Focusing on the latter, the paper draws attention to the steps taken by the RICS to address such matters in the publication of the *Appraisal and Valuation Manual.* In addressing these questions, French and Hague draw particular attention to what the RICS see as the need for all property valuations (whether internal, or for an independent purpose made use of by a third party) to be undertaken within the guidelines set out in the new manual. The benefits of such guidelines for the valuation of property are seen to lie in the fact that adoption of the

<table>
<tr><th colspan="2">Development</th></tr>
<tr><td>Audit Commission Report
CIPFA on Finance
CIPFA/RICS Working Group</td><td>ADC on LAPM
CIPFA on Asset Registers
RICS on LAPM</td></tr>
<tr><th>Initiatives</th><th>Strategies</th></tr>
<tr><td>(Technical)
VFM in the Public Sector
Central Committees
Internal Markets
Information Systems
GIS
Asset Rents under Capital Accounting
Mass Appraisals
Contracting Out and CCT
Private Finance Initiative
(Economics)</td><td>The Three E's
Quality
Enterprise
Competitive
Decentred
Accountable
Corporate
(Culture)</td></tr>
<tr><th colspan="2">Structure</th></tr>
<tr><td>(Informational)
Information Technology
Asset Registration
Property Valuation
Auditing and Review
Performance Measurement</td><td>(Communicative)
Corporatisation
Financial Instruments
Commercial Standards</td></tr>
<tr><th colspan="2">Re-organisation</th></tr>
<tr><td colspan="2">Re-allocation of Resources
Administration
New Model(s) of Service Provision</td></tr>
<tr><th colspan="2">Reform</th></tr>
<tr><td colspan="2">Privatisation
Responsiveness to Consumer Demand
Democratisation</td></tr>
</table>

Figure 1.1 Model of Local Authority Property Management

standards laid down in the manual will first of all: encourage an initial understanding of client's (customer's) needs; promote consistent use of bases and assumptions on which valuations are provided and help achieve good, high quality standards of management. The study also points out the adoption of such standards are necessary because with the introduction of the client-agent split and landlord-tenant type division between central property committees and service users, it has become questionable (even more so under contracting out and CCT), whether the valuation of property holdings can be said to be for internal purposes. As a final point for discussion, the study draws attention to some property management issues underlying the re-organisation of local government and reform of public sector service provision.

Marion Weatherhead's contribution switches attention from initiatives to strategies. Here it is proposed that 'strategies in LAPM' should serve the corporate objectives of local authorities and to achieve this property management ought to 'incorporate real estate' - the resource in question. The study proposes that property management should learn from the incorporation of real estate into local authorities which has taken place in North America and is now beginning to take root in the UK. Echoing the arguments for 'incorporation' found in North America and in the UK (mainly in the private, or newly 'privatised' sector it should be added) the study draws attention to the scale of expenditure on cost outgoings. In the instance of the local authority forming the focus of the study, an estimated 17% of total annual expenditure. A further argument put forward for such a form of 'incorporation' relates to the changes which have taken place to turn land and buildings making up an estate into financial assets. Having made this point, the study goes on to develop a generic model of strategies that incorporate real estate. In doing so Weatherhead suggests the components of the strategies should be economic and cultural and ought not to be over-politicised as in the past this has contributed to the failure for strategies to incorporate real estate into the property management of local authorities. The chapter goes on to detail what steps should be taken to incorporate real estate into strategies for the development of LAPM.

Initiatives

Martin Ralphs and Peter Wyatt consider the benefits that the implementation of geographical and land information systems (GIS and

LIS) can offer local authorities with regard to the management of property. The paper begins by outlining the reasons for recent moves towards the application of information technology (IT) in local authority property management and argues that information used in property management functions i.e. asset registration, property valuation and performance measurement, is largely geo-referenced data. Such data requirements, it is suggested, are handled most effectively by IT applications that include mapping and spatial analysis capabilities such as GIS and LIS. The chapter examines Barking and Dagenham London Borough Council's experience of property management, focusing on the authorities digital land terrier. In taking this form, the study picks up the asset registration initiative and transition from computer-based information systems to the technology of GIS. In particular, it draws attention to the need for common standards in geo-referencing, mapping and spatial analysis and the lessons learnt from Western Australia's attempts to use GIS applications as the informational basis for a strategy towards the communication of data.

Peter Dent's contribution looks at the initiatives taken in the valuation of property. In contrast to Weatherhead, this paper seeks to develop a particular understanding of what is referred to as the 'nature of property management'. Dent seeks to understand the nature of LAPM in terms of the economic, cultural and environmental duties (moral and ethical), the ownership, possession and use of property places upon those responsible for its management. In doing so, Dent draws upon an academic tradition much closer to home and found in the publications of Thorncroft, Denman and Arnison. Adopting the ideal of freedom and liberty, the chapter suggests that property, its ownership, possession and use, should not only be understood in technical or economic terms; for example: either as a legal, commercial or even cultural phenomenon (corporate and financial) for that matter, but in terms of its ability to represent a form of power in the political state of civil society. As a form of power which shifts attention from the question of morals, ethics and duty and reduces them to little more than a methodological debate over the search for a 'technical fix' to problems underlying the economics of specialist, non-market property valuations as outlined by Owen Connellan in his contribution. Here attention is drawn towards the assessment of gross replacement cost, asset rents and capital charges under the different valuations of depreciation available for the management of property held by local authorities.

Strategies

The three chapters presented under this heading represent an attempt to switch attention away from the question of initiatives and towards the strategies of LAPM. As such they pick up some of the issues referred to by Weatherhead and also go some way to illustrate how the moral, ethical issues and questions of duty raised by Dent have been dealt with as part of the asset registration, valuation and performance measurement exercises of property management in local authorities.

Like Dent, the chapter provided by Mark Deakin suggests there is a fault line running through the structure of local authority property management and this is placing a considerable strain on the attempts made by local authorities to adopt the theory and method of property management set out by the AC and CIPFA. To test this hypothesis, the study examines the structure of local authority property management and assesses how well the theory and method of property management assists local authorities in the application of IT and development of computer-based information systems. The study identifies that a number of practical problems have been experienced by local authorities in adopting the theory and method of property management set out by the AC and CIPFA. In particular it demonstrates that local authorities have experienced problems in translating the theory and method of a quality-minded, pro-enterprise, competitive, decentred and accountable culture for property management in to the technology and economics of an information system, corporate strategy and set of financial instruments detailed enough to recognise how the development of a computer-based information system can lead to an improvement in the management of property held by local authorities.

In undertaking a review of the developments which have already taken place, the study suggests that, if anything, there has been a tendency for computer-based information systems to take on the status of asset registers, rather than tools for the valuation of property and measurement of performance. Something the paper suggests is unfortunate and needs to be altered if the limits it places on the valuation of property and measurement of performance are to be overcome. If, that is, the application of IT in the development of computer-based information systems is to provide the (informational) basis for a communicative structure which leads to an improvement in the standards of property management for local authorities along the lines set out by the AC and CIPFA.

Unlike Dent though, Deakin's study resists the temptation to criticise LAPM for its tendency to focus on either technical or economic questions. Instead it seeks to identify the cultural issues by getting inside the moral, ethical and dutiful (i.e. civic) dimensions of the quality-minded, pro-enterprise, competitive, decentralised and accountable strategy put in place to corporatise the management of property in local authorities. This is done by examining how initiatives in the application of IT to property management combine with the quality-minded, pro-enterprise, competitive, decentralised, and accountable (corporatist) view of strategy held by local authorities in the development of computer-based information systems. How, that is, they combine in the development of 'high-tec', 'information rich' computer-based systems, whose innovative technology, economics and culture augment the corporatist view of strategy with the financial instruments (registration of assets, valuation of property, audit, review and performance measurement) also representing the commercial standards upon which the informational basis and communicative structure of LAPM rest.

Neil Martindale's contribution also draws attention to the difficulties of developing strategies for LAPM. As is pointed out, the paper concerns non-operational property. Rather than use loaded terms such as 'commercial' or 'investment', it adopts the label 'tenanted non-residential property' - TNRP and the legal, corporate and financial setting. It compares category bases for property holdings and in particular examines attitudes to the acquisition, management, retention and disposal of TNRP. It notes the confusion between investment and indirect service objectives and expected returns. It discusses the findings of a survey of local authorities centring on the characteristics and management of their TNRP property. The paper states the strategy for TNRP remains undeveloped. To substantiate this, Martindale draws upon the results of questionnaire surveys undertaken to establish how local authorities have developed strategies for the management of TNRP. As the study points out, the survey findings indicate little tangible progress has been made by local authorities in addressing the problem of property management identified by the AC and ADC for TNRP. Indeed, the use of initiatives in asset registration and property valuation (less so in the field of performance measurement) for the generation of capital receipts from the disposal of vacant land and buildings surplus to requirements, is put forward as the only significance exception to this rule. The paper suggests this may be because short-term political expediency too often comes before the economics of, or a long term strategy for the development of the cultural (quality-minded, pro-enterprise, competitive) dimensions to property management in local authorities.

Gaye Pottinger's contribution concerns compulsory competitive tendering (CCT) for property services in the management of local authorities and the private sector response. As the study points out, in the advent of the 1988 and 1992 *Local Government Acts*, tendering for 'white collar' professional services under the provisions of CCT has become common. Following the government's 'competing for quality' proposals, property management has become one of the most common white collar professional services brought into the regime of contracting out and market testing procedures. The study focuses on how legal initiatives centring on the notion of client-customer split, contracting out and CCT, can be augmented into a strategy for a quality-minded, pro-enterprise and competitive management of resources held by the corporations in question. The study stresses the cultural dimensions of the strategic issue in the form of the informational basis for communication (i.e. the intelligent client) and understanding of the motivating factors influencing both the allocation of resources and administration of contracts. It goes on to suggest that while CCT has acted as a catalyst for the development of strategies promoting quality through enterprise and competition, interest from the private sector in all property (architectural, engineering, building and estates) services has eroded as tendering procedures have progressed and it is likely that the old minimum figures for contracts will have to be altered.

Re-organisation and reform

Alex Linkston's contribution strikes a personal tone on the question of re-organisation and reform. His presentation documents the experiences of an authority that has taken the decision to centralise the management of property and support this process of corporatisation with a clearly defined set of initiatives and strategies.

The contributions from Peter Bowers, Geoffrey Heath, Jean Morgan, Peter Reynolds, Beverley Wilson and Joan Wyld, draw attention to heritage issues in LAPM. It suggests many local authorities, particularly those associated with the 'major cities', have a responsibility for maintaining a part of the national heritage, which may be in danger of serious depreciation due to inadequacies in the funding process. Generous nineteenth century industrial magnates bequeathed many of our finest cities with extensive formal and semi-formal parks, all of which require ongoing maintenance. Similarly the reclamation of industrial waste land has resulted in much improved 'open spaces'. National and European funding has supported these capital projects, but has rarely been available to meet the ongoing stream of current costs necessarily incurred. Similarly, the study argues that while major cities typically played a unique role in Britain's industrial development which almost inevitably led to the accumulation of wealth, the authorities responsible for such structures pay heavily in terms of the financing of heritage conservation through the operation of museums and other such services. Today, it is pointed out, local authorities have difficulty in acquiring the requisite financial resources. This is because the system of local authority financing, ostensibly related to 'need', takes no account of these particular demands on resources. In this chapter attention is focused on two sectors of local authority spending where heritage is a particularly important determinant of cost and where the necessary resources are restrained by funding arrangements. The sectors concerned are 'parks and public open spaces' and 'museums and art galleries'. The study reviews the funding system and tests its appropriateness to meet resource needs. It suggests, that under the post - 1990 Standard Spending Assessments (put forward by the AC for VFM and 3 E purposes), there is at least evidence to suggest that expenditure by local authorities to fund services required for the management of heritage property should take account of the city's cultural heritage. The problem lying in the fact that the current system of grant allocation makes no allowance for these factors. If these can be identified and measured more precisely then there is the potential for including them in the grant allocation process. This, it is argued, would result in a grant allocation more closely related to authorities' needs and as an consequence help to ensure that sufficient resources are available to local authority property managers to maintain and enhance a legacy that will benefit generations to come.

Elizabeth Carter's contribution presents the outcomes of a recently completed research project undertaken with the leisure services department of a local authority. The overall aim of the research has been to explore the development of a procedure for evaluating the performance of operational property and to consider the development of appropriate measures. Here operational property is regarded as the assets required to support the organisation's main activities. The study commences by placing the project in context with the findings of the AC report. It continues to set out the details of the case-study and the application of the procedure for property performance evaluation and suggests that the procedure is a constructive attempt to compensate for the shortcomings of traditional estate management practice by identifying and assessing the quality of operational property management in local authorities. The case-study concerns four swimming pools owned by the leisure services department of a local authority. The case-study material is presented against the back-drop of local government re-organisation and reform and the decision by the local authority to set up a central property committee for the 'evaluation of performance and management of resources' in service provision. The strategic significance of the 'evaluative' model is also illustrated through an examination of how it has been made use of to communicate basic information about the poor condition, high maintenance costs of operational assets and means to legitimate a re-allocation of resources by a given administration away from the poorly performing service. To authorise the removal of what is in effect a symbol of locality, a landmark and cultural artefact, via the process of having it declared surplus to requirements and disposed of.

Michael Nevin's study on the private finance initiative (PFI) examines how the technical and economic innovations of PFI can form the basis of an investment strategy for the management of property held by local authorities. The initiative is looked at against the back-drop of the falling allocation of capital for investment on operational property (education, housing and recreation) under Section 94. Conscious that the initiative may not prove attractive in the development of LAPM, Nevin points out that while authorities might adopt a 'wait and see' strategy to the allocation of finance for capital expenditure, far from being a low risk option, such a response is in fact a risky course of action to take. He argues that under any realistic policy scenario, it is unlikely there will be any significant real growth in the finance available for local authorities to spend on capital projects linked to the provision of public services. He proposes that rather than waiting, local authorities and councils should give serious consideration to mobilising additional capital investment through the 'private finance initiative'. Operating on a risk sharing, equity participation basis, Nevin proposes the initiative can form the foundation for a strategy to improve the quality of property in terms of the design, engineering, construction and subsequent management of completed investment projects undertaken in the entrepreneurial spirit of risk sharing, equity participation and competitive advantage the tendering of projects (by subjection of any development proposal to market testing) is able to bring. Ewan Hall's paper provides an account of property management in Scottish Enterprise. As such it provides the opportunity to examine how it might be possible for the pro-enterprise dimension in the development of strategies for the management of property to be transferred across to authorities undergoing local government re-organisation and reform.

Summary

Turning to the more specific points of how well the contributions meet the aims of the book, it is evident that: the review of the institutional framework and development of initiatives is well covered. The issues underlying the registration of assets and valuation of property have to also be seen as being covered in particular detail. The issue upon which more information might have been useful is on the issue of performance measurement. In comparison to the other two initiatives, this is perhaps the least well represented. While both French and Hague and Martindale draw attention to the issue, it is only made the subject of a detailed examination by Deakin and Carter. On the question of strategies, here again a number of chapters draw particular attention to such matters. This is reflected in the chapters appearing under the heading of strategies and in many of the presentations appearing under the title of re-organisation and reform. The question about the structure of LAPM appears to be a more difficult issue to pin down. It demands a knowledge of how initiatives augment into strategies and together the informational and communicative structure the development of property management in local authorities. These outstanding questions surface again under the final chapter, where some pointers as to how it might be possible to develop such a knowledge of LAPM are provided.

References

Association of District Councils (1990a), *Property Management in District Councils - A Good Practice Guide,* ADC, London.

Association of District Councils (1990b), *Efficiency in Welsh Districts Councils - Property Management*, ADC, London.

Association of District Councils (1990c), *Property Management in District Councils - A Good Practice Guide,* ADC, London.

Audit Commission (1988a), *Local Authority Property - A Management Overview,* HMSO, London.

Audit Commission (1988b), *Local Authority Property - A Management Handbook,* HMSO, London.

Audit Commission (1988c), *Management Paper NO.7,* HMSO, London.

Avis, M. and Gibson, V. (1995), *Real Estate Resource Management,* DTI, London.

Avis, M. Gibson, V. and Watts, J. (1989), *Managing Operational Property Assets,* Department of Land Management, Reading University.

Britton, W. , Connellan, O. and Crofts, M. (1989), *The Economic, Efficient and Effective Management of Public Sector Landed Estates,* Kingston University, Surrey County Council, Kingston-upon-Thames.

Brown, R . and Arnold, A. (1993), *Managing Corporate Real Estate,* John Wiley and Sons, New York.

Butt, H. and Palmer, D. (1985), *Value for Money in the Public Sector,* Macmillan, London.

Chartered Institute of Public Finance and Accountancy (1989), *Capital Accounting in Local Authorities - The Way Forward,* CIPFA, London.

Chartered Institute of Public Finance and Accountancy (1991a), *CIPFA Statement - Capital Accounting in Local Authorities,* CIPFA, London.

Chartered Institute of Public Finance and Accountancy (1991b), *Asset Registers,* CIPFA, London.

Chartered Institute of Public Finance and Accountancy (1992), *Capital Accounting by Local Authorities - Report of the Implementation Studies,* CIPFA, London.

Deakin, M. (1997a), 'The development of computer-based information systems for local authority property management: the underlying issue', *Journal of Financial Management for Property and Construction,* vol 2 (1).

Deakin, M. (1997b), 'The development of computer-based information systems for local authority property management: the application', *Journal of Financial Management for Property and Construction,* vol 2 (2).

Elcock, H. (1988), *Local Government: Professionals and Practices,* Methuen, London.

Elcock, H. (1994), *Local Government: Policy and Management,* Routledge, London.

Gibson, V. (1986), 'A management view of valuation in information technology', *Journal of Valuation,* vol 5 (1) :30-40.

Gibson ,V. (1991), 'Who can manage property best: the private or public sector?', *Property Management*, vol 9 (1) .

Gibson, V. (1994), 'Strategic property management: how can local authorities develop a property strategy?', *Property Management,* vol 12 (3): 9-15.

Gibson, V. (1995), 'Is property on the strategic agenda?' *Property Review*, vol 5 (1): 104-109.

Gibson, V. and Carter, E. (1996), 'Is property on the strategic agenda?', *Chartered Surveyor Monthly*, January: 34-35.

Hambleton, R. (1993), 'Consumerism, decentralisation and local democracy', in Roberts, P., Struthers, T. and Sacks, T. (eds) *Managing the Metropolis*, Avebury Press, Aldershot .

Hambleton, R. (1989), 'Urban government under Thatcher and Reagan', *Urban Affairs Quarterly*, vol. 24 (3): 359-88.

Hambleton, R., Hoggett, P. and Tolan, F. (1989a), 'The decentralisation of public services: a research agenda', *Local Government Studies,* January/February: 39-56.

Hoggett, P. (1987),'A farewell to mass production? decentralisation as an emergent private and public sector paradigm', in Hoggett, P. and Hambleton, R. (eds) *Decentralisation and Democracy: Localising Public Services,* School for Advanced Urban Studies, University of Bristol.

Hoggett, P. and Hambleton, R. (eds) (1987), *Decentralisation and Democracy: Localising Public Services,* School for Advanced Urban Studies, University of Bristol.

Joroff, M., Lovargand, M., Lambert, S. and Franklin, B. (1993), *Corporate Real Estate, (Re 2000 Management Team),* Massachusetts Institute of Technology, Cambridge, Massacheusetts.

Lash, S. and Urry, J. (1987), *The End of Organized Capitalism,* Polity, Cambridge.

Lash, S. and Urry, J. (1994), *Economies of Signs and Space,* Sage, New York.

McGuigan, J. (1995), *Culture and the Public Sphere,* Routledge, London.

Martindale, N. (1995), 'Local authority property investment: a virtual reality', *Property Management*, vol 13 (1).

Osborne, D. and Gaebler, T. (1992), *Reinventing Government - How the Entreprenurial Spirit is Transforming the Public Sector,* Addison-Wesley, Reading, Massachusetts.

Scarrett, D. (1983), *Property Management,* E & F Spon, London.

Scarett, D. (1995), *Property Asset Management*, E & F Spon, London.

Stapleton, T. (1986), *Estate Management Practice,* Estates Gazette, London.

Stapleton, T. (1994), *Estate Management Practice,* Estates Gazette, London.

Stoker, G. (1990), 'Regulation theory, local government and the transition from Fordism', in King, D. and Pierre, J. (eds) *Challenges to Local Government*, Sage, London.
Urry, J. (1995),*Consuming Places,* Routledge, London.
Veale, P. (1990), *Managing Corporate Real Estate Assets,* Massachusetts Institute of Technology, Cambridge MA.
Weatherhead, M. (1997), *Real Estate in Corporate Strategy,* Macmillan, London.
Webster, F. (1996), *Theories of the Information Society,* Routledge, London.

PART 1
LOCAL AUTHORITY PROPERTY MANAGEMENT

2 The Development of Local Authority Property Management

Mark Deakin, Department of Building and Surveying, Napier University

Introduction

Ten years has passed since the Audit Commission first published its reports on Local Authority Property Management (AC, 1988a, b and c). Since then, all local authorities have responded to the reports and taken steps to improve the standards of property management in line with the guidelines set out by the Chartered Institute of Public Finance and Accountancy (CIPFA, 1989, 1991a, b and 1992). This paper examines the development of local authority property management in terms of the VFM test: land audits; property reviews and transition towards the 3 E's advocated by the AC and CIPFA. It then goes on to look at the emerging pro-privatisation consensus over the VFM test and questions the transition to the 3 E's has raised about the technical development of local authority property management. The paper identifies the questions about the nature of the development originate from progressive and conservative divisions to do with the theory of property valuation and crisis of legitimation over the economics of the post-war welfare state - the divisions and crisis reflected in the emergence of the new managerialist thesis.

In going on to investigate the 'all pervasive' market reasoning of the managerialist thesis (in both the UK and USA), the paper draws attention to the 'Anglophonic' tailoring and re-engineering of property management, augmentation of initiatives in both the technical and economic basis of the development with the informational and communicative dimensions of the corporate strategy, financial instruments and commerce surrounding the culture of property management in local authorities. Here attention is drawn to the high-tec, economic cum cultural paradigm of an information rich, communicative form of property management and the place it takes in the re-organisation and reform of public services provided by local government under the emerging structures of post-Fordism and neo-Schumpeterian workfare state. The paper draws the investigation to a close by providing some 'sign-posts' in the development of local authority property management.

The VFM test

In the late 1970s it had become generally accepted there was a real need to make large organisations more accountable and subject to a greater degree of audit. With audit came the term 'value for money', what Butt and Palmer (1985) refer to as 'a wide and ambiguous term', but one that, nevertheless, goes a long way to establishing the principle of economy and the use of money as the measure of value attributable to expenditures on goods and services. With the concept of audit and principle of economy came the idea of 'managing better with less', being 'lean, mean, enterprising and competitive'. Based on this managers started to ask the following:

- what accounting procedures are in place;
- how is expenditure audited;
- how could expenditure be made more economic;
- how can the auditing of expenditure be made use of to review the performance of goods and service provision.

In response to this managers started to question whether expenditure met the value for money test. Whether, that is: the accounting and auditing provisions in place are economic and how reviews of expenditure can be carried out to test this. As a consequence a VFM methodology began to develop. It should be noted that the methodology in question has a relatively simple and straight forward philosophy. In its most simplistic form it can be represented as:

- the definition of objectives for the test;
- the detailing of the accounting procedures underlying the provision of goods and services;
- the auditing of expenditures;
- the review of performance.

As a set of inter-related activities the methodology appears quite straight forward. At this level of representation is can be seen as generic, applicable to any situation where accounts are needed and expenditure requires to be audited.

Grounded, as it is in the principle of economy, it is perhaps possible to generalise the objective of the test as value adding - be it in terms of income producing or cost-saving measures. Working within this objective, the test transforms into a management exercise: one that details the accounting procedures for the provision of the goods and services in question; goes on to audit and on further to establish whether such expenditures can be made more economic through a review of performance. It is perhaps this simple and rather straight forward representation of the VFM test that makes it an attractive management exercise. It should perhaps also be noted that the exercise is not one which is limited to the review of performance, because the information generated from the test, its audit and review, can be and often is drawn upon to form the basis of not only a rationalisation, but a thorough and often rigorous re-organisation of the management process underlying the provision of goods and services.

In taking this form, the audit and review issues are represented by the Society of Local Authority Chief Executives (SOLAS, 1986) enquiry into the matter and the Local Authority Valuers' Association (LAVA, 1989) examination of how to manage such exercises. In chronological terms it is a development that is perhaps best marked by Britton, Connellan and Crofts' (1989) representation of such audits and reviews as a form of rationalisation and transition towards the strategic management of property held by local authorities.

Land audits and property reviews

According to Britton, Connellan and Crofts (1989) a land audit or property review, is a process by which systematic attention is given to each interest in landed property by a team of qualified people working to a close brief. Here, the audit and review in question, are seen to represent an essential first step towards attaining good management. In the context of the exercise, 'good management' is defined in terms of the initiatives - in this instance the audit and review - that not only allow the measurement of land and property in terms of 'monetary value', but which also lead to the 'minimum' amount of expenditure on the management of related goods and services.

As they go on to point out, the essential components of an audit and review are as follows. Firstly, it must be supported at both the political level of members, professional officers, directors and executives of the corporation in question. In order to achieve this, it is necessary to 'sell' the idea to those within the organisation whom it will affect and in this connection it is important to state from the outset how the financial proceeds of the exercise are to be distributed within the corporation. Secondly, it must systematically cover all the authority's landed property, regardless of tenure and use. Thirdly, it should cross all boundaries (geographical and departmental) because land audits and reviews are a corporate activity. Fourthly, the first land audit and review should be planned as a single project with a defined time span which should be as short as possible. If this means that it requires additional resources, these should be costed and provided for the project, because if the exercise takes too long, the beneficial effects of the audit and review will be diluted. As a rule of thumb, it is suggested a small portfolio of holdings should be audited within twelve months and a medium-sized holding should be reviewed in three years. It is also proposed that the largest portfolios should be audited within the span of a typical rent review period which is five years.

As they go on to point out: one of the main functions of the land audit and property review should be to establish suitable performance indicators for each property interest and to set up systems for the continuous monitoring of performance according to those indicators. The suggested measures of performance are:

- the amount of net capital receipts from disposals;
- the amount of any increases in receipts from income-producing landed property (eg: investment property);
- the reduction in landed property used by the authority;
- the reduction in running costs;
- the ratio of all receipts and savings to the cost of the audit and review.

From this it is evident that land audits and property reviews centre upon the generation of capital receipts from income producing land and property. An exercise that is geared towards solving the problem of the static estate in local authorities, the subsequent mis-match, under-use and relatively high level of vacancy, by the disposal of land and property the audit and review declares surplus to requirements. While the exercise reduces the amount of land and property made use of by the disposal of poorly performing assets and benefits from the consequent improvement such a form of rationalisation brings about, the problem of running cost control appears to take a low priority in the overall scheme of things. This is to some degree borne out by the fact questions about running cost control only appear towards the bottom of the list. It is perhaps this switch from concern over the generation of capital receipts via the said audits and reviews, to the reduction of running costs that marks the transition from rationalisation to re-organisation under the 3E's and strategic management of property this brings about.

While it is appreciated the distinctions drawn here between VFM, land audits, property reviews, rationalisations, the 3 E's and re-organisation are subtle, they are nonetheless critical for the reason they signify that:

- in responding to the VFM test, the management of property has been augmented by initiatives in land audit geared towards the review of property and assessment of whether land and property held by an organisation meets their requirements, if there is a mis-match, under use of assets, or high level of vacancy;
- in placing a monetary value on the holdings the opportunity cost of land and property ownership is established, along with the price of holding assets that are unsuitable, partially used or vacant;
- the high cost of holding inappropriate assets tends to illustrate the price of owning such resources is too high, uneconomic in real terms, a situation which tends to force a redistribution of land and property through realisation and disposal;
- the outcome of such an exercise represents a form of rationalisation and drive towards economy in the allocation of assets;
- in seeking to consolidate the gains realised from such a form of rationalisation, attention has now begun to switch from the audit and review of holdings as a stock of land and property, towards the stream of expenditure on the goods and services required to manage the assets in question;
- this focuses attention on the static estate (the so-called mis-match, under-use of assets and question of vacant property) and problem of

running cost control - the need for an audit and review of the growing expenditures on the stock and flow of goods and services paid out to cover the cost of managing property;
- following this a number of additional initiatives have surfaced which looked at together represent a deep and thorough re-organisation of property in a drive towards the 3 E's in the management of assets.

It is evident that in taking this form, the movement towards the 3 E's represents a growing interest in the economics of property underlying the initial audit, review, rationalisation and subsequent process of re-organisation forming part of the drive towards a greater degree of efficiency and effectiveness from expenditure on the management of property.

Towards the 3 E's

As already pointed out, Britton, Connellan and Crofts (1989) define good management in terms of: measuring the value of property in monetary terms and employing the minimum amount of expenditure on its management. Having defined 'good' management in such a way, they go on to suggest such a form of property management: deserves the adjectives, 'economic', 'efficient' and 'effective' as the landed property will be maintained on a business-like footing, producing sufficient benefit (performance of duties and attainment of objectives) at minimum possible cost. While economic, the authors also go on to suggest, based on a 'business-like' footing, such a form of management will be efficient because it produces the desired effect (provision of landed property to enable the organisation to perform its duties and attain its objectives) with the minimum possible input of resources. In addition, they also go on to suggest that it will be effective because it will have the desired effect of providing landed property which enables the corporation in question to perform its duties and attain set objectives. As they go on to point out: unfortunately it is not common to find such a form of property management, because in the past the management of property has been subject to two major problems - what they refer to as:

- the static estate and;
- problem of running cost control.

The term 'static estate' is perhaps a little confusing in the sense it introduces another variable into the equation. What is more, it begs the question about the exact nature of the relationship between the estate and landed property: something that also raises a question about the relationship between land and property and why the management focus is not on the former but the latter. As such it is a matter that requires clarification. The term estate is made use of by Britton, Connellan and Crofts (1989) because over the past one hundred years it is the estate which has formed the subject of interest from the academic point of view and it is only over the post-war period that such studies have drawn a distinction between the estate as an ownership of land and other forms of property in terms of fixed and circulating capital - the outcome of this being the appearance of terms such as landed estate or landed property as attempts to highlight the fixed nature of such assets as combinations of land and capital. Again in chronological terms it ought to be recognised that the term estate is often drawn upon where the structure of tenure relates to the landlord's interest i.e. in the ownership of land, the opposite situation being the case where the term property is made use of due to the fact it tends to transcend the interest of the landlord and include the tenant's occupational interest i.e. in the land and capital forming the fixed asset required for operational purposes.

In contrast to the partial, land-based interest of the estate, the term property tends to suggest a more comprehensive representation of the material (land and buildings as forms of fixed capital assets) forming the subject of management. It is this partial, land-based interest that Britton, Connellan and Crofts (1989) evoke in using the term static estate. Here the term static is drawn upon to characterise how such an interest can perhaps best be described and it is from this that we get a number of definitions geared towards the characterisation of the estate in comparison to property management (see Table 2.1).

The authors in question suggest that such an unfortunate characterisation stems, to a large degree, from the lack of consensus in academic circles as to the purpose of the estate and the exact nature of its relationship to property management and while no clear conclusion is drawn in their discussions on the matter, it is evident there is a tendency to associate estate management with the legal and social structure underlying the division of tenure into a landlord and tenant relation, rather than and as opposed to the corporate, financial and commercial dimensions of

Table 2.1 Characterisation of Estate and Property Management

Management	Estate	Property
	Static	Dynamic
	Inert	Active
	Reactive	Pro-Active
	Unresponsive	Responsive
	Partial	Comprehensive

property management. The problem with leaving the subject at the legal and social level of analysis is seen to lie in the tendency it has to put the estate in what is referred to as in a state of 'hypostatis'. In a state, that is, where the estate becomes inert to the developments in its environment and unresponsive to the underlying pressure the market places upon it to change. As a consequence, management under this set of circumstances is seen to be reactive to the demands the market places upon it and tactical in any measures it takes to tackle problems in the legal and social structure of tenure.

In contrast to this and in being seen to take on a more comprehensive form, property management, rather than seeing such pressures as external, attempts to embody such developments and use the dynamics of the market place to become pro-active and responsive to demands for change. The value of having such qualities is seen to lie in the fact that together they allow property management to transcend the static estate forming the legal and social structure of tenure and work with the market to develop a corporate, financial and commercial strategy able to tackle the pressing problem of running cost control. For Britton, Connellan and Crofts (1989) such qualities are seen to be critical because without them it would not be possible to transcend the limitations of the legal and social structure of tenure underlying (and giving rise to) the static estate, or develop the corporate strategy financial instruments or commercial standards required to achieve this. As critical components in the movement towards the 3 E's in property management, such qualities are seen to be indispensable as without them there would not be a corporate, financial or commercial strategy capable of solving the problem of running cost control.

In assessing the response to the call for the development of a strategic approach to property management, the authors point out that professional experts in this field see the options available to them in the following terms:

- do nothing;
- further encourage the breakdown of departmentalism;
- set up new organisational structures to assist the breakdown of departmentalism;
- adopt the principle of a pro-active management of property and view of it as a dynamic resource;
- prepare a corporate statement on property management;
- create a central - preferably computer-based information system for the management of property;
- adopt appropriate accounting procedures;
- audit and review property holdings;
- introduce asset rents as a capital charge for the use of property;
- set up property trading accounts.

If we discount the 'do nothing' option, the list highlights the need to set up new organisational structures capable of breaking down departmentalism, bringing about pro-active management and having the ability to see property as a dynamic resource. A situation the authors are of the opinion will be brought about by the modernisation of property management along the lines of proper registration, audits, review and valuation for the calculation of asset rents and capital charges - not to mention commercial trading of assets. In taking this form, it is evident the discussion has much in common with the initiatives underlying VFM in terms of a search for accountability through audit, review and drive towards economy. Perhaps the critical point of difference in this instance, however, lies in the less partial and more comprehensive nature of the audit and review. The fact, that is, the exercise is not limited to a audit and review of holdings i.e. stocks, but takes on a form which includes the flow of services. In other words: takes on the form of an exercise that searches for not just economy in the management of the standing stock but economy, efficiency and effectiveness in both the income payments and cost outgoings which underlie the stock of holdings and flow of services. Perhaps of even greater significance is the fact that they see this as something which requires proper registration, audit, review and valuation. If, that is, the transition from VFM to the 3 E's is to develop a strategy better equipped to provide a comprehensive, 'quality-minded' management of property held by local authorities.

Strategic management

The discussion of what is referred to as, 'strategic management' seeks to examine what the Institute of Directors (IOD, 1991) refer to as: 'the coming of age for property management; the development of property as a matter of strategic concern to management at the "boardroom" level of chief executives and directorates'. How this has taken place is illustrated in Figure 2.1.

Figure 2.1 illustrates the relationship between the VFM test and movement towards the 3 E's. As such the figure can be read as a set of relationships which for the purpose of explanation break down into three inter-related columns. Read vertically (from bottom to top) the first column shows the VFM test as providing the basis to resolve the issues surrounding the breakdown of the landlord-tenant structure of tenure and subsequent view of property holdings as a static estate i.e. stock of goods not requiring any management expertise - the situation which in this instance has given rise to the problem of running cost control. Under the VFM test, Figure 2.1 shows such problems have led to the application of land audits and property reviews as a form of rationalisation that is seen to be 'enterprising' because of the way in which it exposes the stock of holdings to the workings of competitive environments and in doing so focuses attention on the dynamics of the income production and cost reduction measures available to marketise the management of property (as a stock of goods and flow of services).

As the illustration shows, the shift of attention away from the statics of stocks and towards the dynamics of stocks and flows, has forced organisations to consider the problem of running cost control much more seriously, so much so that the recognition of the problem is seen to have forced a re-organisation of property on the basis of the strategic management represented in the illustration as a movement towards the development of central units, registers, asset valuation and performance measurement. Turning attention to the third column, it is possible to see the structure of modern property management as placing particular emphasis upon what is termed strategic management, with corporate

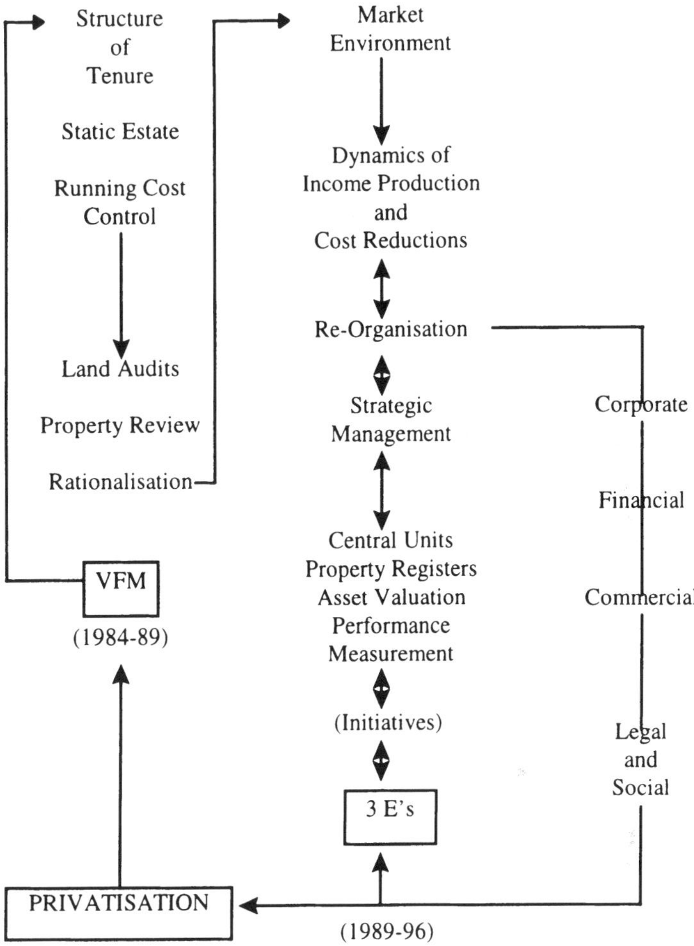

Figure 2.1 Towards Strategic Management

concerns over the setting up of central units, financial considerations about registers, valuation and the commercial standards of performance measurement.

Table 2.2 goes on to represent the three dimensions to the response in terms of the theory, method and practical considerations of strategic management. This illustration can also be read vertically as a set of columns, or horizontally as a number of rows. It seeks to link theory,

Table 2.2 The Three Dimensions

Theory	Method	Practice
Hypostatics	Stocks and Flows	Goods and Services
Dynamics	Competition	Exchange
Modelling	Abstraction	Institutionalisation
Markets	Decentralisation	Pricing
Monetarisation	Accountability	Unitisation
Economy	Efficiency	Technical
Management	Strategic	Allocative
Organisation	Centralisation	Corporate
IT	Information Systems	Communicative
Registration	Computerisation	Audit/Review
Valuation	Income & Cost	Financial
Performance	Measurement	Commercial
Privatisation	Legal & Social Reform	Client- Contractor Split

method and practice by showing the progression of the theory through the method of application to the practical setting.

Figure 2.2 while similar in content to Figure 1.1 differs in form. Figure 1.1 illustrated the logical sequence of events leading from the adoption of VFM. In contrast, Figure 2.2 illustrates two variants on the VFM theme; the 1984-89 carrying out audits, reviews and rationalisations and the post-89 movement from VFM to the strategic management of property and drive towards the 3 E's. It draws attention to the application of welfare economics in terms of income over cost, exchange, technical and economic efficiency, made effective through the strategic response taken by management and as set out in the rest of the illustration. Also in contrast to Figure 2.1, here attention is drawn to the corporate planning, financial budgeting and portfolio analysis forming the strategic considerations as opposed to the subject-based analysis or routine management. Figure 2.3 illustrates how others have approached the subject.

As can be seen, Figure 2.3 identifies the developments underlying the transition from estate to property management over the post-war era. As can also be seen, it characterises the problem property management has

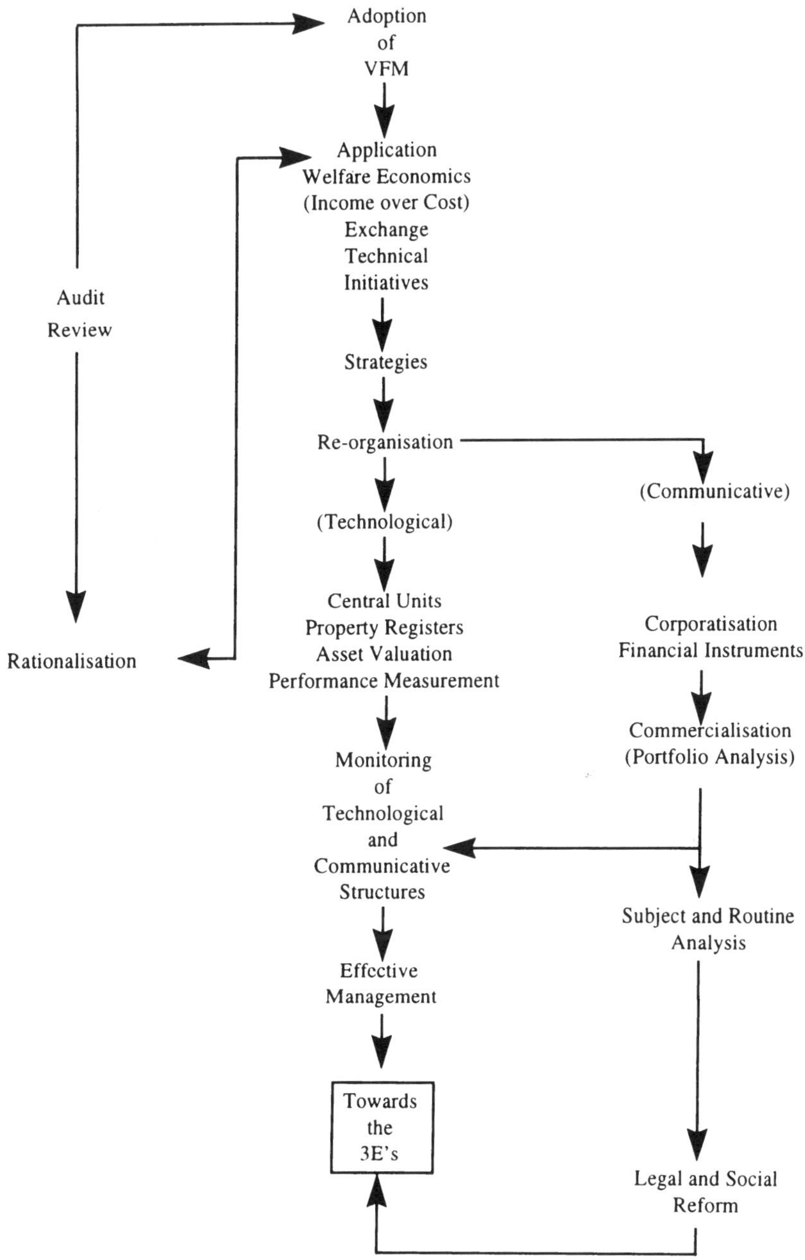

Figure 2.2 Programme of Activities

faced over the period in question as that of the 'static estate'. The static estate and the problems of running cost control, vacant , or under-used premises and mis-match of the demands placed on the management of property relative to supply. It also illustrates that since 1983/84, property management has sought to become pro-active in the management of holdings and develop a number of initiatives which provide a solution to the problems of the static estate. The solution in question appears in the next heading under the title of 'towards a strategic response'. Hence what the diagram draws attention to is the initiatives forming the content of strategies A, B and C listed towards the right-hand side of the illustration.

The initiatives are those responses which attempt to treat property as a dynamic resource, requiring pro-active management. They include: for example; the adoption of VFM as standards of accountability, land audits, property reviews, surveys, measurements and appraisals, the application of information technology, formation of organisational structures and other such measures geared towards the improvement of property management. Strategies A, B and C relate to the strategic responses taken to try and incorporate such standards into the management of property. Here the emphasis is not so much to do with the type of initiative and all its particular requirements (manpower, technical expertise, organisational skills, expenditure, etc) but on where it fits into the overall structure of property management. Where, if you like, VFM, accountability, audit, review, surveys, measurement and appraisals fit into a strategy towards the 3E's. As such, the question is not about what technical merits the initiative offers, but the cost of it and what value it will add to the management of property defined in economic, efficient and effective terms.

In this instance, Strategy A is that part of the response put forward by Britton, Connellan and Crofts (1989) in their examination of property management in the public sector, Strategy B is Avis, Gibson and Watts' (1989) examination of operational property asset management and Avis, Crosby, French and Gibson's (1993) study of property management in terms of performance monitoring. Hence, and as can be seen, the strategic response is one that examines the management of property in terms of operational and investment assets. Strategy C represents Avis and Gibson's (1995) more recent exploration of what they term real estate resource management. The heading Strategies 2, draws attention to the content of strategies A, B and C. In that sense, the strategies which have

Post-war problem	1983/84	1986	1989	1993	1995
	solution	towards a strategic response			
static estate	dynamics	initiatives	strategies 1		
			A	B	C
running cost control, vacant or under-used premises and mis-match of property	towards the proactive management of property holdings	value for money, accountability, land audit, property review, surveying, measurement and appraisal, application of information technology, organisation, income and cost related issues, current cost accounting, asset rents and capital charges as forms of income, consideration of outgoing payments	economic, efficient and effective management	management of operational property assets, performance monitoring of operational and investment property	real estate resource management
			strategies 2		
			corporatisation financial instruments commercial standards		
Estate	Property Management				

Figure 2.3 Developments Underlying the Transition

developed towards the corporatisation of property, development of financial instruments and commercial standards, put forward to solve the problem of running cost control (also, see Weatherhead, 1997).

The emerging consensus

The aforementioned reference to strategies A, B and C, tends to suggest there is some form of consensus emerging over the development of property management in local authorities. To some extent this is true. How true is perhaps the question that ought to be asked. Why? Because the consensus in question tends to be limited to the 'broad picture', not the detail of the development! This of course, begs the supplementary question, what is the emerging consensus? In brief terms, it is the thesis that VFM, land audits and property reviews, represent a rationalisation of property management in local authorities aimed at bringing the standards of services in the public sector into line with those of the private. The idea in particular that in becoming quality-minded, enterprising and competitive, property management in local authorities - the public sector in general for that matter - is compatible, if not equivalent, to that in the private. Compatible in the sense property management in the public sector is based upon the same set of values as those in the private: values such as competition , enterprise and the like and belief that the moneterisation of them in terms of pricing, cost calculations and income projections, will lead to greater economy, efficiency and effectiveness - all of which, it ought to be added, is seen to be a 'good' thing because it is understood to be in the public interest.

As already pointed out, this 'privatisation thesis' - ambiguous in itself - can be seen to represent the emerging consensus. If we look at the main components of property management in local authorities, the consensus on the matter can be seen to break down into disagreements over the detail. The main questions about property management in local authorities relate to:

- the purpose of local authorities under the transition;
- central property units;
- asset registers;
- property valuation;
- performance measurement.

Regarding the first question, few academics or professional experts appear to directly support the idea of privatisation and seek instead to emphasise the merits of VFM and the 3 E's as a form of review and rationalisation. One that is not only seen to re-organise the services the property management division of a local authority can provide in adopting such measures, but also reform the quality of the product on offer (see Britton, Connellan and Crofts, 1989; French, 1994). On the question of central property units, again there appears to be no objection to the principle of centralising the organisation of command and control functions in the property management divisions of local authorities and introducing innovative landlord and tenant-type structures to divide the management of property in such authorities along strategic and routine day-to-day lines. Again, if the said management division is to become the custodian or steward of property held by a local authority, there is no objection to the register acting as an inventory of holdings. Perhaps of greater significance are the questions that have recently been raised over:

- the technical basis, classes and categories of asset valuations;
- the lack of methodological advice;
- confusion over the distinction between costs in use and exchange;
- the distinctive nature of the cost and income approaches to the valuation of property;
- the reduction of property valuation to a financial analysis of annuities, notional interest and depreciation in current cost accounting, capital charging and asset rents;
- the use of such information as a basis to 'evaluate' the stock of assets, streams of services and subsequent rationalisation of holdings;
- the tendency for financial instruments of this type to discriminate - in terms of performance measurement - against cost-based holdings and favour income-producing property.

As can be seen, the questions arise out of the uncertainty and risk, or novelty of the exercise and can be read as a request for further clarification in terms of guidelines, recommended procedures etc. This is particularly noticeable with the first three questions. The subsequent questions are a little more difficult to deal with because they relate to confusion over the technical basis of asset valuations that is subsequently compounded due to resulting methodological problems. It is the question of method that has attracted most attention to date. It is seen to represent a problem of such a magnitude that Young (1994) goes so far as to ask why such an exercise has been embarked upon.

Young (1994) appears to be of the mind that the uncertainties and confusion surrounding the development of property management in local authorities are of such a magnitude they seriously bring into question the logic of the whole exercise. For Young (1994) the introduction of neo-liberal principles about the virtues of competition, enterprise and a greater degree of quantification in the allocation of resources appears to have little significance, neither does the fact such instruments allow decisions about the management of property to reflect the opportunity cost (scarcity and transfer earnings) of income payments, outgoings, capital and interest. If this can be taken to represent the underlying purpose of the exercise, i.e. the introduction of market competition and enterprise in the moneterisation of values (vis-à-vis quantification) then the question which follows is - how is it to be done? How, in other words, is it possible to circumvent the questions raised about the transition to the 3 E's in the development of local authority property management. If we are to answer this we have first of all to recognise it is not an easy undertaking because there are no immediate solutions to the problems in question. Secondly, it has to also be recognised that while the problems appear methodological i.e. about what method to adopt in proceeding to search for such a form of property management, this is only part of the story, for the questions which arise have as much to do with theory as method - the theory of property valuation in particular.

The theory of property valuation

At present, the theory of property valuation is divided along the pro-income line of Baum and Mackmin (1989), Brown (1991), Baum and Crosby (1996) and that of cost (see, Britton, Connellan and Crofts, 1989). The former has its origins in the Fisher inspired thesis of 'income over cost' as a rate of return, while the latter shares Marshall's concern over opportunity cost, scarcity and transfer earnings in the distribution of income as a reward for the 'productivity of capital'. Another initial distinction lies in the tendency for the advocates of the neo-Austrian (pro-Fisher) school of economic thought to adopt a classical notion of liberty under the law of exchange, trade and commerce. While the pro-

Marshallists, like the Cambridge School in general, are sceptical about the theory of an equilibrium under perfect competition and choose instead to focus attention on the imperfect nature of markets as allocative mechanisms. The point in question being represented as the inability of the market to provide public, community or merit goods and services and subsequent need for legal and social reforms if the mechanism is to be economic, efficient and equitable (see, Blaug 1992). The distinction drawn between the two schools of thought is significant because the politics of the modern welfare state tends to divide the valuation of property along progressive and conservative lines.

Progressive and conservative divisions

Under the progressive legal and social reforms of the modern welfare state, the government is required to follow Keynesian doctrine on employment, money and interest so as to manage economic growth through fiscal means. The fiscal means required to fund public expenditure, supplement the market with statutory instruments allowing the regulation of property rights, planning of development, control of land use and provision of public, community, merit goods and services - be it in the direct or subsidised form. The fiscal means - taxation in particular - regulation, planning, control and provision of goods and services also required to re-distribute income in the aim of producing a level of demand sufficient to generate full employment, rising standards of living, the Pareto-optima efficiency criteria and equity condition of Rawlsian social justice. The aims, criteria and conditions that legitimates the management of economic growth, fiscal means, statutory powers and planning underlying the redistribution of income, legal and social reforms of the modern welfare state.

It is a form of management the conservative elements of the neo-Austrian school object to. This is because the Keynesian doctrine of demand management is seen to undermine liberty and freedom and in so doing, replacing the law of consumer sovereignty governing economic growth, employment, money and interest, with the politics of administration. An administrative form of reason seen by the school to represent the antithesis of competition and enterprise due to the 'fact' that its fiscal means for funding public expenditure not only substitutes the freedom of the market with regulation, planning and control, but perhaps more significantly redistributes income (via the various legal and social reforms of the welfare state) in a way which leads to the growth of bureaucracies whose 'extra-market' instruments, regulation, planning and control, turns the demand management of Keynesian doctrine into the cost-push inflation of employment, money and interest. A situation that, for them (and many others for that matter) is seen to mark the end of the pro-growth model of the redistributive welfare state, onset of stagflation, decline in employment and rise in the monetary and interest charges which makes public expenditure on legal and social reform too costly a measure. Not only in the sense of the tax burden required to fund any such measures, but also due to the cost (relative to income) of supplying labour, capital and land in the production of goods and services. Costs seen to be so high as to make the employment of labour, capital and land in the production of goods and services uneconomic and so challenge the pro-growth redistributive logic of legal and social reform under the welfare state.

Legitimation crisis

It is the situation Habermas (1976) refers to as the 'legitimation crisis' of the welfare state. The situation whereby the Keynesian doctrine of demand management results in costs of production which are uneconomic and inefficient in terms of the distribution of income its legal and social reforms produce for employment and the standard of living. For in its advanced stage of development, the welfare state is unable to meet either of these aims, or draw upon sufficient mass support to legitimate any new fiscal measures. Indeed, it is a situation that is seen to expose what Offe (1984) describes as the contradictions of the welfare state and shift to a more conservative administration. One that substitutes 'cost-push' for 'demand pull', monetarist for Keynesian doctrine and reinstates the law of consumer sovereignty in the shift from 'state to market' via privatisation - the so-called deregulation, opening up and liberalisation of property rights in accordance with market competition and enterprise.

It is a situation Bell (1973) refers to as 'post-industrialisation' and others for example, Giddens (1990), Lash and Urry (1987, 1993) and Jessop (1993) term the crisis of Fordist mass production under the Keynesian welfare state. The crisis Lash and Urry (1987, 1993) and Jessop (1993) refer to not only in legal and social, but economic terms and see as representing the transition to post-Fordism and the neo-Schumpeterian workfare state (see Jessop, 1993 in particular). The transition that incorporates and overseas the dismantling of the welfare state, disengagement of government from the management of economic growth, deregulation of markets, fostering of competition and enterprise, removal of fiscal measures, loosening of planning and development, redistribution of the tax burden, control of money supply and interest rates via tight public expenditure. Whether this shift has taken place under Thatcher or Reagan, the new discursive reality traversing the state can be described as a pervasive 'managerialisation' discourse, which aims to make marketisation the driving force of an enterprising and competitively successful public sector. It is clearly linked to the proliferation of managerial panaceas issuing from the USA during the 1980s, claiming to offer genuinely novel 'business' solutions to the problems accumulating from the need to adapt organisationally to rapidly changing and confusing market conditions.

The new managerialism and market reasoning

The most profound accomplishment of this discourse may not be that it literally rolls back the state in order to release the full blast of market forces but, rather, that it inserts a new managerialism and market reasoning into the state and state-related agencies of the public sector, in effect calling upon organisations that are not themselves private businesses to think and function as though they were. The effect of these powerful and normalising discourses is to make it virtually impossible to think outside of them. This may be illustrated by a book which, in the early 1990s became a major codification for new managerialist theory and practice in the public sector on both sides of the Atlantic, Osborne and Gaebler's (1992) *Reinventing Government.* Drawing on the ideas of management gurus such as Drucker and Peters, their managerial principles are drawn from practical experiments conducted by US city governments in response to the 'tax revolts' of the late 1970s and more broadly, the structural transformations brought about by the transition to post-Fordism. Under tight budgetary constraints and faced with radically transformed economic circumstances, it is proposed that governments have to become much more 'enterprising' then they had been during the 'bureaucratic-industrial' era. The 'principles' of the theory Osborne and Gaebler (1992: 19-20) put forward for good management are as follows:

> Most entrepreneurial governments promote competition between service providers. They empower citizens by pushing control out of the bureaucracy, into the community. They measure the performance of their agencies, focusing not on inputs but on outcomes. They are driven by their goals - their missions - not by their rules and regulations. They redefine their clients as customers and offer them choices - between schools, between training programs, between housing options. They prevent problems before they emerge, rather than simply offering services afterwards. They put their energies into earning money, not simply spending it. They decentralise authority, embracing participatory management. They prefer market mechanisms. And they focus not simply on providing public services, but on catalysing all sectors - public, private and voluntary - into action to solve their community's problems.

Although Osborne and Gaebler deny asking for government to be 'run like a business', their ideas undoubtedly originate from the ideas about corporatisation being adopted by city governments and the local authorities they represent.

The discursive moment in the UK and USA

It is a 'discursive moment' that McGuigan (1996) describes as a shift towards the philosophy of 'VFM' and the '3E's' under post-Fordism and the movement towards a neo-Schumptereian workfare state, characterised by an increasingly pervasive market reasoning and managerialist rhetoric from the late 1970s to the present and foreseeable future. The UK examples of this have already been set out and appear in the form of Butt and Palmer (1985); Britton, Connellan and Crofts (1989); Avis, Gibson and Watts (1989) and Weatherhead's (1997) research. The US position has not yet been set out and while influential in the research of Avis, Gibson and Watts (1989); Avis and Gibson (1995) and Weatherhead (1997) is worth examining for the fact its case studies include Ford's own response to the crisis in question. The research in question includes that of Veale (1988), Joroff, Lovargand, Lambert and Franklin (1993). The standard textbook representation is provided by Brown and Arnold (1993).

In the case of the USA, the emphasis is not so much on the transition from estate to property management, as the corporate real estate and initiatives making up what is termed the 'strategic management of the fifth resource'. As Joroff, Lovargand, Lambert and Franklin (1993) point out, in the early 1980s corporate managers, consultants and researchers set to work in transforming four major resources - capital, manpower, technology and information. Until now however, real estate has not figured in this transformation. What they suggest is that real estate represents the corporation's last under-managed resource. These conclusions are drawn from surveys undertaken in 1981 and 87 respectively. Now it is argued, leaders in the field of corporate real estate, recognise this under-development of the subject and are participating in the search for a strategic management of the fifth resource. The reasons put forward for this are as follows:

- mergers;
- outsourcing;
- divesture;
- downsizing.

Taken together these changes are seen to signal a deep and thorough economic re-organisation. An economic re-organisation so deep and thorough, it is argued that if corporations are to remain profitable, they must change from the mass production of the past and become more competitive - through cost cutting, rationalisations (mergers, divestiture, downsizing, outsourcing) - and enterprising in 'tailoring' appropriate responses to the developments in question.

Here the 'tailoring' of the appropriate response is taken to represent the development of corporate real estate management in general and the corporate management of real estate as the fifth strategic resource in particular. In essence, the research identifies two dimensions to the development; the first being the design and organisation of real estate units; the second being the financial management of the resource as a form of corporate strategy. Both these dimensions are then underpinned by an examination of how IT automates real estate and acts as both the informational and communicative structure for its corporate management. The research identifies five stages to the evolutionary development of corporate real estate units, they are as follows:-

- taskmaster - supplies the corporation's need for physical space as requested;
- controller - satisfies senior management's need to better understand and minimise real estate costs;
- dealmaker - solves real estate problems in ways that create financial value for the business units;
- intrapreneur - operates like an internal real estate company, proposing real estate alternatives to the business units that match those of the firm's competitors;
- strategist - anticipates business trends, monitors and measures their impacts; contributes to the value of the corporation as a whole by focusing on the company's mission rather than focusing only on real estate.

Putting these tasks into the evolutionary development of corporate real estate management, Joroff, Lovargand, Lambert and Franklin's (1993) represent the engineering approach of the 'taskmaster' as the traditional role of the real estate manager - the skills and expertise that correspond to the 'static estate' in the UK example. The 'cost minimiser / controller' is also taken to represent the response of real estate managers to decline. It is the 'deal-maker' stage that is taken to represent the start up of real estate corporate management and its subsequent growth and maturity under the 'intrapreneur' and 'strategist' stages. As illustrated in Table 2.3, it is at this 'deal-maker' stage that VFM and the 3E's appear in the transition from the traditional to contemporary situation and where real estate becomes the corporate management of the fifth strategic resource. Table 2.3 also introduces the financial dimension to corporate estate management in the form of the fourth and fifth columns relating to both capital costs and pricing.

Learning from Ford's re-engineering

While the research by Joroff, Lovargand, Lambert and Franklin's (1993) is based on case-studies drawn from Kodak, IBM, Hewlett Packard, Kraft and Sun Microsystems - effectively from corporations across the whole industrial structure - Ford is put forward to exemplify how, under this

Table 2.3 Development of Corporate Real Estate

Initiatives/ Strategies	Decision Criteria	Products	Capital Cost	Pricing	Evolutionary Stage
Engineering Approach (Taskmaster)	Business unit wants	Taj Mahals and palaces *RE costs out of control*	Absorbed as corporate costs	Accounting for cost	Tradition (Static Estate)
Cost Minimisation (Controller)	Traditional control standards	Low cost palaces *Cost savings but no competitive standards*	Business units pay depreciation	Cost Accounting	Decline (Cost Control)
Market Cost and Usage Standards (Dealmaker)	Market economics drive RE decisions	Spec building quality *Lower costs and competitive standards*	Business units may pay opportunity cost of capital	Value Adding	Start up (Value for Money)
Market Design Approach (Intrapreneur)	RE unit makes decisions like a RE company	Spec building design standards leveraging needs with the market *Savings and profits*	Business units pay market rent	Real estate market pricing	Growth (Economy)
Business Strategy Approach (Strategist)	Business strategy drives R E decisions	Innovative buildings and location strategies *Savings, profits and strategic advantage*	Business units must justify market rents	Capital market pricing	Maturity (Efficient and Effective Management of a Portfolio)

organisation's corporate management, real estate becomes the fifth strategic resource. This is illustrated by the following quote:

> Ford Motor Land Development Corp. is an unusual kind of real estate organisation. Created in 1970 to develop some 2,300 acres of land in Dearborn, Mich., the unit spent the first 17 years of its life as a real estate developer operating with the benefit of its alliance with a major tenant, Ford Motor Company.
> [Task master / Controller]
>
> In 1987 it began to accept responsibility for corporate real estate services for Ford Motor Co on a world-wide basis and for the development of dealership properties. The gradual transformation from real estate developer to real estate services group was recently completed by its acceptance of European real estate operations and world-wide construction responsibility. These two steps completed the merger of the development group with Ford's internal real estate services.
> [Deal Maker]
>
> Ford Land uses its development background to educate its business units on the real value of space. Bob Jackson, president and COO of Ford Land, says that some business units have begun to examine their occupancies and land holdings and ask Ford Land whether they can capture hidden value from their real estate, having seen the results in other areas of the company.
> [Intrapreneur]
>
> Ford Land is also sensitive to the issues raised at the level of the Intrapreneur. Ford's internal training centre long occupied a 1929 school building. Due to substantial increases in demand for training from Ford and supplier companies, the training unit sought new space. A greenfield development site was identified and planning was well underway when it became clear that a Ford-operated banquet facility posed an attractive alternative to new construction. In recent years alternative facilities opened in the area, including hotels and a private club. By deciding to shut down a profitable but redundant operation, the banquet facility, Ford Land demonstrates the value of accumulating ever more sophisticated real estate strategies.
> [Strategist]
>
> They tripled the training centre capacity at only a 30% increase in cost, and made the kind of decision that capital markets have come to expect more frequently. Ford had a profitable operation in the banquet facility

> but the returns to that capital will be substantially higher in the alternative use. This kind of efficiency should get rewarded in the share pricing mechanism.
>
> Ford's decision shows a portfolio approach to asset management. By looking at assets in combination, the team at Ford saw that conversion of the banquet facility to a training centre would have at least two positive synergistic effects. First, the hotel occupancy in the immediate vicinity would be enhanced, and second, the kitchen facilities at the adjacent club could be used to service the training centre, putting those resources to more efficient use. While using a portfolio approach and satisfying capital market demands, Ford also serviced the goal of cost minimisation.

It is this 'evolutionary shift', or re-engineering of Taylor's *Scientific Management* that is of interest to Lash and Urry (1987, 1994) and Urry (1995) in their examination of the shift towards much more 'reflexive' systems of producer services in the USA, Germany and Japan. Here attention is drawn to the high design, discursive skills and expertise (theoretical rather than practical knowledge) underlying the IT systems of the less vertical (hierarchical) more horizontal (flatter) communicative structures for the development of such 'small batch' (tailored) producer services. To producer services, whose response to the economic re-organisation has been to transcend both the static estate and need for cost-control by becoming more competitive and enterprising in developing the cultural dimension to corporate management. The cultural dimension to corporate management, which in adopting the financial instruments and IT of horizontal, more flatter communicative structures, is forced to face the risk and uncertainties that characterise the market.

As such, and as Lash and Urry (1987, 1994) and Urry (1995) point out, the developments in question are not just a response to economic re-organisation, but like McGuigan (1996) and Webster (1997) suggest, in promoting quality rather than quantity, enterprise and competition are also cultural phenomena and can only be understood as part of the discourse on the new scientific principles of corporate management (the so-called managerialist thesis) under post-Fordism and the neo-Schumpeterian workfare state (Jessop, 1993). Albeit, in this instance, the discourse on its application to corporate management and the development of real estate as the fifth strategic resource.

It is perhaps a little ironic that in the case of corporate real estate management, it should be Ford who provides the 'best' example of a response to the crisis of Fordism under the welfare state and in taking the form it does also provides a new model of corporate real estate management not only for the private sector, but for city governments as local authorities. The case study also goes a long way to demonstrate just how all pervasive the marketisation is. For as the example illustrates, it provides a new model of corporate real estate not only for the private sector, but the management of city governments as local authorities under the post-Fordist, neo-Schumpeterian workfare state.

Tailoring the UK response

If for the moment, it can be assumed that property may be substituted for real estate, it becomes evident that Gibson's (1986, 1991, 1994 and 1995) research (along with Avis, Gibson and Watts, 1989; Avis and Gibson, 1995) mirrors that currently taking place in the USA and represents an attempt to examine the relationship between IT, the corporate and financial dimensions to the management of property. As such it attempts to redress the imbalance, or asymmetric relationship that has previously existed between initiatives and strategy. In doing so, it centres attention on the role of initiatives in the development of corporate strategy and the financial dimensions of property management.

There can be little doubt that the research undertaken by Gibson, Avis, Gibson and Watts, opens up a number of possibilities for those with a particular interest in the development of property management in local authorities. It is valuable for the fact the research introduces the technical concerns over the informational basis of IT applications, the communicative structures of corporate strategy and the financial dimensions of property management. The programme of research can perhaps best be seen as a sign-post marking a significant development in the transition from estate to property management in local authorities. For what it does is switch attention away from the technical and economic concerns over the informational basis of IT applications for asset registers, property valuation, auditing, review and performance measurement (initiatives) to the culture of communication surrounding the corporate strategy and financial dimensions to the management of property in local authorities. It is this theme that Weatherhead (1997) also develops in her studies of corporate strategy and finance in IBM, BT, Marks and Spencer, Sainsbury's and Boots.

While significant and marking an important step forward, the research has to be put into context: firstly; there are some obvious difficulties over the 'Anglophonic' use of the terms real estate and property: secondly; the research tends to 'downplay' the technical and economic concerns about initiatives in the informational basis of communicative structures in favour of the cultural question surrounding the corporate strategy and financial instruments required for such purposes: thirdly; as a consequence, the management thesis tends to 'blur' any distinction between values in terms of the technical, economic and cultural composition of either the informational basis, communicative structures, corporate strategy, or financial instruments in question: fourthly; all the publications from this school of thought illustrate an ambivalence towards the public sector.

It is perhaps Hambleton (1990) and Cochrane (1993) who best draws attention to the significance of the new manageralist thesis in the sense that in attempting to 'turn professionals into managers', it produces a set of experts who are unaware, insensitive and poorly educated as to the forms of public service provision (also, see Lash and Urry, 1993; Urry, 1995). The fact that structures of provision i.e. the combination of initiatives and strategy can be pro-private and public, central-administrative, bureaucratic, decentralist-market, consumer-orientated, based on uniform, or plural values, elitist or popularist, is something that tends to be missed by advocates of the managerialist thesis. It is a set of possible responses and re-organisations Hambleton (1990) summarises as:

- the radical right strategy of cutting, reshaping public spending and promoting privatisation;
- the reform of public services as the management of strategies for improving responsiveness and meeting consumer's needs;
- reform of public services conceived of as a political strategy for empowering the consumer and citizen in order to strengthen democracy.

While Hambleton (1990) draws upon Hoggett's (1987, 1989) thesis on the crisis of the long-standing association between Taylorist-type organisations and Fordist-based mass production, the subsequent demise of a strong, centralist welfare-state and shift towards post-Fordism (see Stoker, 1990 and Cochrane, 1993), what is noticeable is the degree to which all three forms of response to the new 'high-tech, economic cum cultural paradigm' of 'information rich communication', focuses upon the question of strategy. In this sense the technology, economics and culture of the informational basis and communicative structures underlying the corporate strategies and financial instruments management adopt to reform public sector service provision by either radically cutting, improving responsiveness or strengthening of democracy (also, see Urry 1995; McGuigan, 1996 and Webster, 1997).

The influence of the first form can be traced back to Peters and Waterman (1982) and Osbourne and Gaebler (1992) in terms of the USA, with Butt and Palmer (1985) providing the UK examples. The emphasis here being on the cultural dimension to the development and in that sense the use of language, theory and method by management in the design and modelling of the corporate strategy and financial instruments required to either privatise, improve or democratise the provision of public services.

It is an issue Gibson (1991) reflects on in asking the question of who manages 'operational' property best? Interestingly, after noting the similarities between the two sectors, Gibson (1991) finds the operation of the corporate strategies and financial instruments make it difficult to establish whether one sector provides a greater degree of VFM or meets the 3 E's better than the other. It is a question Martindale (1995) has also asked in relation to 'investment' property. The difficulty with this form of investigation lies in the fact it tends to focus on general trends in structures of information and communication (in this case those underlying the development of property management in local authorities) rather than particular experiences. As a result, the research into the privatisation of property management has no reference point from which to measure the economies that surface as a consequence of drawing upon the technology in question or developing the required informational basis and communicative structures.

To date it appears there is no research within the new managerialist thesis, as exemplified by Avis, Gibson and Watts, which has attempted to look at the AC reports or activities of CIPFA as a means to improve the responsiveness to consumer needs. While this ethic appears to be that 'embedded' in the earlier research of Britton, Connellan and Crofts (1989), the report in question only serves to document the early stages of the transition from estate to property management in local authorities and is unable to establish the degree to which corporate strategy and financial instruments have combined with the initiatives in question to improve the quality of public services and become more responsive to consumer needs. In that sense make the services in question meet the VFM test and 3 E's assessment. It is a line of enquiry Deakin (1997 a,b) has sought to further by providing particular case-study examples of the response in question. By, in this instance, examining how the initiatives and strategies combine with the technology and economics of a pro-quality, enterprise-minded culture and decentralised market whose informational basis and communicative structure is competitive enough to resolve the running cost control problem underlying the VFM test and transition to the 3 E's in the management of property held by local authorities.

While it is noticeable the third issue Hambleton (1990) refers to is one that has attracted little, if any attention, it does go to highlight a further forgotten dimension of the new managerial thesis. The fact the issues underlying the development of property management in local authorities do not only concern the informational basis of communicative structures - be they to do with the technology, economics or culture of initiatives and strategies, but in representing the democratic rights of consumers in civil society, are also about the politics of public sector service provision (see Hambleton, 1993). Given it is probably going to be this political dimension that will surface in the ongoing re-organisation and reform of local government along the lines of questions about 'civic responsibility' and the empowerment of citizens as the consumers of public services, it is a matter the exponents of the thesis ought to perhaps 'build' more firmly into the corporate strategy and financial instruments drawn upon for the development of property management in local authorities.

It should perhaps also be noted that while there is an obvious Anglophonic dimension to the developments in question, little if anything is known about the situation in Europe. While some useful information on the evolving system of property management has been made available by Avis and Gibson (1995) and Adair and Downie (1996), at present this research does not extend the work of Joroff, Lovargand, Lambert and Franklin (1993) or the studies by Lash and Urry (1993) of Germany (even Japan for that matter). Consideration of the situation in Europe and the Pacific Rim require further investigation.

Some sign-posts

Although the task of giving due consideration to this much neglected dimension of property management in local authorities is not an easy one, a number of points can be drawn from the foregoing discussions:

- put into context, the developments in question represent a major challenge for local authorities and one that is particularly difficult for them to meet due to the fact the Taylorist form of organisation and bureaucratic management of technology, under Fordism and the welfare state, has (during the post-war development of the public sector in particular) tended to be routine, habit forming and centre upon the commercial transactions of buying and selling estates;
- the shift towards the development of initiatives and strategies represents a transition from estate to property management in local authorities;
- over the past eight years or so, most headway has been made in the development of initiatives to introduce IT in the registration of assets, valuation of property, audit, review and measurement of performance to meet the VFM test and establish the 3 E's;
- in contrast, there has been a noticeable absence of expertise available to assist in the cultural development of both the corporate strategy and financial instruments required to form the framework for such initiatives, tests and criteria;
- it is the financial instruments for the management of property that represent the most problematic issue, for while considerable progress has been made on the registration of property, unease exists over the relationship between the cost and income approaches to valuation (Marshall and Fisher respectively) due to the breakdown of post-war consensus over the technology and economics of the welfare state and inability of the discourse on enterprise and competition to provide either an informational basis or communicative structure which represents an acceptable alternative;
- at present the discourse centres around the financial instruments of valuation and distinction between exchange, use value and income foregone in terms of opportunity cost from the marketisation of property management;

- the notion of opportunity cost is being used to simulate the market in the public sector, generate cash flows, annuities and capital charges;
- the developments move the transition beyond land audits and property reviews and towards a form of strategic management that represents a deep and thorough re-organisation of property management in local authorities;
- these developments are not peculiar to the UK but are mirrored by the evolution of corporate real estate management in the USA. In both the UK and USA it is the marketisation of management as applied to property or real estate that is all pervasive and it is this development which is being made use of in the transition from the static estate and problem of running cost control;
- the irony of this lies in the fact it is the tailoring and re-engineering of Ford that is leading the way in the response to what is known as the crisis of Fordism under the welfare state, economic re-organisation and development of producer services forming part of the transition towards the corporate management of real estate/property as a strategic resource. The tailoring and re-engineering that is in many instances being used as a model for the deep and thorough re-organisation of real estate/property management in city governments and local authorities throughout the USA and UK;
- the development of the producer services in question mark a major discursive shift towards a more 'reflexive' understanding based on theoretical knowledge, systems design, modelling and testing (the building of meta-information data-bases and communicative structures as expert systems). It also breaks with the hierarchically divided bureaucracy of standardised public service provision in the post-war welfare state (dominated by planners, rather than surveyors) and introduces what are termed 'post-Fordist structures', with flatter, more horizontal arrangements, addressing the risk and uncertainties of enterprising, more competitive and decentred-market regimes for the management of property held by local authorities;
- while the developments can be seen as a response to the crisis of Fordism in the welfare state - in the form of the fiscal tightening, cut-back in public expenditure, search for VFM and 3 E's under 'zero-sum' budgets, the lack of data currently available on the transition makes it difficult to establish whether the initiatives and strategies underlying the emerging high-tech, economic cum cultural paradigm of the

information rich and communicative form of property management in local authorities, represents a drive towards privatisation, improvement in responsiveness, or movement towards a greater degree of democratisation.

This goes some way to set out the significance of seeing the development of property management in local authorities as a combination of initiatives and strategies. The issue is also significant for a further reason; for the fact that in dealing with the organisation of resources, it has become an even more salient aspect of property management in local authorities due in part to the environment of zero sum budgets, funding shortages, capital spending restrictions, standard spending assessments and service cut backs which accompany the re-organisation of local government. The emphasis here being not on the development of additional initiatives, but of strategies for radical cutbacks, improving responsiveness and democratisation of public sector service provision in the climate of tighter economic circumstances, efficiency drives and effectiveness tests. In contrast to the developments in the initiatives and strategies already referred to, this has to be seen as a matter that is of particular significance for the question of local government re-organisation and reform and represents a terrain which has not yet been mapped out.

References

Adair, A. and Downie, M. (1996), *European Valuation Practice: Theory and Technique*, Chapman and Hall, London.

Audit Commission. (1988a), *Local Authority Property - A Management Overview*, HMSO, London.

Audit Commission. (1988b), *Local Authority Property - A Management Handbook*, HMSO, London.

Audit Commission. (1988c), *Management Paper NO.7*, HMSO, London.

Avis, M., Gibson, V. and Watts, J. (1989), *Managing Operational Property Assets*, Department of Land Management, Reading University.

Avis, M. and Gibson, V. (1995), *Real Estate Resource Management*, DTI, London.

Baum, A. and Crosby, N. (1996), *Property Investment Appraisal*, Routledge, London.

Baum, A. and Mackmin, D. (1989), *The Income Approach to Property Valuation*, Routledge, London.

Bell, D. (1973), *The Coming of Post-Industrial Society,* Heinemann, London.

Blaug, M. (1992), *Economic Theory in Retrospect,* Cambridge University Press, Cambridge.

Britton, W., Connellan, O. and Crofts, M. (1989), *The Economic, Efficient and Effective Management of Public Sector Landed Estates,* Kingston University, Surrey County Council, Kingston-upon-Thames.

Brown, G. (1991), *Property Investment and the Capital Markets,* Chapman and Hall, London.

Brown, R. and Arnold, A. (1993), *Managing Corporate Real Estate,* John Wiley and Sons, New York.

Butt H, and Palmer, D. (1985), *Value for Money in the Public Sector,* Macmillan, London.

Chartered Institute of Public Finance and Accountancy (1989), *Capital Accounting in Local Authorities - The Way Forward,* CIPFA, London.

Chartered Institute of Public Finance and Accountancy (1991a), *CIPFA Statement - Capital Accounting in Local Authorities,* CIPFA, London.

Chartered Institute of Public Finance and Accountancy (1991b), *Asset Registers,* CIPFA, London.

Chartered Institute of Public Finance and Accountancy (1992), *Capital Accounting by Local Authorities - Report of the Implementation Studies,* CIPFA, London.

Cochrane, A. (1993), *Whatever Happended to Local Government?,* OU Press, Buckingham.

Deakin, M. (1997a), 'The development of computer-based information systems for local authority property management: the underlying issues', *Journal of Financial Management for Property and Construction,* vol 2 (1).

Deakin, M. (1997b), 'The development of computer-based information systems for local authority property management: the application', *Journal of Financial Management for Property and Construction,* vol 2 (2).

Elcock, H. (1988), *Local Government: Professionals and Practices,* Methuen, London.

Elcock, H. (1994), *Local Government: Policy and Management,* Routledge, London.

French, N. (1994), 'Asset registers and asset rents for local authorities : a viable property management tool', *Property Management,* vol 12 (3).

Gibson, V. (1986), 'A management view of valuation in information technology; *Journal of Valuation,* vol 5 (1) : 30-40.

Gibson ,V. (1991), ' Who can manage property best: the private or public sector?', *Property Management,* vol 9 (1).

Gibson, V. (1994), 'Strategic property management: how can local authorities develop a property strategy?', *Property Management,* vol 12 (3) : 9-15.

Gibson, V. and Carter, E. (1996), 'Is property on the strategic agenda?', *Chartered Surveyor Monthly,* January: 34-35.

Giddens, A. (1990), *The Consequences of Modernity,* Polity, Cambridge.

Habermas, J. (1976), *Legitimation Crisis*, Heinemann, London.

Hambleton, R. (1989), 'Urban government under Thatcher and Reagan', *Urban Affairs Quarterly*,vol 24 (3): 359-88.

Hambleton, R. (1993), 'Consumerism, decentralisation and local democracy', in Roberts, P. , Struthers, J. and Sacks, J. (eds) *Managing the Metropolis*, Avebury Press, Aldershot.

Hambleton, R., Hoggett, P. and Tolan, F. (1989), 'The decentralisation of public services: a research agenda', *Local Government Studies*, January/February: 39-56.

Hoggett, P. (1987), 'A farewell to mass production? decentralisation as an emergent private and public sector paradigm', in Hoggett, P. and Hambleton, R. (eds) *Decentralisation and Democracy: Localising Public Services*, School for Advanced Urban Studies, University of Bristol.

Hoggett, P. and Hambleton, R. (eds) (1987), *Decentralisation and Democracy: Localising Public Services*, School for Advanced Urban Studies, University of Bristol.

Institute of Directors. (1991), *Director's Guide to Property*, IOD, London.

Jessop, B. (1993), 'From the Keynesian welfare to the Schumpeterian workfare state', in Burrows R. and Loader, B. (eds) *Towards a Post-Fordist Welfare State*, Routledge, London.

Joroff, M., Lovargand, M., Lambert, S. and Franklin, B. (1993), *Strategic Management of the Fifth Resource: Corporate Real Estate,* (Industrial Development Research Council), Massechusetts Institute of Technology, Cambridge MA.

Lash, S. and Urry, J. (1987), *The End of Organized Capitalism*, Routledge, London.

Lash, S. and Urry, J. (1994), *Economics of Signs and Space*, Sage, London and New York.

Local Authority Valuers Association. (1989), *Effective Property Management through Review*, LAVA, London.

McGuigan, J. (1996), *Culture and the Public Sphere*, Routledge, London.

Martindale, N. (1995), 'Local authority property investment: a virtual reality', *Property Management*, vol 13 (1).

Offe, C. (1984), *Contradictions of the Welfare State,* Hutchinson, London.

Osborne, D. and Gaebler, T. (1992), *Reinventing Government - How the Entreprenurial Spirit is Transforming the Public Sector*, Addison-Wesley, Reading, Mass.

Society of Local Authority Chief Executives. (1986), *Our Heritage - Property Management in a Local Authority,* SOLACE, London.

Stoker, G. (1990), 'Regulation theory, local government and the transition from Fordism' in King, D. and Pierre, J. (eds), *Challenges to Local Government*, Sage, London.

Taylor, F. (1967), *The Principles of Scientific Management.* Norton Library, New York.

Veale, P. (1988), *Managing Corporate Real Estate Assets*, Massachusetts Institute of Technology, Cambridge MA.

Weatherhead, M. (1997), *Real Estate in Corporate Strategy*, Macmillan, London.

Webster, F. (1996), *Theories of the Information Society*, Routledge, London.

Young, P. (1994), 'Market valuation with no market', *Journal of Property Valuation and Investment*, vol 12 (3) : 9-27.

3 Local Authority Property: Asset Registers, Valuation and Property Audits

Nick French, Department of Land Management and Development, Reading University and Louise Hague, Estates Surveyor, Hampshire County Council

Introduction

In 1988 the Audit Commission for Local Authorities in England and Wales published their results of a study of local authority property management (Audit Commission, 1988a and 1988b). In that report, it was noted that the full extent of local authority property holdings was unknown. In many local authorities, not only was the value of the holdings unknown, but there was uncertainty over the actual extent of ownership within the council's portfolio. The Audit Commission reports therefore recommended that all local authorities should undertake a comprehensive review of their property holdings to form an asset register for each respective council.

Since that date, the majority of local authorities have established their own systems for the registration of assets and, to a lesser or greater extent, have undertaken a full valuation of all their property holdings. In most cases the valuations have been undertaken on a desktop basis in accordance with the regulations laid down by the Royal Institution of Chartered Surveyors - RICS (in consultation with the Chartered Institute of Public Finance and Accountancy - CIPFA) and as contained in the Statements of Asset Valuation Practice (Old Red Book) and the Manual of Valuation (Old White Book). Most authorities are now involved in a rolling programme of up dating these valuations formally in accordance with the new regulations contained in the RICS *Appraisal and Valuation Manual.*

Effective property management

Good management of all local authority owned property assets is of equal importance as the management of other resources within the council. For the effective, efficient and economic delivery of services, it is vital that all property holdings are utilised to the best advantage. This requires that the property provider and the property user are both fully conversant with the value of the property holding and that a rent/charge is made accordingly. The Audit Commission stated that 'good property management' is not an end in itself. It must clearly respond to the policies and objectives of the service areas. These, in turn, will relate to the policies of the council as a whole.

Good property management should also ensure that by identifying the value in use of an asset, it will be possible to determine if that property is being used effectively. Properties that are too large for their required use are inefficient, both in terms of annual running costs and, more importantly, in terms of the opportunity cost of capital for the areas which are not used to their full capacity. In addition, there may be further repercussion in other resource areas apart from the property itself: for example; an under-occupied school may still require a fixed number of teachers to deliver an acceptable balance of subjects under the national curriculum, resulting in a staff/pupil ratio lower than the council's standard. Similarly, the physical characteristics of a building might adversely affect the effective delivery of a particular service. For example, a library in a traditional 1930s building might not be suitable for the new demands placed on the service due to advances in information technology and a lower quality service might result.

The Audit Commission report found that, historically, local authorities have adopted a largely passive approach to property management which resulted in a concentration on service delivery whilst ignoring the resource implications. In short it was found that there is no strategic property management undertaken by the majority of local authorities. However, it is recognised that the role and function of local authorities is changing; partly as a natural evolution, but more in response to external economic and political pressures. Decreasing capital allocations from central government, changes in the population demographics, moves toward service delivery by non-traditional suppliers and local government re-organisation are just a few influences affecting all local authorities.

The asset register must therefore be viewed as a comprehensive information source which feeds into this process. A comprehensive asset register should be seen as the first step by local authorities in meeting the criteria of 'best practice' as part of an authority-wide property strategy. It is important to recognise that asset registers will be required to support any new form of capital accounting that might be introduced over the next few years. It is in this context that the role of asset registers, and asset rents, must be assessed. It should be stressed that whilst some of the external pressures might be peculiar to local authorities, many private companies in the United Kingdom are reviewing their property holdings in a similar way (Gibson and Watts, 1989; Avis et al, 1993 and Hillier Parker, 1993). In the last few years a number of large operational companies in the United Kingdom have chosen to segregate the management of their property holdings from the day-to-day running of their core business. This has either been achieved by forming property sections within the main company structure or in some cases the hierarchy has been more clearly defined by the formation of subsidiary companies feeding into the parent company. The operational arm would then pay the property subsidiary an open market rental for each property that they occupy. This is not dissimilar to the property review currently being undertaken by local authorities.

From a private sector viewpoint, the advantage of separating the property function from the core business is twofold. Firstly, it allows the performance of each operational outlet to be measured on the same basis; a rental would now be deducted as an operational cost on both freehold and leasehold properties. Secondly, the investment performance of the properties themselves can now be measured. Both of these are laudable objectives, but the measurement of performance is not as straight forward as the theory might suggest. The 1993, '*Property Management Performance Monitoring*' report by Oxford Brookes University and The University of Reading (Avis *et al*, 1993), highlighted the lack of information available to judge (benchmark) the performance of the property asset. A property investment might be used to assess the performance of the freehold asset, but there are very few benchmarks by which the performance of the operational use can be judged. Indeed, it concluded that there were many areas of operational property performance which are not capable of measurement in quantitative terms and an objective qualitative monitoring procedure would have to be developed.

Given that the nature of corporate property holdings in the private sector tends to be more homogeneous than an equivalent local authority portfolio, it would be reasonable to expect that the problems of performance measurement experienced by private corporations will apply equally, and possibly to a greater extent, to the more diverse and specialised holdings of local authorities. Indeed, the exercise of identifying criteria to be used to judge the performance of local authority property (in terms of the efficient use of the land and buildings) might be inappropriate in certain circumstances. In New Zealand the municipal authorities have already undertaken a similar exercise of identifying and valuing the local authority property portfolio, but have extended the requirement to include the determination of an annual 'financial return 'of each asset. This might seem to be a useful measure of performance as the annual return is a readily understood benchmark, however, how does one assess the financial return of an asset such as a park or conservation area? (Young, 1994). There is a great danger that pure financial measures are used inappropriately to judge the performance of 'social' assets. This is not to say that the asset register, and associated asset rent exercise should not be undertaken. It should, however, be carried out in the knowledge that it is not a panacea to effective property management. It must be seen as an integral part of an all encompassing property strategy which will addresses the issues of measurement and monitoring.

The asset register

The exact form of an asset register to be adopted by a local authority has not been prescribed and, as such, each authority has developed its own format in accordance with existing records held by that authority. However, the general principle is contained in the non-mandatory, guidance notes '*Asset Registers - a Practical Guide*' which have been published by (CIPFA). The guidance notes state:

> Asset Registers are records of all fixed assets whose value is material. Their function is to provide the information about assets needed for their financial management, operational management and servicing; and to support fixed assets as shown in the balance sheets. Asset registers thus include a wider range of information than computerised property records, and substantially more than the inventories kept primarily for assets of lower value.

There is no necessity for all the information to be held on a single register, although for many authorities this will be the most convenient and sensible approach. The lack of a defined mandatory approach on an authority wide basis, might allow a quicker implementation of the registers in the short term, but will ultimately result in a lack of compatibility of systems and approaches between authorities which could lead to substantial problems during the current local government re-organisation. Initial research (French, 1994) would suggest that very few local authorities are liaising with each other to try to ensure a consistency of approach.

An asset register is more than a simple agglomeration of existing information. Indeed one of the principal recommendations of the CIPFA Guide was that a asset registrar should be designated to oversee the process. CIPFA propose that the registrar should be responsible for the identification of assets and existing records; the assessment of the suitability of those records to the requirements of the asset register for that particular authority and, having determined the extent of available information, the registrar would then need to ensure that any additional data required is assessed and collated. The asset register needs to be sufficiently simple to allow effective interrogation (computerised or manual) yet sufficiently comprehensive to ensure that the register is capable of meeting demands placed on it by any future (unknown) capital accounting policy. It should therefore include:

- all property owned or occupied (with a note on tenure);
- infrastructure assets (highways, coast defences, monuments etc.);
- council housing and other local authority housing (e.g. service tenancies);
- specialised buildings (leisure properties, crematoria, abattoirs etc.);
- leased property and properties where authorities have user rights;
- buildings under construction.

In addition to the property assets, the register should also record other material assets such as mechanical plant, vehicles, equipment and (the catch-all of) other valuable capital assets.

The implementation of the asset register

As previously noted, there is a substantial disparity between the extent and nature of existing record systems in different authorities. Some authorities had the advantage of building upon previous property review registers, others have undertaken the review process for the first time. Where organisations have had to establish asset registers from a limited information base, the following steps have normally been adopted:

- identification and assessment of existing information sources: most local authorities have purpose designed records of their property holdings. The legal register of deeds; the terrier of property (written and map based) normally allocated according to holding committee; and the statutory register of surplus land (in accordance with the 1980, *Local Government, Planning and Land Act*);
- documentary research of records: to identify who owns what property; where are the boundaries of the holding (are they disputed ?); what is the legal position regarding tenure ?
- physical inspection of the assets: to assess the physical condition of the property; to determine the extent and nature of current usage; to collate all information required to undertake the capital valuation of the asset.

The CIPFA publication on '*Asset Registers*' suggests certain data sets which will be required for each site, each establishment, each building (including those under construction) and any ancillary equipment, plant or vehicles. This paper will not consider the detailed logistics of establishing and implementing an asset register. It is concerned with the valuation of the assets identified and the decapitalisation of the assessed capital value to an asset rent figure.

The valuation issues

In January 1993, CIPFA formally endorsed proposals for a new system of capital accounting by local authorities. It has expressed the wish for the new system to be introduced in the 1994/95 financial year. The current system of capital accounting is inconsistent in its treatment of fixed assets. The decision of how to treat a particular asset for accounting purposes is determined by the means by which the purchase or construction of that asset has been financed. This has resulted in arbitrary and inconsistent charges to service revenue accounts and thus it is impossible to make any reasonable or meaningful assessments as to the true 'cost' of providing services from particular property assets. Such a system is incompatible with the tenets of an effective property management strategy. It is therefore important that the new system of accounting for fixed assets provide a firm basis for comparable reporting of financial performance by local authorities. The aim is to promote better accountability for the use of scarce capital resources and the better management of the property portfolio.

The accounting basis for the new system will be current value (cost) on the basis of revaluations every five years. Current value is defined as the assets current value to the business in their existing form. The basis of the valuation in this case should reflect the underlying accountancy principle that the business will continue and will be profitable for the foreseeable future by continuing to use the (property) assets currently held for that purpose. The value of those assets is equivalent to the replacement cost of those assets in their existing state, the 'deprival value'. In practice this will be the replacement cost adjusted to reflect the condition of the existing asset. This is termed the 'net current replacement cost' (NCRC). In some circumstances the NCRC will exceed the 'recoverable amount', (the 'net realisable value' (NRV)) which in simple terms is the price at which the asset can be sold in the open market. This figure would reflect either the existing use or likely alternative use which ever produced the higher capital receipt. Accordingly, CIPFA's proposals simply require assets included in the balance sheet at current value to be included at the lower of NCRC and NRV.

Initially the valuations undertaken would have conformed with the non-mandatory requirements of the old White Book, VGN 8A and B which were intended to provide guidance to 'valuers who are instructed to prepare valuations of fixed assets held by local authorities'. However, as of the 1st January 1996, the revised and updated RICS *Manual of Appraisal and Valuation* came into effect and all valuations since that date should have been carried out in accordance with those provisions, unless the valuer determined a specific reason why the Red Book should not apply. The principle aims of the new manual are stated to be:

> to encourage initial understanding of client needs and establish whether the professional advisor is competent to meet them; to promote consistent use of bases and assumptions on which valuations are provided; to help valuers to achieve high standards of professional competence; to promote the provision of comprehensible valuation reports; and to ensure published references to valuations are clear, accurate and informative.

Although many local authority valuers have argued that the Red Book does not apply to them due to the Section One exception:

> valuations by internal valuers solely for internal use by their organisations i.e. where no part of the Report, any information therefrom

> and/or the valuation figure is to be seen by or communicated to any third party.

This, in the opinion of the RICS, is a dangerous policy. All local authority information can come into the public domain and thus on that basis alone it will be prudent to follow the provisions of the Red Book. Similarly, with the internal division of 'service provider' and 'client departments', it becomes increasingly difficult to determine what counts as 'internal use' and what is being provided to 'any third party'.

The manual is not principally concerned with valuation theory or methods but with the mechanics of practice including the assembly, interpretation and reporting of information relevant to the task of valuation. The manual contains 22 Practice Statements with 14 appendices and a further 18 Guidance Notes with 4 appendices. The first 7 Practice Statements will be essential reading for all valuers and establish the relationship between the valuer and the client. The remainder deal with valuations for specific purposes.

Bases of valuation

Practice Statement No 4 defines 10 bases of valuation with a further 4 in respect of plant and machinery. Those most relevant to local authority valuations are as follows:

- market value;
- open market value;
- existing use value;
- depreciated replacement cost;
- open market rental value;
- open market value.

The majority of the bases of valuation are not new. However, where a new definition has been introduced (Market Value), the sister definition of Open Market Value has also been modified slightly.

Market value is defined as:

> the estimated amount for which an asset should exchange at the date of valuation between a willing buyer and a willing seller in an arms length transaction after proper marketing wherein the parties had each acted knowledgeably, prudently and without compulsion.

Problems with the choice of valuation base

One of the principal concerns when undertaking a valuation of a local authority asset is the appropriate basis. In many cases, there is a clear indication of the basis to be adopted, however in others the distinction is not so precise and different valuers might adopt different bases accordingly. This problem is exacerbated when the valuation is a mass appraisal exercise restricted to desktop analysis (a logistical necessity due to the resource and time constraints placed on many authorities when undertaking the initial property audit). In such cases, the distinction between the value of the asset in use (normally carried out on a DRC basis) and the value of the asset in exchange (carried out on a MV and OMV basis) can be quite extreme (DRC normally being significantly higher the OMV). Whilst the DRC figure can be justified in valuation terms, if an asset is revalued in the register from a MV basis to DRC basis, the asset charge resulting being fixed (normally 6 percent of capital value) will also change significantly. As the client department will then have a much larger charge placed against the use of a particular asset they will question the uplift.

Properties will either be classified as operational or non-operational assets. Operational assets are those held and used (or occupied) for the direct delivery of services by the authority itself (e.g. schools, libraries, council offices, etc.). Non-operational property would include assets held by the authority but not currently utilised by them (e.g. development land, leased property and surplus property). Within these two broad classifications a further criterion, specialised and non-specialised property, will apply. Specialized properties, as the name suggests, are properties for which there is no recognized market. Non-specialized properties are those for which there is a general demand and thus would sell in their existing, alternative or modified use, on the open market.

Requirements in respect of operational property

The purpose of valuations of operational properties is to record the current value of the asset to the authority in its provision of services. This is equivalent to the accounting basis of NCRC noted above; in short the valuer is asked to determine the cost of replacing the asset if the authority was deprived of that asset today. The value will therefore be OMVEU in the case of properties which can be readily acquired on the market (i.e. non-specialized properties) or DRC in the case of property types for which there is no recognized market (i.e. specialized properties). Where assets are specialized DRC is the most frequently used basis.

Requirements in respect of non-operational property

In the case of properties which are held for non-operational purposes (e.g. investment properties, development land banks, and land surplus to requirements), the basis is uniform; it is open-market value. However, in considering the valuation, the valuer must have regard to realistic alternative uses. Having taken this into account, the value will reflect the most probable selling price if the property was available for purchase on the open market today.

Although the valuer will be responsible for the valuations provided, it is the chief financial officer (CFO) who is the 'client' in the valuation process. Full information should be provided to the 'client' in the form of:

- the date of the last valuation (properties are to be revalued at least every five years, or when a change (or cessation) of use/occupation occurs);
- the basis of valuation;
- an explanation of the programme of revaluations where appropriate;
- the date of valuation, the valuer and his/her qualifications.

From this information, the local authority will be able to determine the appropriate asset rent for each property. Apart from the advantages of allowing greater strategic property management by revealing the occupational cost to the client occupier by way of the asset rent, the determination of capital values for all assets allows the authority to monitor the opportunity cost of providing services from particular properties. This might lead to a rationalization of holdings, where the disposal value outweighs the current utility value.

Such assertions must be viewed with a cautionary note, as not all uses can, or should be, valued in financial terms. The legacy of the 1980s is a belief that everything has a financial value and that assets with an inherent social value have a price. This may be good property management in a (private) profit-making organization, but is such a rigid approach appropriate to all public services?

Charging internal asset rents

This is not to say that lessons cannot, and should not, be learned from the private sector. As noted previously, there is an increasing trend for private corporations to disengage their operational property requirements from the property ownership rate. Recent research has shown that many corporations have split the function between an internal landlord and internal tenant, the latter paying an internal asset rent to the former (see Hillier Parker, 1993). In this sector, although there is a plethora of different (quasi) legal agreements, the general principle is that the internal rent should be equivalent to the open market rental value in a normal at-arms-length transaction. The benefits of such a system are:

- the encouragement of a more cost-effective use of property. It stops property being regarded as a free resource, encourages better property practices and helps to identify surplus property for disposal;
- the facilitation of performance measurement of service departments as each user is made aware of the direct cost of their occupation, thus highlighting any inefficiencies;
- the identification of property occupancy costs as a constituent part of the total cost of production/service provision;
- the facilitation of general budgeting and financial planning by highlighting the opportunity cost of occupation.

All these advantages can apply equally to local authority property, subject to the caveat of ensuring that the performance measurement benchmarks are not exclusively financial. The private sector has recognized the need to judge operational use by more qualitative methods;

the public sector must ensure that similar appropriate benchmarks are also developed for their use.

In connection with this matter, the CIPFA has established the following principles:

- service revenue accounts should be charged with a capital charge or asset rent for all fixed assets used in the provision of the service;
- as a minimum such charges should equal the annual provision for depreciation, where appropriate, plus a capital financing charge determined by applying a nominal rate of interest to the amount at which the asset is included in the balance sheet.

Recent discussions with a cross-sectional sample of local authorities would suggest that there is no consensus on the appropriate 'nominal' rate to apply to decapitalize the asset value. Current guidance would suggest that each local authority has discretion in choosing its own rate, and while this would then be applied consistently across that particular authority's portfolio, a neighbouring authority (which potentially could merge with the first authority at reorganization) could use a totally different percentage. Again, this highlights the importance of authorities working together in an attempt to standardize methods.

Despite the possible lack of consistency between authorities, the determination of asset rents by such a decapitalization model makes sense in the case of specialized property. However, in the case of non-specialized properties, market rentals would be available. It therefore seems obtuse to introduce a hypothetical rental calculation for such properties. Surely, the opportunity cost of their occupation should be based on the true rent in the market? However, the principle in terms of property management is useful and it must be recognized that the whole implementation process of asset registers and rental determination is under constant review. Any incongruities or anomalies should be addressed as part of this monitoring process.

Asset rents as a management tool

As of the 1994/95 financial year, client departments will be charged an asset rent for all the properties which they occupy. Initially, the budget debit that will appear in their service revenue account will be matched by an identical credit (rental subsidy) as a 100 per cent contribution towards the rental payment. Thus the true financial impact of asset rents will not be immediately apparent. It will be a paper transaction. The hope is, however, that the process of supplying this information will concentrate the mind of the service department on the actual cost of its current occupancy. In cases where authorities have been using this technique prior to the 1994/95 requirement, it has been possible to use the asset rental procedure as part of an incentive-driven rationalization process within the authority. User committees are charged a rent for all property; if they surrender part of their holdings they are allowed to use the rent 'saved' for other purposes. Of course any system of incentives which focuses on recycling (capital or) rent can only encourage the full use of property where the asset rent saved is sufficiently high to stimulate the redistribution of resources. Low asset rents will have less significant impact unless the corresponding running cost figure is excessively high. This would argue for a high percentage to be adopted as the decapitalization factor. One of the problems of such an incentive-driven management system is that, ultimately, it can be seen to reward those service providers which have been least efficient in the past.

An alternative, and more proactive use of the asset rental system would be gradually to reduce the rental subsidy on properties which the property department has identified as being under-utilized. This would then force the service provider to consider appropriate and more cost-effective means of providing a property. This form of audit is not formally being proposed at this stage, the logical outcome of the process is that end users should be charged for the properties that they occupy, and it is for them to examine their specific space requirements critically. This could be done by giving up part of the under-used space and remaining in a rationalized smaller area, or they could vacate the property completely and move to new premises. Ultimately, this could include taking a lease of a non-council building. The introduction of this possibility reinforces the assertion that asset rents should, as far as possible, mirror true rents in the market on similar lease terms. It is paramount that, when assessing internal asset rents, they (where appropriate) reflect market rent reviews, market covenants and normal division of repairing liabilities. If they do not it could make non-council property (in the case of non-specialized property) appear disproportionately under or over-priced. It should be remembered that the way in which asset rents are used as a property management tool will vary according to the political agenda and local requirements. It is important that the role of property as part of the service provision is not divorced from the overall strategy of the particular local authority.

Conclusion

This paper has brought together some of the principal elements which are affecting the implementation of an asset register, together with the associated determination of asset rents. In the new world of compulsory competitive tendering, this presents private practice (and competing local authorities) with a unique opportunity to contribute to the valuation of all local authority property holdings. More importantly, the new capital accounting procedures to be adopted by local authorities require a more proactive involvement of the property management professional; again this is an opportunity for all involved in property management.

Whilst there are, and will be, continuing problems with the valuation of property which is principally specialised in nature, one of the benefits which is developing, due to the quantification of the cost of property usage, is that property resourcing is now forming part of the business agenda. Property as a resource has become more important. This in turn now requires local authority valuers to explain and advise the client departments in a more informative and detailed manner. Today there is a greater need to communicate the basis of the valuation to the client department. Ultimately, as the client departments themselves are become more accountable for their individual expenditure they will want greater value for money and will rationalise their property holdings on the basis of information communicated to them by managers.

References

Audit Commission for Local Authorities in England and Wales (1988), *Local Authority Property -A Management Overview,* HMSO, London.

Audit Commission for Local Authorities in England and Wales (1988), *Local Authority Property -A Management Handbook,* HMSO, London.

Avis, M., Braham, R., Crosby, N., French N., Gibson, V., Temple, M., Whitman, B. (1993), *Property Management Performance Monitoring,* Oxford Brookes University and the University of Reading, GTI/Oxford Brookes, Oxford.

Avis, M., Gibson, V. and Watts, J. (1989), *Managing Operational Property Assets,* University of Reading.

Chartered Institute of Public Finance and Accountancy (1991), *Asset Registers - A Practical Guide,* CIPFA, London.

French, N. (1994), 'Asset registers and asset rents for local authorities: a viable property management tool', *Property Management*, vol 12 (3).

Hillier Parker (1993) '*Charging out Internal (Asset) Rents; Internal Property Management Accounting Practices*', Corporate Real Estate Research Papers No.1.

Royal Institution of Chartered Surveyors (1996), *RICS Appraisal and Valuation Manual,* RICS, Coventry.

Young, T. (1994), 'Market valuations with no market', *Journal of Property Valuation and Investment*, vol. 12 (3).

4 Local Authority Property Management Strategies

Marion Weatherhead, Gardiner and Theobald Management

Introduction

This paper proposes that local authorities should be seeking to ensure that in all areas of their operations the role of real estate is included when they are developing corporate strategy. As information technology and connectivity developments release operations from location and time, corporate operations have a much greater choice of accommodation. This has brought real estate into the strategic equation where businesses seek competitive advantage and local authorities seek efficient services attuned to local needs. The paper reviews the financial issues and looks at where local authorities can learn from the experience of corporate business. The main body of the paper reviews ways in which local authorities are and can work towards developing corporate strategy incorporating real estate. The paper is illustrated with examples taken from the business world and the London Borough of Bromley.

Property management strategies

Property management strategies are developed to focus real estate resources and costs on serving corporate objectives, by methods such as ensuring real estate holdings are not excessive, match the organisation's needs and are not overly expensive. Going beyond the confines of property management strategies is another approach which is to initiate the development of *corporate strategy which incorporates real estate.* Under this scenario real estate will be used best if it is considered alongside other resources when planning what an organisation could/should achieve, what it wants to achieve and how it will be achieved.

It should be the aim of property managers to strive to see this happens in our local authorities. All too frequently the corporate strategy is published and then the real estate implications are considered which is not the way to achieve the best solutions. Acquiring and disposing of real estate takes time - sometimes years - and transaction costs are high. More importantly strategy will be more workable if all aspects of implementation are considered during formulation. The incorporation of real estate into local authority strategic planning requires property experts who understand local authority finance and the work of the different council departments. Likewise chief officers, and especially finance directors, need to understand real estate and the property market. Local authorities frequently excel at including real estate in their strategic planning. However mostly this has been confined to projects, such as town centre redevelopment with a sizeable real estate content, rather than the more mundane activities of local government.

The author has been researching the role of real estate in the corporate business sector. Although there are differences, there is also much that is similar. The results of my research are published in '*Real Estate in Corporate Strategy*'. This paper draws upon the research to highlight some of my findings and place them in the local authority context. To help do this the paper will draw on information provided by the London Borough of Bromley.

The London Borough of Bromley was previously used as a case study in 1988 by the Audit Commission in their report *Local Authority Property: A Management Handbook*. Then the focus was on the reuse of redundant property - and the example was the conversion of a surplus teacher training college into a Civic Centre. Bromley has remained under the same political control and, apart from a short break had been under the same Council Leader, Councillor Dennis Barkway, for 24 years until his retirement due to ill health. Such continuity is an uncommon occurrence in modern local government. So Bromley has been unusual in being able to develop and implement long term policies - there was plenty of scope for strategic planning.

The author is grateful to the officers, especially the Chief Property Officer, Frank Whiting and John Lellow from the Borough Treasurer's Department who helped my investigations. It should perhaps be pointed out at this stage that in writing the paper no attempt is made to provide a comprehensive case study of Bromley - reporting that would be far too long winded! Some illustrations are used to show the effects of central government policies, others because they are examples of good practice or innovative thinking.

The transfer of ideas

Strategists need open minds and lots of ideas. Improvements and developments in many fields are frequently not the result of a completely new idea. They arise from the transfer and adaptation of ideas from another source such as different industries, different countries or different users. Those who want to do the best to serve their local community will be searching for new ways forward. Those seeking to improve the services are more likely to be successful if they employ methods that have been tried successfully elsewhere. This avoids complete innovation which tends to frighten people. Adoption or adaptation of tactics previously used elsewhere, if fully understood, should reduce risks to manageable proportions.

While some of what has happened in the corporate business field will not be useable in the same form within local authorities, much will be relevant. However, what follows does not wish to promote the notion that government, whether local or central, should mirror business. Government is a different process with different objectives but along the way both commerce and government use similar resources and real estate is significant for both. Ideas developed in corporate business have relevance to the public sector.

The changing use of real estate

Real estate has long been a major corporate resource but until recently it has not attracted much attention beyond the property world. Now things are changing. First in the USA and now in the UK, corporate business is slowly becoming more interested in the investments they make in real estate.

Until the 1990s most businesses had little choice about their real estate operational assets because various other aspects of their operations more or less dictated their location. As Joroff et al (1993) has pointed out, these were circumstances where deal-making was the most valuable skill for a real estate manager. Traditionally real estate education has dwelt on knowing about buildings and understanding the property market. More recently focus has been on additional skills such as facilities management, appreciation of building obsolescence and for those working in property investment - improved understanding of the development process and financial markets. These skills are still required but now those dealing with corporate real estate resources (whether for private or public bodies) need to add strategy and finance skills. There are many reasons for this but paramount is the 'information age'.

We can see information technology and connectivity changing the way we live and work. Some are resisting but as the report of the City 2020 Symposium held in Paris in 1995 pointed out - the technophobes of 1990s will be gone by 2020 Whether those that need only a cup of coffee and a laptop to work - at home, in the air, anywhere - will be the norm can be open to doubt (and fear of cabin fever), but already a lecturer in his office at MIT in the USA, can teach a class in Singapore (Mitchell, 1995).

It is a change that cannot be ignored and it is far reaching - organisations are being freed from location and time because information can be delivered to most places instantly. It is a process that is becoming cheaper day-by-day. Even goods are travelling faster - 24 hour delivery for direct mail (by telephone, fax or internet and payment by credit or debit card) is commonplace. 'Just-in-time' production methods have goods passing through the manufacturing process so quickly they hardly have to be stored.

Of course, not everything is flexible and new constraints are developing - for example, 'just-in-time' manufacture works best if the suppliers are close to the main assembly plant. Nevertheless, overall more businesses are free to locate anywhere. Once location is not obvious and becomes a matter of choice it also becomes a matter for strategic consideration as one solution may led to greater success than another. An additional push for change in corporate business has been the recession, property slump and the switch from high to low inflation. These have all contributed to change in the 'own or rent' equation which has culminated in changes to real property law.

Real estate costs and value

Research has revealed that for the average business 40 percent of the assets are real estate and that real estate is responsible for about 17 percent of costs. (Currie and Scott, 1991; Bannock and Partners, 1994). For local authorities the amounts involved are massive. The Audit Commission put the replacement value (ie no land content and excluding let buildings) of local authority owned and occupied buildings at over £75 billion in 1988 and suggested that many individual councils have portfolios worth over £250 million (Audit Commission, 1988).

The 1995 Accounts for Bromley reveal operational buildings valued at nearly £250 million plus investment properties valued at nearly £125 million which together represent 78 percent of the Council's long term assets (see Figure 4.1). Employing resources of this magnitude warrant the utmost consideration even if in areas of lower land values the percentage is not so high for the same volume of property.

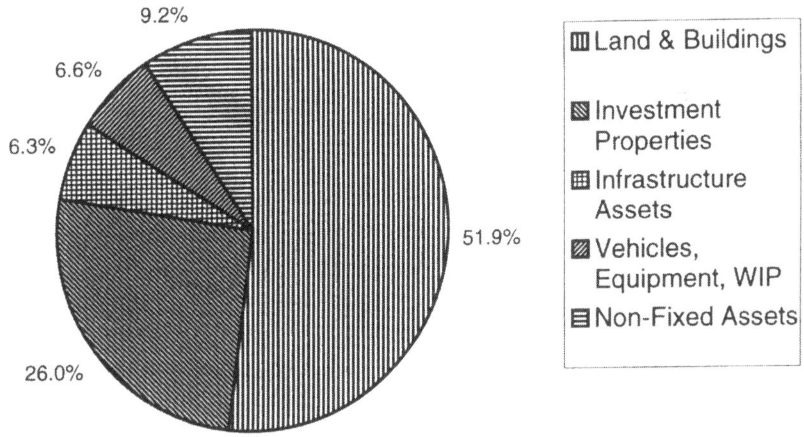

Figure 4.1 London Borough of Bromley 1994-95
Consolidated Balance Sheet: Long-Term Assets

Real estate and finance

The financial structure, and the influences on that structure, are very different between business and local authorities. Both are subject to government policies. In business this is mainly through taxation and capital allowances. Whatever the comments of the business community, taxation changes rarely dominate corporate business decisions in the way government interferes in local government.

Governments use local authorities as one of the major tools to influence economic growth and stability - most notably the level of the Public Sector Borrowing Requirement (PSBR). Control is achieved by restrictions on the expenditure of local authority capital receipts and restrictions on the use of their reserves. All income from the sale of capital items is removed from the financial control of the committees responsible for the sales and becomes part of an authority's general coffers. Its re-use is then under the control of finance committees within the remit allowed by central government. Consequently any effective review of the need and use of property within local authorities lies with the main Council (ie the political caucus) rather than individual committees.

Asset values

Local authority accounting methods have changed to reflect more accurately the value of the assets on the balance sheet and the amount used to support each service. In 1994 CIPFA's *Code of Practice* was implemented. It replaced historic cost accounting for local authorities with a current value based balance sheet. This has been a major improvement on previous methods. Then property which had been acquired without loans did not even feature in the balance sheet. Under the new arrangements properties must be valued on an existing use basis which for many buildings such as schools means using depreciated replacement cost rather than any form of market related value. It means that the figures in the balance sheet have limitations. This is especially the case when it comes to appraising the potential or otherwise of the local authorities' estates.

Transfer of the Bromley Council's housing stock to a housing association brought in capital receipts sufficient to pay off all the Council's debts. After this sale and prior to the implementation of current value accounting in the balance sheet, those properties that had been purchased by a loan were still shown in the balance sheet at a value equal to the loan. Those purchased outright from revenue were never shown in the accounts - no matter what the cost. It all seemed even sillier when Bromley did not have major long term debt! It is history now, but when accountancy systems have promoted such nonsense in recent memory, it must be difficult to get anyone to take the financial aspects of property management issues seriously.

Capital charges

Capital charges are another aspect of the changes aimed to bring some realism to local authority accounting. But the reality is that the users of the buildings - the politicians on the council committees and the departmental chief officers and staff - have no real incentive to seek to reduce the charges because their committee/department receives no immediate benefit in return by way of extra spending possibilities. There is little to gain by being prudent. The charges are formula driven and, frequently, even more unreal because they are mostly based on depreciated replacement cost values and not market values. Additionally they are notional - an accounting procedure - they are not a cost that has to be met by the local community from council charge and business rates taxation. The formula for capital charges includes two components one to equal interest payments and another to cover depreciation.

Bromley has implemented a planned maintenance programme which aims to ensure that the real estate maintains its existing value. The costs of the planned maintenance programme are included in the accounts in place for the depreciation payment element of the capital charges formula. Implementation of the planned maintenance programme is still in the early stages with reviews of the computer system, the balance between professional and occupier involvement and decisions on what is unplanned maintenance and what constitutes improvement, all still being redefined in the light of experience. Like most local authorities, the programme comes under attack when additional expenditure demands encourage the tendency to nibble away at maintenance budgets. However the planned maintenance programme does seem to be drawing attention to these issues rather more than under previous financial arrangements. As it is based on the needs of the individual buildings the programme will highlight those that are expensive to maintain.

Local authorities and business

Clearly local authorities are not in the same position as businesses because they operate to serve one geographical area. Most of their real estate is based within their boundaries. Each local authority is seeking to assist the lives of those living and working in its environs. This means that they often select to use real estate in less obvious locations because one of their policies is to pump-prime development in deprived areas. When local authorities operate in this way, their 'market driven' strategies will be the opposite to the norm!

The reasons for real estate ownership by local authorities are varied. Bromley Council is the landlord for five farms. These are let at market rents which reflect the special lease conditions related to maintaining public access and enhancing the benefits of the green belt. In these circumstances ownership has been deemed essential to achieve the wider objectives. Although locational freedom has been a major factor in making real estate assets of greater strategic significance, other factors such as tenure, type and use of buildings have also gained greater importance. These factors are just as relevant to local authorities as businesses.

Many goods and services used by local authorities are bought-in, some have always been purchased but for some services such as council charge collection buying-in (or outsourcing) is a new arrangement. When a good or service is purchased the provision of real estate for undertaking the production or service falls to the supplier and not the local authority. Outsourcing removes the direct involvement in real estate from local authorities. The public finance initiative (PFI) is another way of distancing public bodies from property risks. Decisions to use outsourcing (or PFI) are, in part, real estate decisions, just as the decision by Marks and Spencers plc to outsource distribution was, in part, a real estate decision (Weatherhead, 1997).

Bromley was one of the first authorities to outsource the exchequer function and when this took place the staff who transferred to the new contractor, Capita Managed Services Ltd, moved from the Civic Centre into one of the town hall buildings and staff from there came into the Civic Centre. Bromley then received a rent of £160,000 pa from Capita for use of part of the town hall. Later rationalisation, including the transfer of the housing stock (and staff) to a new housing association, enabled the Council to remove the staff from the second part of the town hall which was then let to the local further education college. This time the rent was £125,000 pa and Bromley College gained a town centre site which was a convenient location for many residents enrolled on courses. Both arrangements brought revenue income with less restrictions than capital receipts and maintained the authority's long term control over the old town hall, a building with a strong civic image.

Despite the accountancy differences, philosophically there are few differences between the approach of many businesses and local authorities to real estate. Historic cost accounting for some or all of a business's assets is still common and many business managers do not give much thought to the real value of their real estate - they see it as a necessary evil. Consequently the differences between businesses and local authorities will be more relevant to the tactics of implementation than the overall issue of seeking to gain the greatest possible contribution from real estate, a major resource, in achieving an organisation's objectives.

Developing corporate strategies incorporating real estate

The ideal situation is that an organisation's strategy is developed by people who understand all aspects of its operations and the environment in which it operates. They should also have the skill to interpret economic and other forecasts, or better still be able to initiate forecasts which are modelled on their organisation's circumstances now and in the future.

Corporate strategy incorporating real estate should use economic models and other forecasts for:

- the property cycle;
- national/local levels of real estate investment;
- national/local rent levels
- national/local property markets.

For most businesses and local authorities this is a dream - it just doesn't happen. In fact most don't even dream about it! Nevertheless without seeing or setting this target, local authorities are making progress towards this ideal as they step up systems to develop and implement specific real estate strategies. Now they need to lift their sights higher to ensure that they move further along the path and start to incorporate real estate into the formulation of corporate strategy. This will involve real estate experts being included in the team developing the corporate strategies for matters such as introducing improvements to community safety or developing a sports strategy. These fringe areas would previously have been considered without a great deal of thought as to how the use or otherwise of real estate could help success.

Each local authority will have its own different objectives. Even though government policies and the current environment will push many councils in the same direction, they will have different resources and different needs. Corporate strategy, or corporate plans as they are more commonly called by local authorities, will be different but many of the influences and the tactics used to implement them will be similar. The following will concentrate on the philosophical considerations and practical methodologies that will help local authorities make the best use of their real estate.

The philosophy - leadership

For many authorities real estate has been in the background, a necessary evil because education, care for the elderly, libraries etc cannot be provided without accommodation. When real estate has come to the forefront it has often been to present an image of the importance of a town by the building of a magnificent town hall. Many of these are superb and have succeeded in promoting the economic standing of the community and attracting new businesses and residents. Many splendid medieval, Victorian and even modern buildings are regularly used to entertain and influence political, business and even world leaders. Local heroes are still presented to citizens from town hall balconies.

Between the extremes of 'necessary evil' and 'grand magnificence' many ordinary buildings have the potential to make a greater contribution to community life than just providing accommodation. This needs the commitment of the leaders of the local authority - the politicians and the chief officers - who are the people with the power and the incentive to make changes and to ensure that real estate matters are drawn into the implementation of strategic policies. This is no different from business. All the companies studied for my book had made profitable competitive advantage from real estate because they brought real estate issues to the centre of their businesses and made them the responsibility of senior management.

When senior managers (and politicians) constructively illustrate the importance they place on a particular area of their operations, others tend to follow. It may not be easy. Staff and councillors will probably need the support of new management structures, they may need training, they may need cajoling in order for change to take place. Without the clearly demonstrated support of senior managers and political leaders, especially for those managing real estate from day-to-day, it will almost certainly remain the case that real estate issues are disregarded by the majority of staff who are not property experts. Such neglect leaves real estate resources open to abuse by those who seek personal satisfaction from their control of real estate. Such individuals seek to be managing the biggest facility and gaining the best offices for their staff. This is not dissimilar to the culture at IBM UK Ltd when, in the early 1980s during periods of high profits, local managers indulged in space - it was an indication of success which staff sought to achieve alongside their salaries. Those days are now history and use of space at IBM UK Ltd is focused on supporting the acquisition of profitable business by helping staff meet customers' needs.

Methodologies

Reviewing businesses that have made innovative use of real estate revealed that there seems to be prerequisites or stages to reaching the position where incorporating real estate into main stream corporate planning is workable. This suggests that a local authority will need first to be producing:

- plausible corporate strategy;
- an understanding of its real estate holdings;
- a corporate real estate strategy.

Corporate strategy

If real estate is to be managed so as to serve the needs of the local population these needs, and how they are to be served, must be well publicised. This means that the authority must have a corporate strategy or plan.

To be strategic, this needs to be more than the spending objectives for the coming year - it should contain the ambitions and needs of the council for its area in the coming years. Given the time it takes to adjust the size and use of an estate, change (if required) can be achieved more effectively when time is allowed for planning and implementation. Frequent political change and hung councils are situations where long term strategies can be difficult although agreement and compromise on some matters may make the focus on individual long term policies possible.

The strategic theories and analytical tools used to extract useful information for developing the local authority plan will be much the same as those used by business strategists. Many strategic methods are generic and have been imported into the business world from the writings of those desperate for success including Sun Tzu, a Chinese army commander 2000 years old, and Machiavelli, a Renaissance Italian Prince, gaining and holding power in troubled times. Some will say nothing changes! More recent writings, often by American business school professors, offer much that is helpful. However although they provide many useful thoughts and ideas, they tend to be focused on the needs of commercial business so will be less directly suitable for local authorities.

Knowing the real estate

It is impossible to include real estate considerations in corporate strategy if the real estate assets are not known and understood. The asset registers are a step along this path, as is the move to current valuation on the balance sheet. However to make progress it is essential to move beyond the statutory valuations and undertake some 'what-if' calculations to seek out real estate resources that have potential for other uses which could increase their value. This does not mean the value has to be realised just that those who make the decisions should understand the full picture. Local authorities may seek out real estate holdings with other potential such as historic associations, the capacity to develop urban 'country parks' or to promote urban regeneration. Knowing and understanding an authority's real estate involves rather more than the facts and figures of an asset register.

Additional to information on value and potential, is a need to understand fully the existing state of each real estate holding. The most comprehensive way is to undertake a portfolio audit. This was done by BT plc and was the foundation of all the real estate changes they have since undertaken. The review of each property focused on cost, value, efficiency and quality (see Figure 4.2).

Corporate real estate strategy

Most commonly the real estate issues are considered after the publication of the corporate plan. It helps if it is easy to extract from the plan those matters which are relevant to real estate management. Also worthy of consideration by real estate managers will be any strategies related to issues, such as customer needs or service quality, where real estate

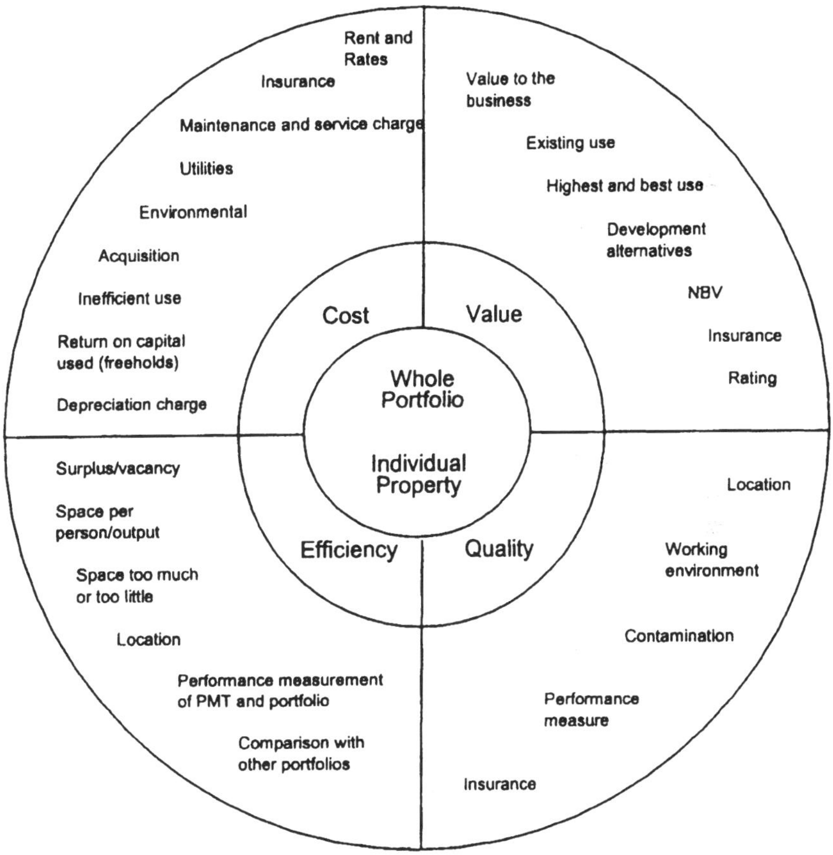

Figure 4.2 Portfolio Audit Seeks to Identify Information in the Cost - Value - Efficiency - Quality Sectors

changes may help execute the plan. The drawing together of information from a review of existing real estate and the real estate requirements of the corporate plan should make it possible to produce a corporate real estate strategy. This will be the basis for real estate management from day-to-day. In dynamic authorities the corporate real estate strategy will include plans for improving real estate management and for developing new real estate practices to match the changing needs of the business. Frequently at this stage real estate managers and their facilities managers begin to look at other organisations to see if their own performance at least matches that elsewhere. This can be useful but there is little point in focusing on matters such as occupancy costs if the properties themselves are not serving the authority's needs.

A corporate real estate strategy may also include consideration as to whether IT advances and other operational possibilities could reduce the need for real estate. Real estate downsizing most frequently occurs when staff numbers reduce but may also arise because space standards and working practices change. The changes at BT plc started in this way. They began a massive downsizing programme because IT advances made much of their operational property and their staff redundant. As a result BT's real estate costs fell by nearly 20 percent per annum between 1990 and 1995 and they are reducing the estate by 250 000 m^2 to 300 000 m^2 each year.

Since 1987 all Bromley Council committees have been obliged to report annually to the Policy and Resources Committee on their land and property holdings so that any potentially surplus land or under-utilised buildings could be drawn to the attention of the Land and Property Sub-Committee. This sub-committee has then reviewed property holdings. Over the years sales of surplus buildings have provided a steady flow of capital receipts which, after government formula calculations, provided access to sufficient funds to maintain the capital programme. More recently it has become apparent that in future there will be less surplus land and buildings available for sale.

In 1995 a Property Division was established under a Chief Property Officer which provides valuations and estates, architecture, mechanical and electrical engineering, quantity surveying and building maintenance services. Some services are provided through direct service organisations (DSO), others by directly employed staff. The Division covers most of the Council's property needs. One exception is a sites and premises section within the Education Department which acts as an informed client for the local authority's primary schools (all but one senior school are Grant Maintained). A Civic Operations Manager working to the Borough Secretary handles accommodation allocation and porter services in the Civic Centre is another exception. As is the Social Services Department which handles the residential homes but specialists are not employed as the properties are subject to a management agreement with an external carer.

The Property Division has valued all the properties for the asset register, calculated the capital charges, implemented a planned maintenance programme and is now about to lead a property review. Details of this review are still to be published but it seems likely that it will cross committee boundaries and set up a system for reviewing the authority's real estate needs on a geographical basis under guidance from the Property Division. My impression is that the review team will keep close contact with the central political and managerial core of the authority. Until the Committee report is published nothing more is known. There is little evidence to suggest the outcome of the review will be a dogmatic 'sell everything' policy but at this point it is worth recalling the comments in the Audit Commission's (1988) *Local Authority Property: A Management Handbook.* They highlighted that generalisations or dogma, such as strategies to either immediately selling all surplus property or, conversely, holding on to freeholds because of a belief that public ownership benefits a community, are not an adequate basis for effective management.

Strategy not tactics

More and more local authorities are introducing hot-desking - the arrangement where staff who are not always in the office share desks (Weatherhead, 1997). At other times they work at home, in their cars, in hotels or at clients offices etc. A variety of flexible working arrangements have been put in place by various UK employers. It is important to appreciate that hotdesking is a tactic which can be used to assist the implementation of an organisation's strategy. If hotdesking is used without the supporting facilities and management framework the desired results may not arise.

Organisations where it was first introduced such as IBM UK Ltd and BT plc used purpose built accommodation and they are still monitoring effectiveness and fine tuning the arrangements. Both have reduced real estate expenditure during the 1990s but in both cases this had more to do with staff reductions than hotdesking. The benefits of hotdesking have not been so much from cheaper accommodation costs but as a component of flexible working practices which have interrelated with information technology systems, management and process systems and the accommodation. In BT plc this package has been named as Workstyle 2000 (see Figure 4.3). The result has been working practices that are much more sensitive and responsive to customer need.

At IBM UK Ltd a key factor in their success was that the real estate changes were not seen as an end in themselves, but as a contribution

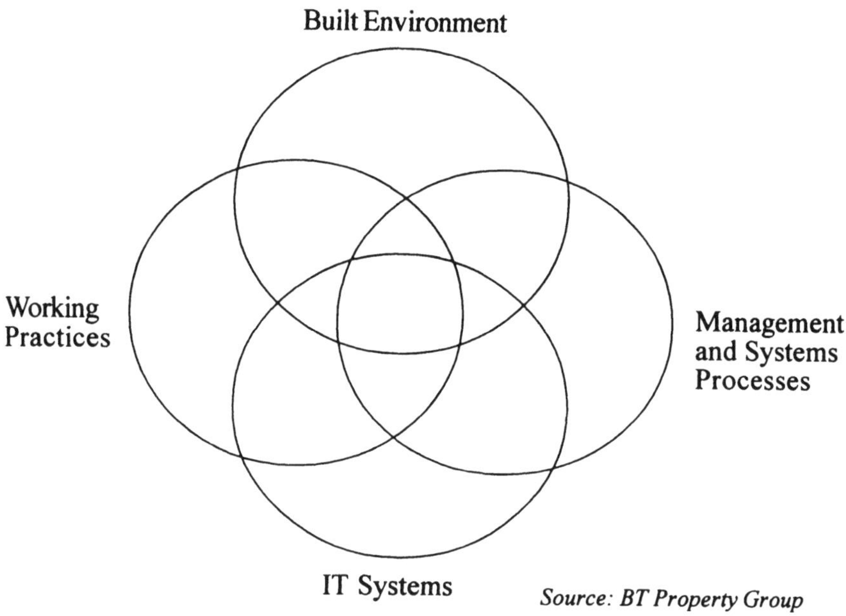

Source: BT Property Group

Figure 4.3 Workstyle 2000

towards helping the sales staff meet their targets - which in the early 1990s were essential for the survival of the business.

An indication that introducing such working practices involves expenditure can be seen from BT's capital expenditure on land and buildings. From the introduction of its new real estate policies in 1990 capital expenditure dropped rapidly in line with corporate downsizing.

Since the development of the Workstyle 2000 project, capital expenditure began to increase because the refitting of existing buildings will not produce the required facilities for modern working not just in offices but also warehouses, workshops, depots etc (see Figure 4.4). So while some buildings have been rented, capital expenditure has increased but as an integral part of the achieving corporate objectives.

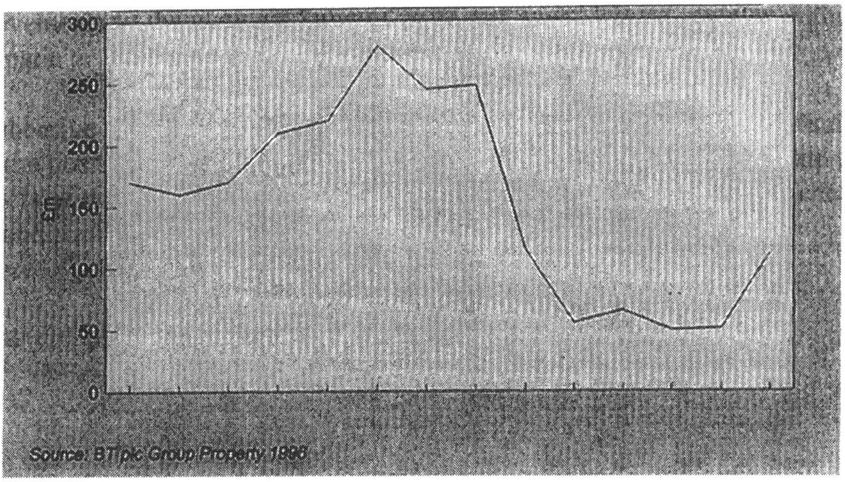

Figure 4.4 Capital Spend on Land and Buildings by BT plc

Corporate strategy incorporating real estate

Authorities that have a sophisticated corporate real estate strategy are only a small step away from beginning the process of creating, from inception, corporate strategy *incorporating* real estate. This involves including real estate expertise in the team developing the corporate plan. The team can then incorporate real estate considerations into policies related to all the Council's work, such as, operations management, outsourcing, delivering child care etc. It can range across issues such as whether the real estate contributes to the quality of the service, the convenience of staff, the desired operational methods and even the culture of the authority.

When the centre of the organisation is including real estate in all the decision making processes, individual committees and departments will be caught up in a culture and value system focused on being prudent and innovative with real estate resources. If the politicians and senior managers ensure incentives to use real estate wisely and for the benefit of the local population this is more likely to occur. Many main stream strategy theories and methods are capable of incorporating real estate issues. Examples of these are illustrated in *Real Estate in Corporate Strategy* together with a structure for the stages of ensuring corporate strategy incorporates real estate. Including real estate experts in corporate strategy preparation should be more far reaching than involving them only to cover matters such as comprehensive redevelopment plans, proposed bids for lottery or EU funds, links into other regeneration schemes or working out PFI Schemes that concentrate on real estate.

In some matters such as the comprehensive redevelopment of Bromley town centre with an indoor shopping mall, a bypass road and pedestrianised precinct, it is clear that real estate expertise has already been involved at the highest levels of strategic planning. Not only has Bromley been improved, the deal struck with the developers brought the authority a substantial commercially based rental income from the completed shopping centre. Real estate is also a key component of Bromley's latest major development proposals which aim to restore Crystal Palace Park to much of its Victorian splendour with a new concert bowl, improvements to the National Sports Centre and a new leisure complex within a refurbished park.

The comprehensive audit of all council property expected to commence the beginning of the autumn of 1997 will put Bromley in the position to be able to take the next step and incorporate real estate directly into all aspects of strategic planning. It will help if incentives are introduced to encourage councillors and staff to 'think property'.

Conclusions

Undoubtedly other local authorities will wish to approach these issues in different ways because they have different political agendas, different facilities and different financial positions. Whatever these considerations, the local authorities that are going to serve their electorates best will:

- have real estate expertise at the highest levels of management and political briefing;
- know and understand all aspects of their real estate;
- plan to make sure all real estate decisions (and indecision) serves to implement their policies;
- attempt to move towards including real estate issues in their strategic deliberations.

References

Audit Commission (1988), *Local Authority Property: A Management Handbook,* HMSO, London.

Avis, M. and Gibson, V. (1995), *Real Estate Resource Management: A Study of Major Occupiers in the UK,* GTI Specialist Publishers Ltd with Oxford Brookes University and the University of Reading.

Bannock, G. and Partners (1994), *Property in the Boardroom: A New Perspective.* Hillier Parker and Graham Bannock and Partners.

Bromley. (London Borough of) (1995), *Annual Report and Statement of Accounts: 1994-95,* London Borough of Bromley.

Business Publishing (1996), *The City in 2020: The Official Report of the Symposium held at Disneyland, Paris,* Business Publishing.

Chartered Institute of Public Finance and Accountancy (1993), *Code of Practice on Local Authority Accounting in Great Britain 1993 - A Statement of Recommended Practice,* CIPFA, London (Note: 1996 edition now in use).

Chartered Institute of Public Finance and Accountancy (1994), *Capital Accounting by Local Authorities: Asset Registers an Update,* CIPFA, London.

Currie, D. and Scott, A. (1991), *The Place of Commercial Property in the UK Economy,* Centre for Economic Forecasting, London Business School.

Joroff, M. et al (1993), *Strategic Management of the Fifth Resource: Corporate Real Estate,* Industrial Development Research Foundation, USA.

Mitchell, W. (1995), *City of Bits: Space, Time and their Infobahn,* MIT Press, Cambridge, Mass.

Weatherhead, M. (1997), *Real Estate in Corporate Strategy,* Macmillan, London.

PART 2
INITIATIVES AND STRATEGIES

5 The Application of Geographic and Land Information Systems to the Management of Local Authority Property

Martin Ralphs, School of Surveying, University of East London
Peter Wyatt, School of Valuation and Estate Management, University of the West of England

Introduction

The aim of this paper is to consider the benefits that the implementation of geographical and land information systems (GIS and LIS) can offer local authorities with regard to the management of their property assets. The paper will begin by outlining reasons for recent moves towards the application of information technology (IT) in Local Authority Property Management (LAPM) and argue that information used in property management functions is largely geo-referenced. Such data is handled most effectively by IT solutions that include mapping and spatial analysis capabilities such as GIS and LIS. To demonstrate this, the case study of Barking and Dagenham London Borough Council is described, focusing on their digital land terrier and its application to Local Authority Property Management. The paper will also go on to describe the Western Australia Land Information System (WALIS) and its application in a local government environment. This system is an example of how information sharing between local and central government organisations can add value to data sets collected and maintained by each, reduce duplication of effort and offer a more consistent service. WALIS is an initiative that was developed at the local level and is similar to GIS and LIS development in local government throughout the UK.

The paper will conclude by suggesting that to implement successful systems like WALIS appropriate data referencing and integration standards are required. The Land and Property Gazetteer Working Party, with a strong local authority influence, were responsible for the creation of British Standard 7666 which introduces standard referencing methodologies for streets, land parcels and address information. Migration to this standard by local government and central government data providers, such as the Valuation Office and the Land Registry, will present new opportunities for integrated property management. This paper will examine these developments and outline recent initiatives for the integration of property information and dissemination at a national level, namely the National Land Information System (NLIS) pilot in Bristol and the Scottish Land Information System (ScotLIS).

IT in local authority property management

The following will examine the developments in LAPM following the Audit Commission's enquiry and assess whether the initiatives put in place remain appropriate after the re-organisation of local government. It is important to consider IT initiatives in this light because often they depend on collaboration and support across departments and changes to structures can lead to organisational and operational problems. For example, the issue of regularly updating changes is relevant during local government re-organisation because of the substantial movements in the holdings of property by local authorities and departments therein.

In its memorandum of evidence to the Audit Commission the Royal Institution of Chartered Surveyors recommended (RICS, 1987) that:

- local authorities should adopt a more corporate approach to property management;
- a central property department is recommended;
- a central database of property owned and leased by the authority is essential to allow performance indicators to be constructed and to permit more informed decision-making; and
- a central property database could be used for estate management, development, and by maintenance and service departments.

Clearly the RICS felt that the property portfolio is a key area of management policy within a local authority and therefore suggested a move towards a 'property' department with a dedicated property information system, rather than having the property functions dispersed among legal, treasurers', environmental services and other departments. This would allow performance indicators to be developed and more informed property decisions to be made. The Chartered Institute of Public Finance and Accountancy (CIPFA), in its report on local authority asset registers, supported the recommendations of the RICS regarding the need for a central database of property owned and occupied by local authorities (CIPFA, 1991).

When the Audit Commission published the findings of its review of LAPM, it did so in two documents. First, the overview (Audit Commission, 1988a) highlighted a lack of information about property in many authorities. For example, it was commented that many authorities did not know what they owned. It was therefore suggested that a property committee should be formed within each authority and one of its main responsibilities would be to bring together information on the authority's property holdings. The second document, the Audit Commission's handbook on LAPM (Audit Commission, 1988b) recommended all authorities to bring their land and property terriers up to date and maintain a reliable index of property deeds. The Commission suggested that unique property reference numbers (UPRNs) should be used to link terrier information to financial and other information systems. The use of UPRNs that contain map co-ordinates (a national grid reference for example) offer an opportunity for local authorities to implement information systems that store, manage, analyse and display property information geographically. This is an opportunity that many authorities have taken up.

Property data in a spatial context

The Audit Commission reported concern about the paucity of property information in many authorities (Audit Commission, 1988b) and suggested core information that should be recorded in a property database, with links to financial and other information systems (Audit Commission, 1988a). The Commission stated that 'the importance of an up-to-date and comprehensive terrier cannot be overstated since it is the starting point of much property management work'. Information regarded as essential is illustrated in Figure 5.1.

This type of geographical information is well suited to input and analysis using GIS and LIS and several authorities now use this technology to maintain their land terriers. The advantages of GIS and LIS over paper-based systems are described by Lilburne and Rix (1991) and can be summarised as; an ability to handle changes in features over time, an opportunity to tailor the database to suit different types of user, provision of authority-wide access to a corporate resource, geographical analysis of property information and high quality map production. The transition from a paper-based to a GIS-based land and property terrier represents a shift from a static inventory / index system to a dynamic, integrated property management system.

Since the Audit Commission's report on local authority property management in 1988 (Audit Commission 1988a) there has been substantial investment in GIS and LIS by local government. This has been assisted by the recent Service Level Agreement with the Ordnance Survey.

Many implementations of GIS and LIS in local government have been aimed at improving planning-related functions such as planning application procedures, the recording of planning histories for each land parcel and the administration of local land charges. Some authorities are using GIS and LIS to assist in their emergency and disaster planning procedures and one county council has used a GIS to help manage traffic flow and provide visitors with route information. The application of GIS and LIS to local authority property management is also regarded as an effective use of data collected as part of the statutory functions undertaken by local authorities. Applications include:

- the identification of under-utilised property and its proximity to over-utilised property or premises that are in need of refurbishment;
- impact assessment of development proposals on neighbouring properties;
- space and facilities management (for example the calculation of grass-cutting area prior to tendering for work);
- the mapping of property values for planning and development purposes;
- the mapping of vacant land; and
- modelling the environmental impact of proposals for housing development.

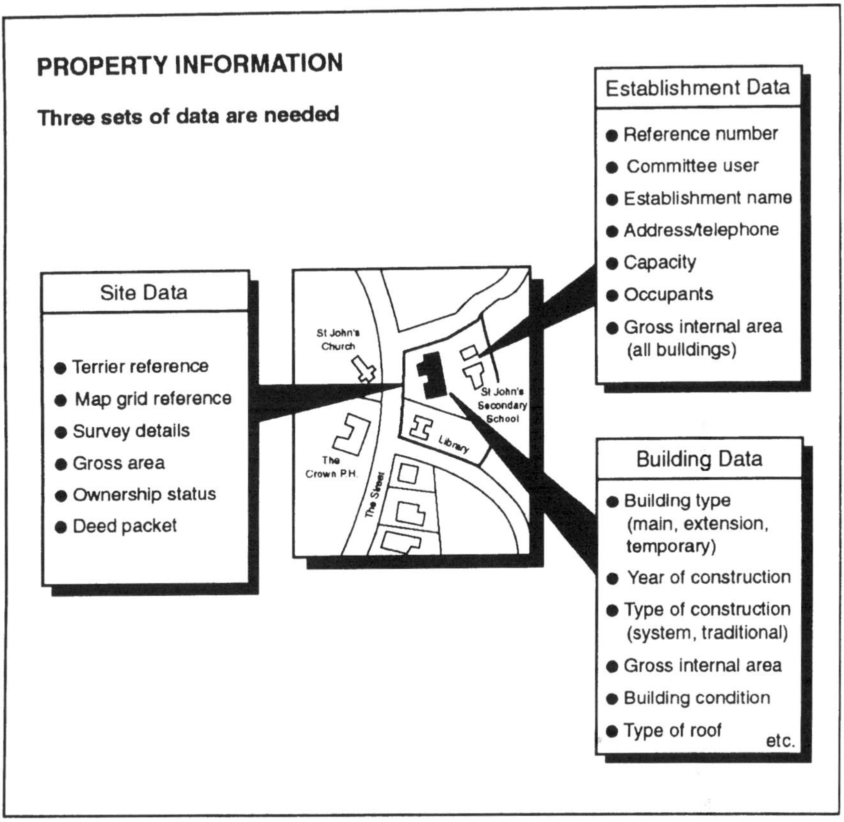

Figure 5.1 Property Information for LAPM
Source: Audit Commission (1988a)

The application of GIS and LIS in practice

A survey of the handling of property data in the Eastern Thames Corridor revealed some of the important issues surrounding the implementation of GIS and LIS within a local authority environment (Lopez, 1992). Many early applications of GIS in local government suffered from common problems:

- lack of finance;

- lack of a corporate information strategy;
- lack of comprehensive GIS feasibility and cost-benefit systems;
- emphasis on technical rather than institutional and data-related issues;
- high cost of digital data and manual data conversion;
- no mandate to share data; and
- problems were highlighted regarding the use of government statistics where certain data were not suitable for local government functions due to inappropriate scale, detail or accuracy.

Information 'islands' developed between which data was rarely shared and independent databases designed for one function were created rather than networked as part of a corporate resource. The survey showed that departments were not sharing data to a large extent and those that tend to be were doing so on a project-by-project basis. A lack of central guidance exacerbated the problems encountered by individual authorities.

In support of the evidence submitted to the Audit Commission by the RICS (RICS, 1987) the survey of local authorities in the Eastern Thames Corridor revealed that the land terrier was regarded as one of the key coverages to be included in the plans for a corporate information strategy. As the level of computing skills within local government increase, users are realising that constraints to information flow are creating obstacles to IT development. It was argued in the survey report (Lopez, 1992) that local authorities should assess their departmental data requirements, work towards corporate data standards and a policy of sharing information before implementing a GIS. Recent developments are contributing to the development of GIS and LIS implementations in local government. The service level agreement, agreed between the Local Government Management Board and the Ordnance Survey allows local authorities to purchase digital map data at a discounted price. Despite the absence of a mandate to develop data standards, representatives from local government have been instrumental in publishing the BS7666 property referencing standard, discussed in more detail below. Such standards encourage departments to view data as a corporate resource and also encourage local authorities to move towards a national property data referencing standard.

Case study - the London Borough of Barking and Dagenham

The London Borough of Barking and Dagenham (LBBD) has 57 sets of property data and 70 percent of their information relates to council - owned property. The authority is engaged in six types of property activity:

- management of council property ownership;
- control and regulation of property related activities;
- council building management;
- infrastructure development and maintenance;
- service planning and marketing; and
- local property taxation and electoral registration.

In 1991-2, the council devised a strategy for property management incorporating GIS technology. This is ongoing, and involves the implementation of five components:

- a core referencing system;
- a computerised land terrier and associated systems;
- a property regulation database, health and consumer services system and a new land charges administration system;
- a planned maintenance system and related building management systems; and
- an infrastructure management system.

The central feature of the strategy was the development of a 'federal' approach to property information within the context of a corporate standards framework. It was recognised that benefits could be gained from the co-ordination of information resources that were used by related processes, but that detailed co-ordination of all aspects of property information was unrealistic and unnecessary. The decision was taken to move forward within a framework of common referencing standards, so that the objective of closer integration of information across the authority could be pursued while practical considerations of day-to-day operation were also taken into account.

The authority decided that the problems and costs of taking forward a corporate information management strategy were outweighed by the benefits arising from the resulting opportunities for data sharing and reduction of data duplication (London Borough of Barking and Dagenham, 1996a).

Implementation of the strategy

London Borough of Barking and Dagenham (LBBD) has made significant steps towards the implementation of its corporate solution. The initial phase of development has concentrated on the Land Terrier and corporate Master Address File (MAF). The council used to operate a range of addressing systems, which was seen as a source of potential problems when any linking system was adopted. The MAF should resolve this issue by providing a standard, regulated system of address referencing and will be completed by April of 1997. The MAF will be compliant with British Standard BS7666 Part 2, the Specification for a National Land and Property Gazetteer (BSI, 1994).

The Land Terrier computerisation is well underway. Council House Sales data capture will be completed by March 1997. Significant financial benefits have already arisen from the Land Terrier update through the cleaning of manual records. LBBD has purchased the Sysdeco GIS package and developed this as a data capture and property management tool. Most of the Land Terrier data capture will be complete by 1998 and the associated Property Management System is already operational, dealing with the lettings administration of the entire commercial property portfolio owned by the authority. Once Land Terrier data capture is complete, the Property Management System will be integrated with it, bringing together lettings information with land titles and deeds.

Even though it is incomplete, the Land Terrier has already made a significant contribution to the workings of the authority. The effective administration of council house sales information has been a primary source of benefits. LBBD has 21,000 council house sales operations to administer, each with its own set of restrictive covenants. These properties were sold off variously by LBBD, the Greater London Council (GLC) and the London Borough of Redbridge. By using the MAF and

GIS mapping to identify these properties, LBBD has saved money and generated new income by recognising errors in the title registration process, speeding up the process of inventory by colour coding and mapping properties digitally and flagging up potential benefits from existing covenants on sold properties.

One of the first applications that will come on-stream from the terrier implementation is a new Land Charges administration system. This will encompass information resources from the Planning, Health and Legal Services departments relating to planning and building controls, highways management and grants available for properties. By bringing together information resources from these different departments, the administration process should be made more efficient. The authority is also considering integrating Census of Population information with the terrier database for planning and development purposes.

Use of 1920s digital mapping information to capture land parcel boundaries

An interesting application of digital mapping arose in the capture of parcel boundaries for the land terrier. Prior to the 1930s and 40s, much of the Borough comprised agricultural land. Field boundaries were used to demarcate the extent of many of the council's older land titles and deeds and these have long since been destroyed by urban development. One of the problems faced by the authority was to reconcile ancient land titles and deeds with the existing urban landscape. The solution devised was to utilise digital Ordnance Survey County Series maps from the 1920s and 1930s which show the field boundaries, and to reconcile these with the existing digital cover of the Borough. This approach was an effective way of identifying the exact location of older land titles, and has been praised by HM Land Registry (LBBD, 1996b).

Looking abroad

An interesting example of inter agency co-operation at the state government level is provided by the Western Australian Land Information System (WALIS). This project illustrates the benefits and some of the problems encountered in attempting to take forward a multi agency information sharing exercise. WALIS was started in 1981 because of recognised inefficiencies and data duplication that was occurring amongst land information holders in Western Australia (Western Australia State Government, 1990). The value of land information resources there is estimated to be in the order of billions of Australian dollars, with tens of millions spent on annual maintenance. Co-operation, and a computerised Land Information System were thought to offer a better technological and managerial solution to the integration and management of this resource (Burke, 1993).

Much of Western Australia is under considerable developmental, environmental and social pressure. Accurate, consistent and current land information is required to manage land resources. However, different agencies collect different, specialised sets of information. WALIS sought to build upon this by promoting the sharing of information among agencies, with the expert agency in each topic area being responsible for collating data from that area. WALIS involves a consortium of government agencies and local government working together to integrate and improve access to state land information. It does not involve a central system, but a network of distinct computerised components operated by individual government agencies, which was found to be a more practical approach (Burke, 1993).

A large number of agencies participate in WALIS, including conservation, planning, energy generation, environmental protection, valuation, land administration and emergency service departments. In order to make sure that the management of the system is successful, the management structure allows mechanisms for agency participation and clear allocations of accountability (Burke, 1993). Figure 5.2 shows how the management structure is currently organised.

WALIS is administered by whichever agency is currently hosting the Integrated Land Information Programme (ILIP) and the chief executive of that agency becomes accountable for the project and responsible to the Minister for Lands. Day-to-day management is delegated to the director of ILIP, who also chairs the WALIS Council. The ILIP office co-ordinates development, develops WALIS strategy, operates an information directory, maintains central computing resources and provides specialist advice for the WALIS community. The Executive Policy Committee works alongside ILIP and sets policy and priorities while the WALIS Council is the focus for agency co-operation.

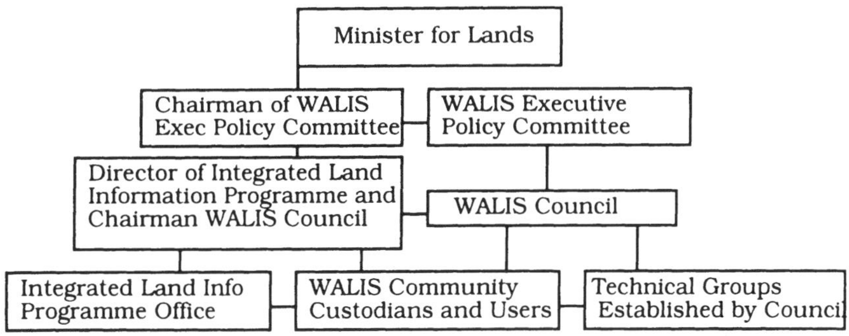

Figure 5.2 Current Management Structure for WALIS
Source: Burke (1993)

Sharing land information resources

WALIS is built on the premise that each agency collects information for which it has a high level of expertise and shares this with other agencies. In 1992, a series of policies were introduced to assist with this. These policies included:

1. A national policy on data transfer and pricing of land related data for all levels of government (Federal, State and Local). This had the following main points:

   a) all datasets have a clearly defined custodian;
   b) land related data is transferred from the custodian to other WALIS participants at marginal cost (cost of transfer). Such data may not be made available to third parties outside WALIS without the consent of the custodian agency; and
   c) a current directory of available data and custodians should be available nationally.

2. The policy that all agencies should share their information at the cost of extraction and distribution.

A dataset custodian is responsible for the maintenance of that dataset, implementation and compliance with standards and maintaining entries in the Land Information Directory relating to the data. Custodians are now working to develop standards for data description, classification, format, quality, structure and accuracy (Burke, 1993). Users outside the custodian organisation liaise with the custodian in detecting errors, defining standards and advising about future requirements. The custodian system means that each agency bears a small proportion of the overall load and concentrates on the maintenance of those resources that it is best qualified to administer.

Examples of current WALIS initiatives include the Land Information Directory, a computerised index to land information in Western Australia, the Pastoral and Agricultural GIS, which is used for crop management and land conservation support, Land Information Access, which provides on-line cadastral information and Integrated Forest Management, which integrates water resources, landscape visualisation, vegetation data and flora and fauna data. In future, a large increase in local government participants in WALIS is expected, and increased co-operation with the private sector is also likely. By bringing together a range of agencies working with spatial information, the WALIS initiative has brought substantial benefits through data sharing, data fusion, standards implementation and inter-agency co-operation.

The need for co-ordination and standards

In the UK, users of geographical information within a GIS environment are becoming increasingly aware of the need for standards of spatial data specification, description and transfer if the substantial benefits of GIS data integration are to be fully realised. Recent Federal government initiatives in the United States are moving toward a National Spatial Data Infrastructure (Federal Geographic Data Committee, 1993) that will facilitate the integration of federal and local government spatial information resources. Similarly, the recent spatial data standards development work by the Commission of the European Communities (see

CERCO, 1991, for a discussion) demonstrate that the role of standards for geographical information in aiding data fusion is very significant.

A lack of standard practices adds to project costs or prevents key projects from being taken forward (Rowley, 1992). In Britain, the Interdepartmental Group on Geographical Information (IGGI), central government's co-ordinating body for geographical information, has recently examined the potential for integrating the plethora of spatial units that are currently utilised within central government. In a paper describing this initiative, Garnsworthy and Massingham (1995) explain that much of the spatial data collected by central government might be useful for more than one purpose, but that inconsistency in spatial referencing frameworks, excessive complexity, lack of accuracy and differences in times of measurement mean that integration is often impossible, They suggest that the establishment of geographical data standards will greatly facilitate data sharing initiatives and bring substantial benefits in optimising the use of existing information and reducing data duplication.

Local authorities and the drive for spatial data standards

Local authorities are spearheading the development of standards for spatial data referencing, driven by their internal requirements for integrated geospatial information resources. The Local Government Management Board has been instrumental in working with the Association for Geographical Information (AGI), British Standards Institution and others on the development of the standards for spatial information that come under the banner of British Standard BS7666 (BSI, 1994). These are:

1. BS7666 Part One, Specification for a National Street Gazetteer and associated Computerised Streets and Road Works Register, providing a standard referencing framework for all streets in the UK.
2. BS7666 Part Two, Specification for a National Land and Property Gazetteer, providing a standard referencing framework for all land parcels in the UK and means of linking them to external data resources.
3. Specification for a Standard Address Format, providing a standard methodology for the recording of address related information.

BS7666 Part 4 (Specification of a dataset for recording a Public Right of Way) will be launched on November 14, 1996. The impetus for this new part arose because many local authorities were experiencing difficulties in fulfilling their obligations to record public rights of way. The benefits of using an IT solution to maintain definitive maps and statements of public rights of way were realised by many authorities and the working party responsible for developing BS7666 felt that duplication of effort could be minimised if the design of recording procedures for rights of way were standardised. This would also lead to other benefits such as ready exchange of data.

Each of the components of BS7666 provides a valuable resource for information integration, and the acceptance of the suite of specifications as a British standard and subsequent undertaking by Local Authorities to adhere to them is a significant step forward. Construction of BS7666 is progressing across the country. A completed database of BS7666 information will be a substantial resource, providing an integrated base framework for building geographical information resources at the national level.

Standards for data description

Another type of standard that is seeing widespread application is concerned with the description of spatial information. 'Data about data', or 'metadata', is now recognised as having a key role to play in the effective transfer of information resources from one place to another. The Americans have developed a Federal Government standard for describing geospatial information (FGDC, 1994) which has been adopted by all Federal government organisations and many other local government and executive agencies under the auspices of their National Spatial Data Infrastructure programme. Development of a similar European standard is currently underway.

Meta information standards will allow users of geographical information to evaluate the usefulness of data resources from other organisations for their own applications. The issue of data quality, and the suitability of data for specific uses is now being raised in the GIS community. If expensive mistakes are to be avoided, this type of information is essential because it allows potential users to evaluate information resources before they purchase or use them.

In recognition of the need for data quality information, the Association for Geographical Information has recently published a set of guidelines on spatial data quality and how to determine which aspects of quality are important given different user objectives (AGI, 1996). This publication is a much needed introductory document to the pitfalls of using and bringing together spatial information from different places.

The future

There are several initiatives under way that seek to widen the use and application of property information using GIS and LIS. Many of these initiatives originated at the application level in a similar way to that of the WALIS described above. Developments in IT have not occurred in isolation from their application. The main issue has been to try to ensure that the developers of these systems adhere as far as possible to common standards. In this way the initiatives that are briefly described below are achievable.

The absence of an integrated LIS in the UK has been recognised and there have been calls for comprehensive access to property data collected by various organisations and integrated using a common property referencing standard. The idea was propounded in a project called Domesday 2000 (Dale, 1991) which put forward the case for a National Land Information Service (NLIS) that would integrate data sources relating to property ownership, use and value. A market potential survey was undertaken and revealed a substantial market for integrated access to property information sources. Research continued under the auspices of the Domesday Research Group and a demonstrator system was developed with funding from the RICS. This led to a pilot NLIS, developed for part of Bristol and which is currently being expanded from two postal districts to the whole of Bristol (Smith, 1996). The project has been successful in using the property referencing standard, BS7666, to integrate data from various government departments and will investigate ways of including non-addressable property in order to gain one hundred percent coverage for the study area. Bristol City Council are hoping to use the system for the administration of local land charges and the Land

Registry plan to develop an on-line conveyancing application of the NLIS pilot. KPMG are due to report at the end of this year on the economic and financial viability of a national land information service that will offer integrated access to property use, ownership and price data. In parallel with NLIS, a similar initiative is under way in Scotland, called ScotLIS.

The Secretary of State for the Environment has endorsed two recommendations of the Association of Geographic Information and the Inter-departmental Group on Geographic Information. They are to develop:

1. The National Geospatial Database (NGD). NGD is an initiative that is being led by the Ordnance Survey and is defined as an over-arching framework that should facilitate the integration and dissemination of geospatial data sets that are maintained by various organisations (Nanson et al, 1995). It is envisaged that services like NLIS and ScotLIS would ease the development of such a system - being the practical application of a philosophy of data trading using common standards and adding value by combining disparate data sets.
2. A new Geographic Information Standards Statement for government departments and agencies.

Other developments such as the Spatial Information Enquiry Service (SINES) and the Standard Geographic Base for the UK (a set of core spatial references) are forcing suppliers and consumers of property information to focus on how to structure IT and information management policies so that maximum value is obtained from data collected. The emphasis is shifting from single-purpose to value-added data sets.

References

Association for Geographical Information (1996), *Guidelines for Geographic Information Content and Quality*, AGI, London.

Audit Commission (1988a), *Local Authority Property: A Management Handbook*, HMSO, London.

Audit Commission (1988b), *Local Authority Property: A Management Overview*, HMSO, London.

British Standards Institute (BSI) (1994), *Spatial Data-Sets for Geographical Referencing* : *BS 7666*, BSI, London.

Burke, A. (1993), 'The Western Australian Land Information System', in *Proceedings of the Urban and Regional Information Systems Conference,* URISA, United States, vol 1: 31-44.

CERCO Permanent Technical Group (1991), 'Organisational chart of geographic data standards and its application to project MEGRIN', in Koen, L and Kölbl, O., *Proceedings of the OEEPE Workshop on Data Quality in Land Information Systems,* OEEPE Official Publication No. 28, OEEPE, Frankfurt, pp.157 - 174.

Chartered Institute for Public Finance and Accountancy (1991), *Asset Registers - A Practical Guide,* CIPFA, London.

Dale, P. (1991), 'Domesday 2000: the professional as a politician', in *Proceedings of the AGI 91 Conference,* Association of Geographic Information, Birmingham.

Federal Geographic Data Committee (FGDC) (1993), *Vision for a National Spatial Data Infrastructure : a Strategic Plan for NSDI,* FGDC, United States.

Federal Geographic Data Committee (FGDC) (1994), *Content Standards for Geospatial Metadata,* FGDC, United States.

Garnsworthy, J. and Massingham, R. (1995), 'Geographic information standards in government', in *Proceedings of the Association for Geographical Information Conference,* Birmingham, AGI, London.

Lilburne, L. and Rix, D. (1991), 'The use of GIS in local government property records', *Mapping Awareness and GIS Europe,* vol 5 (10): 16-21.

London Borough of Barking and Dagenham (1992), *Land and Property Information Strategy,* unpublished consultancy document, London Borough of Barking and Dagenham, London.

London Borough of Barking and Dagenham (1996a), *GIS Review,* unpublished consultancy document, LBBD, London.

London Borough of Barking and Dagenham (1996b), *The Property Database Project,* Legal and Property Division, Chief Executive's Department, LBBD, London.

Lopez, X. (1992), *Data exchange and spatial information flows within local government in the Eastern Thames Corridor,* South East Regional Research Laboratory, Birkbeck College, University of London.

Nanson, B., Smith, N. and Davey, A. (1995), 'What is the British National Geospatial Database', in *Proceedings of the AGI Conference, Association of Geographic Information, Birmingham,* AGI, London.

Rowley, J. (1992), 'A strategy for geographic information standards', in *Proceedings of the Association for Geographic Information Conference,* Birmingham, AGI, London.

Royal Institution of Chartered Surveyors (RICS) (1987) *Property Management in Local Authorities: Evidence to the Audit Commission,* RICS, London.

Smith, P. (1996), 'The NLIS in 1996: the pilot project expands', *Mapping Awareness,* March : 22-24.

Western Australia State Government (1990), *An Integrated Land Information Program*, ILIP Office, Perth, Australia.

6 Managing Public Sector Property Assets: Valuation Issues

Peter Dent, School of Real Estate Management, Oxford Brookes University

Introduction

This paper is divided into two parts. The first part considers the nature of local authority assets within the context of overall management objectives. This leads on to the second part, a detailed analysis of research undertaken to examine the compilation of asset registers, the methods for the valuation of these assets, the appropriateness of such methods and the resulting explanations of value.

Until recently it seems that many authorities failed to keep a comprehensive record of their holdings. Whatever the reason for this, it is apparent that in order to undertake an active approach to the management of such assets, information in sufficient detail on the whole portfolio is the first priority. This must then be backed up by an efficient means of access to that information. In the UK, CIPFA and the RICS have worked together to draw up guidelines for authorities to undertake the task of preparing asset registers and valuing all their property holdings in line with the RICS's Statements of Asset Valuation Practice and Guidance Notes and its Manual of Valuation Guidance Notes (now incorporated into the RICS *Appraisal and Valuation Manual*). This exercise had to be completed by all authorities by April 1995. It is an exercise which hopefully will achieve greater accountability, economy and a more efficient resource use. Despite these guidelines, there is some doubt about the methodology used in completing the valuations. This paper, based in part on postal questionnaires and interviews, questions the validity of asset valuations in the public sector and whether more appropriate means of appraisal may be found in other disciplines.

The nature and management of local authority assets

The management process, at the most basic level, has been defined as the process which converts information into action and in the context of property management, Thorncroft (1965) describes it as: 'the direction and supervision of an interest in landed property with the aim of securing the optimum return, this return need not always be financial, but may be in terms of social benefit, status, prestige, political power or some other goal or group of goals'. This suggests that property ownership is about power; not simply the power to secure a return on an investment, but the less tangible power of status and control. It is also about the freedom to express that power. This has most clearly been seen in the past in terms of political alignments, although, over the course of the last 100 years, there has been a move away from the concept of freedom expressed in political terms to a 'new idea of liberty' which is political only in the sense that the role of the state is understood as essentially a matter of protecting the rights of individuals. Among the most important of such rights is property (Ryan, 1987). This sense of power and freedom engendered in property ownership is also concerned with responsibility and the idea of 'moral authority' referred to by Arnison (1984) when considering the role of property in social relationships.

Whilst the individual must accept some responsibilities for the ownership of private property, in the public sector such ownership and associated responsibility has much wider social implications. This is the case because local authorities 'provide the infrastructure on which economic, social and environmental development is based' (Local Government Information Unit, 1992). As such their aspirations and assets (homes, schools, roads etc.) create the framework within which the overall well-being of a community will be determined.

The nature of the property assets held by a local authority can be identified under three main headings for management purposes (see Audit Commission, 1988):

1. Direct service property. This relates to those properties occupied in the course of providing a specific (sometimes specialist) service e.g. schools, crematoria etc. This is usually to fulfil a statutory requirement.
2. Tenanted property. This generally relates to investment property which the authority can let in an open market and obtain a commercial

return. However it also includes property let to support other economic or social activities (for example, employment opportunity, community groups etc.).

3. Vacant property. This category includes both land and buildings which are either surplus to requirements or acquired in advance of development, redevelopment or the completion of a public scheme (e.g. highway improvement, public open space etc.).

In addition to these broad categories local authorities will also 'own' infrastructure assets such as roads and footpaths.

In the context of the management function of local authorities this breakdown has a clearly identifiable logic. But, when it comes to providing values for the assets, categorising assets by methodology may suggest a different grouping. This raises concerns about the appropriateness of the way in which data on property assets is currently presented within the overall management structure of the authority.

Asset registers and asset values

> In the last decade... it has thus become more important than ever that the valuer of property assets should conform to certain recognisable and acceptable standards in the approach to valuations, their use and their presentation... Such a valuer (will have a) responsibility to the public (Bowie, 1976).

Whilst the call to establish local authority asset registers and assess asset values is much more recent than this quote (the quote itself was made in the wake of the general debate on inflation accounting) it was made at a point in time when responsibilities for, and reliance on, valuations were starting to become an important issue for the property profession. But still today (20 years later) it is debatable whether there are 'recognisable and acceptable standards' to follow for valuers of local authority assets despite the number of guidelines available. It is also potentially divisive to allocate a monetary value as the sole measure of such an asset's worth when the purpose of ownership is outside the financial sphere. But with the current exercise now complete this is how it may look.

From the point of view of CIPFA '...the proposals are aimed at improving the quality of published information, which may stimulate further investigation/review to ensure that the local authorities' assets are managed and utilised efficiently and effectively' (CIPFA, 1990). Clearly it is a significant benefit to an authority's management function to maintain a register of ownership and a portfolio database. What is more open to question is the validity of notional values derived through methods that sometimes rely on arbitrary inputs.

The justification for undertaking the exercise seems to have its origins in The Layfield Report (1976) where reasons for asset valuation include: (1) for comparison with outstanding loans; (2) to discharge accountability to the public for their use by ensuring the best use is made of the assets, and (3) for resource allocation and priority setting. This might suggest more efficient resource allocation and a performance measure over time. But unless the difficulties of providing values for some public assets are overcome (or at the very least acknowledged and qualified values given) then serious distortions may exist in the outcomes reported in the accounts and used potentially both within the authority and externally.

From the results of the surveys undertaken for this paper it is apparent that despite significantly improved information availability and the guidance provided from the various accountancy and valuation bodies, there is still a degree of uncertainty firstly about the appropriate method/base and secondly about some of the finer detail in specific cases. Of course much methodological detail is usually left to the judgement of the individual valuer, but now those 'guidelines' are mandatory as opposed to prescriptive, such uncertainty tends to militate against any judgement, however well-founded, that veers too far away from these guidelines.

Methodology

In an earlier article (Dent and Bond, 1993) some of the limitations of conventional bases of valuation were highlighted. Most valuation methods are based on the assumption that property is held for financial gain (either direct in the case of investment property or indirect in the case of owner occupied holdings). This may not be the case with local authorities who have a role of providing services to the local community.

Whilst the provision of these services relies to some extent on the generation of revenue, there is no financial profit motive and, because of the nature of the asset and its use often there is no clearly definable market. Nevertheless, local authorities are now under pressure to 'value' their assets. CIPFA require all fixed assets to be included in the consolidated balance sheet at current value. In this context this is defined as their net current replacement cost except in the case of infrastructure and community assets. Here infrastructure assets are defined as 'fixed assets which are inalienable assets, expenditure on which is recoverable only by continued use of the asset created. Examples being highways and footpaths'(Annex A GN11 RICS, 1995 Amendments 2 March, 1996). Community assets, on the other hand, are - assets that the local authority intends to hold in perpetuity, that have no determinable useful life, and that may have restrictions on their disposal. '... The test for a community asset is whether it is alienable'. These two groups of asset do not need to be valued as such but simply recorded at historical cost.

There will generally be no real technical problem in arriving at appropriate values for non-specialised, non-operational assets as, by their very nature, there tends to be a clearly defined market within which value criteria can be assessed. On the other hand, value issues surround the more specialised, operational property. Generally, the recommended approach for the valuation of such property is to use a depreciated replacement cost even though there is a lack of enthusiasm for it within the valuation profession, according to the RICS. In fact, because it is based on a building cost figure, and on terms, it is assumed, that would have been agreed prior to the start of construction (see Practice Statement 4.8.2 RICS, 1995), in times of significant contract price change the end figure may be misleading for the purpose required.

This has been explicitly demonstrated by Garry Hicks (1993) when tender prices dropped between 1989 and 1993 by approx. 25 percent leading to a commensurate overvaluation on a specialised building. Because of this built-in timelag there will always be a misalignment such that the asset's assessed value is unlikely to be its deprival value. In the case of local authorities this is particularly relevant bearing in mind the nature and size of assets involved. This particular issue is not insignificant in itself. However, when taken in the context of the overall exercise of attempting to quantify the unquantifiable (or rather, quantifying but using inappropriate measures to do so), this can compound the arbitrariness of the approach. Whilst it is acknowledged that an accounting theory is central to any culture, it has to be recognised the parameters of such theory are not restricted to monetary values. Taking such a restrictive view may well distort (knowingly or unknowingly) outcomes as 'it may be that the (basically irrational) selection of a single dimension and a single goal (whatever it may be) is a powerful incentive towards the manipulation of one's environment' (Gambling, 1974).

In the case of local authorities, serious doubt has been expressed over the application of an approach which uses a monetary test of profitability. According to Notton (1990), 'where no test of profitability exists against which to measure deprival value the figures appearing in the balance sheet representing the worth of the asset to the business cannot be stated as 'values'. In the guidelines published so far public properties not occupied or held primarily for profit are to be valued using the depreciated replacement cost approach. The resultant figure should be a value 'expressed as subject to the prospect and viability of the continuance of the occupation and use' (Practice Statement 4.8.6 RICS, 1995).

The appropriateness of this phrase (or equivalent as appearing in The Manual of Valuation Guidance Notes 2nd edition 1989) was questioned in the Britton, Connellan, Crofts' report (RICS/Kingston Polytechnic, 1991). The assumption here is that the authority intends to hold on to the asset and continue the use to which it is put for, at least, the short term. The calculation also assumes viability. This suggests that regardless of what value is produced using this approach an asset should not have a value which jeopardises the continuance of its use. The term 'viability' has been defined as 'capable of maintaining its life or the life of its kind' (Oxford English Dictionary).

In the context of a property asset held primarily for investment this could relate to either the flow of net benefits or the potential net realisation price of the asset. In fact there will usually be an element of both in the assessment. But in the case of a local authority the purpose of 'maintaining the life of an asset' is essentially non-monetary (i.e. it is most usually to maintain a service).

On the face of it, therefore, substituting viability for profitability in the guidelines does not provide an effective answer. In another context, however, it has been suggested that 'financial measures of performance will only be effective if they are complemented by non-financial expressions of output and impact' (CIPFA, 1978). This takes the discussion of such assets away from measurement solely through quantitative techniques into the wider arena which includes qualitative judgements of social and environmental impacts. Whilst this is certainly within the aegis of every local authority it does not appear to be the intention behind the RICS's or CIPFA's guidelines. In fact, whilst CIPFA identify three alternative methods of measuring current value (i.e. 'entry value', 'exit value' and 'value in use') they concentrate exclusively on the first two in their *'Guide to Valuation'* (1994) whereas the value in use approach would seem to be the most adaptable to include the wider issues.

Research undertaken

Against this background the author undertook some primary research of local authorities and their advisers into the issues surrounding the valuation of their assets. The intention of the research was to carry out studies into the experience in the UK to assess the overall exercise.

Research procedure

A pilot study was undertaken with a small sample of local authorities to assess the extent of the exercise to produce asset registers within the stipulated timescale, whether the end result was considered beneficial and what effect the whole exercise had on resources. This study was followed by a postal questionnaire to all local authority valuation officers in the UK. In total 227 authorities were contacted. The results that follow are based on a response rate of 55 percent. The initial data analysis included the calculation of means and percentages by response categories for all questions to provide an overview of response patterns. This information helped to identify the proportion of public assets owned by local authorities and to determine the extent of any problems highlighted in the approaches taken to record and value these.

Results of the local authority survey

Asset register

It seems that one of the main issues, and a major impetus for the whole exercise, was concern over the lack of data held by authorities on their property holdings. Whilst some authorities maintained a comprehensive record of their assets the suggestion was that many did not know the extent of their ownership. CIPFA's report on the 'Implementation Studies' (CIPFA, 1992) also indicated that some discrepancies might have existed.

In the case of Solihull, for example, '...not all properties were insured; sold properties were still insured; and water bills were being paid in respect of demolished properties...'. The overall inference was, however, that probably most authorities had all the necessary information but it was not collated in one central location. It was also apparent from the pilot study that not all departments within individual authorities were aware of the importance of the task of compiling and maintaining an asset register/terrier and the significance of the information required to be included.

From the pilot study, no authority indicated that it was proposing to inspect every property specifically for this exercise. Most were intending initially to centralise and rationalise existing data with the longer term objective of completing a more extensive survey and valuation on a rolling programme. Some of those questioned had employed temporary part time staff to assist in this, others had increased their staff complement. However, because of budgetary constraints, most authorities were relying on existing staff to take on increased workloads or rather give lower priorities to other duties (for example, day-to-day management).

The necessity and use of computers seems to be determined very much by the level of computer literacy of the person directly responsible for the collation of the information. For example, a small authority with a relatively straightforward task had developed a sophisticated database as the asset register, whilst a much larger authority with a more complex portfolio was hoping to complete the task, at least, initially using existing paper based records. From the postal questionnaire responses, approximately two thirds of respondents had a computerised database, leaving a third still relying on hard copy alone. On the question of reviewing the information held on database the results show that 36 percent of authorities update their records on a continuous, day-to-day basis.

Assets owned

It is interesting to note that only property holdings are required to be valued in the UK. This includes both operational and non-operational. Plant, equipment and vehicles, infrastructure and community assets (parks, cemeteries, non-operational heritage property etc) do not require valuation, but are recorded at historical cost. The UK has managed to avoid many of the problems associated with valuing such assets as infrastructure by not requiring them to be valued. This perhaps is in acknowledgement of the difficulties involved with determining realistic figures for such assets.

Table 6.1 Details of Asset Recording

Factor	%
Is a record of assets owned kept	
Yes	98
No	2
Type of Database Maintained	
Computer	69
Hard copy	
Both computer and hard copy	

Valuation of assets

The regularity of asset valuations was of interest to determine if there is consistency in this between local authorities. Further, it was of interest to determine if the local authorities are fully aware of the purpose for carrying out such valuations. Given that the majority of local authorities value the assets for a financial reporting purpose which occurs on an annual basis, the regularity of valuation would indicate how up-to-date the figures shown in these reports are. Obviously, the older the valuations, the less relevant they may be to present day circumstances, which could potentially jeopardise the usefulness of the figures indicated in the reports for management purposes.

The results indicate that 92 percent of authorities regularly value their assets. The interpretation of what is considered 'regular' seems to be five yearly, with 83 percent of respondents updating valuations on this basis. No doubt cost would be a reason for this less frequent updating but it is also likely that this is the case because it is the minimum requirement in the guidelines.

Table 6.2 Update of Information Recorded

Factor	%
How often is the Register Updated	
Continuously, day-to-day	36
Regular	33
When needed, reactive	30
Annually	0
Two-three yearly	0
Never	1

Table 6.3 Asset Valuations

Factor	%
Are Assets Valued Regularly	
Yes	92
No	8
Regularity of Valuation Updates	
Annually	13
Two yearly	1
Three yearly	12
Four yearly	3
Five yearly	83

Table 6.3 Asset Valuations continued

Factor	%
Purpose of the Valuation	
(i) Legislation	39
(ii) Annual book-keeping	51
(iii) Insurance	2
Asset Management	2
Other	6

While it does appear that local authorities are aware of the purpose for having the valuations completed, it is of concern that they are using these for other purposes in some cases. Given that a valuation is undertaken for a particular purpose and the methodology adopted is based on that purpose, the valuation figures may not be relevant, or the methodology appropriate, for another purpose and to use them for such could be providing misleading results. Financial reporting is now required annually by legislation so annual bookkeeping and legislation options may be considered by some respondents to be one and the same.

Table 6.4 The Valuers Employed

Factor	%
Valuer Status	
In-house	84
Independent	16
Both-in-house & Independent	0
Verification of In-house Values	
Yes	0
No	100

In this section of the survey authorities were asked about the status of the valuers undertaking their valuations and whether these valuations are independently verified. The purpose of these questions was to determine the objectivity of the valuations and their appropriateness to the task, as well as to identify the independent valuers involved. There is no requirements to have values verified. This may raise questions on the overall objectivity of the exercise. It was not surprising, therefore, that no authority sought external verification.

Valuation methodology

As already mentioned, not all asset classes are required to be valued in the UK. For property holdings specific guidelines are provided as to which method to use for each asset separately listed. For example, depreciated replacement cost is the method to use to value such properties as schools, leisure centres, fire stations, cemetery buildings etc. termed operational, specialised property.

Table 6.5 Valuation Methods for Property

Factor	%
Method	
Sales Comparison	32
Replacement Cost	33
Income/DCF	20
Other	15

Guidance provided

All those interviewed were aware of the valuation guidelines and their implications. Most had seen the additional information booklets produced by CIPFA. This was supported by the responses from the questionnaire. However, most considered that their authority could have been more supportive in allowing staff to attend training and awareness courses and seminars.

Table 6.6 Guidance Provided

Factor	%
Extent of Guidance	
None	5
A little	12
Some	58
A Lot	25

The most significant difficulty identified was concerning the valuation of non-market specialised properties and the cost approach recommendations. Some of these difficulties have been alleviated by the CIPFA publications but some specific cases still cause uncertainty (for example, civic and heritage buildings).

Appropriateness of the valuation exercise

The majority of the respondents consider that the valuation methods outlined in the questionnaire are appropriate for the exercise being undertaken. Of those that responded by saying they consider either none, or only some of the methods to be appropriate, the reasons most commonly cited for this were that cost and historic government values do not adequately reflect value.

Only approximately two thirds of the respondents consider that the values derived are an accurate reflection of the value of local authority's assets. These lower-than-expected results would indicate that for some respondents the valuations are not meeting the purposes for which they are required. Reasons cited include the inaccuracy of the valuations, no alternative uses were included, no opportunity costs were shown and, in some cases, there may be two different values (i.e. authority and community values) and not just one, as assumed. Despite, therefore, up to 37 percent of the respondents considering that the valuations are not an accurate reflection of value, 92 percent considered that the valuation exercise, as a whole, was useful in achieving the purpose for which it was required.

Table 6.7 Appropriateness, Accuracy and Usefulness

Factor	%
Appropriateness of the Methods	
Yes	91
Some are, others are not	0
Unsure	2
No	7
Accuracy of the Valuations	
Yes	63
No	33
Unsure	4
Usefulness of the Valuation Exercise	
Yes	92
No	7
Unsure	1

Suggestions for how the task could be better achieved included the need for accurate condition surveys and information on asset running costs to be supplied, an increased timescale allowed for undertaking the valuations, greater liaison between authorities, the need to find an alternative to depreciated replacement cost and the use of net realisation 'values'.

Conclusions

Most local authorities keep an asset register, with two thirds of the respondents using a computer database for this. Authorities update their registers regularly (i.e. on a day-to-day basis) but are not so efficient with their valuation updates, these being mostly five yearly.

Most respondents use in-house valuers and over three quarters of the respondents considered that the valuation methods recommended were appropriate and the valuation exercise was useful in achieving its purpose.

It is clear, however, that the process of recording and valuing local authority assets for financial reporting purposes is still evolving. From this study it would appear that much work is still needed to achieve the initial purpose of greater resource efficiency. The guidelines emanating from CIPFA and within the RICS Manual are constantly under review. However, now that the deadline to complete the asset registers has passed, the pressure to a large extent has been removed and resources can be re-allocated. Over the next five years on a rolling programme all assets will have to be valued in line with the requirements in the RICS Manual. What has not, as yet, been addressed by authorities is the appropriateness of the methods prescribed for the large number of non-market, specialised property assets held by authorities.

Whilst, therefore, this research has highlighted the problems involved with the recording, valuing and reporting of local authority assets within the UK, it is clear that although, from the foregoing, the professional bodies involved are taking action to help overcome these, additional work is needed to achieve more authentic valuations for some specific assets. Research is continuing in an effort to develop a more appropriate methodology. Work currently underway with colleagues both in this country and abroad may enable a truly valid international valuation model of such assets to be developed.

Note

This paper is a modified version of a paper presented at The RICS Cutting Edge Conference in Bristol in September 1996. That paper was undertaken in conjunction with Sandy Bond at Massey University, New Zealand and drew comparisons between the experiences of UK authorities and public bodies in New Zealand.

References

Arnison, C. (1984), 'Masters and tenants: leasehold tenure as a mechanism for moral governance,' in Chiddick, D. and Millington, A. (eds), *Land Management: New Directions*, Spon, London.

Audit Commission (1988), *Local Authority Property. A Management Handbook* HMSO, London.

Bond, S. and Dent, P. (1996), 'Public sector property assets: management objectives and valuation methodology', *Cutting Edge,* RICS, London.

Bowie, N. (1976), 'Valuation of company property assets', *Chartered Surveyor Urban Quarterly,* vol 4 (1).

Britton, W., Connellan, O. and Crofts M. (1991), *The Cost Approach to Valuation*, RICS/Kingston Polytechnic.

Chartered Institute of Public Finance and Accountancy (1978), *Social Accounting*, CIPFA, London.

Chartered Institute of Public Finance and Accountancy (1990), *Capital Accounting in Local Authorities: Final Report of the Capital Accounting Steering Group,* CIPFA, London.

Chartered Institute of Public Finance and Accountancy (1992), *Capital Accounting by Local Authorities - Report of the Implementation Studies,* CIPFA, London.

Chartered Institute of Public Finance and Accountancy (1994), *Guide to Valuation,*CIPFA, London.

Dent, P. and Bond, S. (1993), 'Public property holdings: evaluating the asset', *Property Management,* vol. 11 (4).

Gambling, T. (1974), *Societal Accounting*, George Allen & Unwin Ltd, London.

Hicks, G. (1993), 'Overvaluation of specialist buildings', *Estates Gazette,* 9331.

HMSO (1976), *Local Government Finance,* Cmnd 6453.

Local Government Information Unit (1992), *Local Government in the 1990s. A Discussion Document on the Role and Function of Local Authorities*, LGIU, London.

Notton, W. (1990), 'Public sector property assets', *Estates Gazette*, 9013.

Royal Instutition of Chartered Surveyors (1990), *Statements of Asset Valuation Practice and Guidance Notes* (Third Edition), RICS, London.

Royal Institution of Chartered Surveyors (1992), *Manual of Valuation Guidance Notes,* RICS, London.

Royal Institution of Chartered Surveyors (1995), *Appraisal and Valuation Manual,* RICS, London.

Ryan, A. (1987), *Property,* Open University Press, Buckingham.

Thorncroft, M. (1965), *Principles of Estate Management,* Estates Gazette, London.

7 Valuation of Specialised Public Sector Assets

Owen Connellan, School of the Built Environment, Glamorgan University

Introduction

Local Authorities are now required to produce asset valuations for accounting and management purposes. Specialised property, for which there is little or no market, has to be valued under the RICS Red Book using the Depreciated Replacement Cost (DRC) basis. This paper reviews the consequent requirements of Local Authorities and the valuation techniques available for producing capital and rental figures, including the latest 'S Curve method'. This paper derives from a comprehensive *Valuation Manual* prepared by Britton and Connellan (1997).

CIPFA requirements on capital accounting

Local Authorities have been required to prepare asset registers and to value these assets following *Sections 41 and 42 of the Local Government Act 1989* and subsequent regulations. These called for the introduction of a code of practice for the preparation of a statement of accounts which presents fairly the financial position and transactions of a local authority. The response to this is embodied in the *Code of Practice on Local Authority Accounting in Great Britain* prepared by the Chartered Institute of Public Finance and Accountancy (CIPFA, 1993) whereby local authorities are required to prepare a register and valuation of all their land and property '*with a material value*' for inclusion in their balance sheets from 1994/5. Subsequent valuation instruction advice from CIPFA (1994b) requires the authorities to carry out the valuations in accordance with the RICS *Appraisal and Valuation Manual* (RICS, 1995 [Red Book]).

The purposes of valuations

These asset valuations are part of a move to a common accounting approach aimed at ensuring a measure of conformity throughout local authorities. The valuations will give rise to capital charges in service revenue accounts for all fixed assets used in the delivery of services.

The need for revaluation

The 'first pass' valuations have now been carried out and the more onerous task of revaluation now looms ahead for local authorities.

Sources

The subsequent *Red Book* references will be mainly to *Practice Statements*, (PS) and Appendices, or to *Guidance Notes*, (GN) and Appendices thereto. Compliance with these *Practice Statements* is mandatory upon members of the RICS, ISVA and IRRV (subject to the right to justify departure). *Guidance Notes* provide further material and information on good valuation practice. Following the advice and recommendations contained in the *Guidance Notes* is not mandatory but in practical terms the whole of the Red Book is likely to be regarded as best practice.

Guidance Note 11

GN 11.2.2 refers to the *Code of Practice* (CIPFA, 1993) which sets up the current local authority accounting system and goes on to say: '[the system] requires nearly all fixed assets to be included in the consolidated balance sheet at current value, defined as their net current replacement cost, other than infrastructure assets and community assets, which should be recorded at historical cost'.

GN 11.4 states: the valuer may be asked to carry out any or all of the following activities:

- agree, if requested, the categorisation of assets prepared by the authority;
- classify the assets to be valued;
- carry out inspections and prepare valuations;
- estimate the remaining useful life of assets to be valued; and undertake revaluations periodically as required by the client in accordance with the *Code of Practice on Local Authority Accounting*.

GN 11.5 states the reasons for the valuations as: for inclusion in the financial statements of the authority, and to provide a basis for the assessment of capital charges for the use and consumption of the assets. GN 11.6.1 states: the [CIPFA] Code requires that operational assets including operational land and buildings (except infrastructure, other than certain water and drainage properties in Scotland) should be included in the balance sheet at the lower of net current replacement cost (NCRC) and net realisable value (NRV) in existing use.

Categorisation and classification of properties

GN 11 Annexes A and B define Non-operational Assets as: fixed assets held by a local authority but not directly occupied, used or consumed in the delivery of services. Examples are investment properties and assets that are surplus to requirements, pending sale or redevelopment. It defines: Operational Assets as: fixed assets held and occupied, used or consumed by the local authority in the direct delivery of those services for which it has either a statutory or discretionary responsibility. Community Assets as: assets that the local authority intends to hold in perpetuity, that have no determinable useful life, and that may have restrictions on their disposal. It also goes on to define Infrastructure Assets as: fixed assets which are inalienable assets, expenditure on which is recoverable only by continued use of the asset created. Examples are highways and footpaths.

GN 11.9 states : for valuation purposes local authority property usually falls into the following groups:

- Non-operational property (i.e. investment, surplus and development property) is valued on the basis of (open) market value (MV/OMV);
- Operational, non-specialised property, valued on the basis of existing use value (EUV); and

- Operational, specialised properties, valued on the basis of DRC.

A summary of the categorisation, classification and valuation is provided in Figure 7.1.

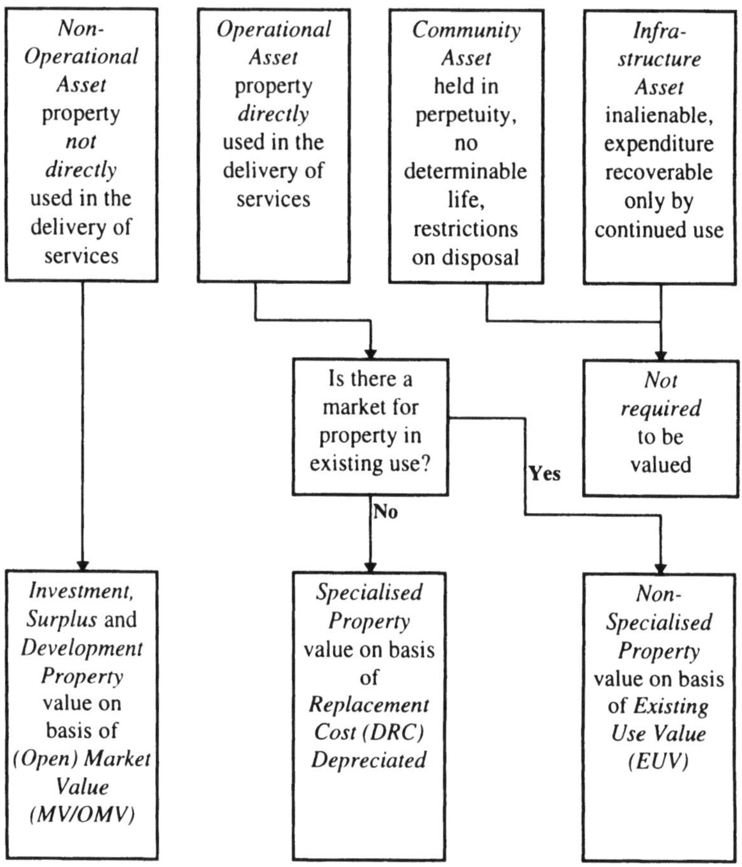

Figure 7.1 Classification and Valuation Treatment of Assets

Specialised property

Specialised Properties are defined in the Red Book as: those which, due to their specialised nature are rarely, if ever, sold on the open market for single occupation and as a continuation of their existing use, except as part of a sale of the business in occupation. Their specialised nature may arise from the construction, arrangement, size or location of the property, or a combination of these factors, or may be due to the nature of the plant and machinery and items of equipment which the buildings are designed to house or the function, or the purpose for which the buildings are provided.

GN 11.10.1 states: the use of much local authority property often brings it within the category of 'specialised property' It is the appointed valuer's responsibility to determine whether each property is 'specialised' or 'non-specialised' and to value as required by PS 3.

Depreciated replacement cost [DRC]

PS 3 is entitled '*Purposes of Valuations*' and PS 3.5 deals with specialised properties. PS 3.5.1(b) includes the following statement: the (DRC) basis is used to arrive at the net current replacement cost required for accounting purposes for those properties in respect of which there is a lack of demand or market. In each case where the valuer is considering the use of the DRC basis of valuation he must be satisfied that it is not practicable to prepare a reliable valuation on the existing use value basis.

PS 3.5.2 goes on to say: except in respect of public sector property DRC must always be expressed by the valuer as subject to adequate potential profitability of the business compared with the value of the total assets employed. The valuer, following consultation with the directors or, in the case of the public sector, the instructing body should decide whether any further deductions should be made to reflect the client's advice as to the inability of the business to carry the property in its balance sheet at the full DRC value.

PS 3.5.4(b) states: in the case of specialised properties in public ownership not occupied primarily for profit, where the test of adequate potential profitability is not available, DRC should be expressed as having regard to the prospect and viability of the continuance of the occupation and use.

DRC is defined in PS 4.8.1 as: the aggregate amount of the value of the land for the existing use or a notional replacement site in the same locality, and the gross replacement cost of the buildings and other site works, from which appropriate deductions may then be made to allow for the age, condition, economic or functional obsolescence and environmental factors etc; all of which might result in the existing property being worth less to the undertaking in occupation than would a new replacement.

PS 4.8.2 states: the cost to be estimated is not to erect a building in the future but that to have the building available for occupation at the valuation date, the work having commenced at the appropriate time. PS 4.8.3 states: the depreciated replacement cost (DRC) basis of valuation is used for the valuation of specialised properties. It is a method of using net current replacement costs to arrive at the value to the undertaking in occupation of the property as existing at the evaluation date, where it is not practicable to ascertain existing use value. However GN 11.10.3 states: where the DRC basis is adopted, the authority may require also a valuation for a realistic alternative use in connection with its asset management strategy and policy. There are, therefore, three elements required in order to perform a valuation on the DRC basis - the value of the land in its existing use, the gross replacement cost (GRC) of the building and the appropriate deductions from GRC for all types of obsolescence and depreciation.

Site valuation

There are some fairly detailed provisions relating to the valuation of the site within a DRC calculation in PS 4.8.7 but these can be distilled into a set of decision-based rules which are shown in Figure 7.2. Thus, in relation to sites for primary schools, for example, in the majority of cases the schools will be located in or immediately adjacent to the residential areas which they serve. In that case, the basis of valuation for the school site and its playing fields will generally be residential value.

There is no straightforward definition of GRC where it might be expected in the Red Book, that is in PS 4.8, and its meaning has to be constructed by inference from the various provisions relating to it. The closest textbook parallel for the valuer is the building and site improvement costing which goes into a residual valuation, subject to a number of provisions specific to the task in hand such as the use of modern substitutes.

It would appear that a building falls into one of two categories, the first a reconstruction of the existing building exactly as it was originally constructed, which is termed for the purposes of this paper as replacement, and the second a modern building with what is termed in PS 4.8.8(b) above as 'equivalent service capacity'. For this latter category various expressions are used in the Red Book but these have been treated as synonymous and the single expression 'modern substitute' is used to cover all of them.

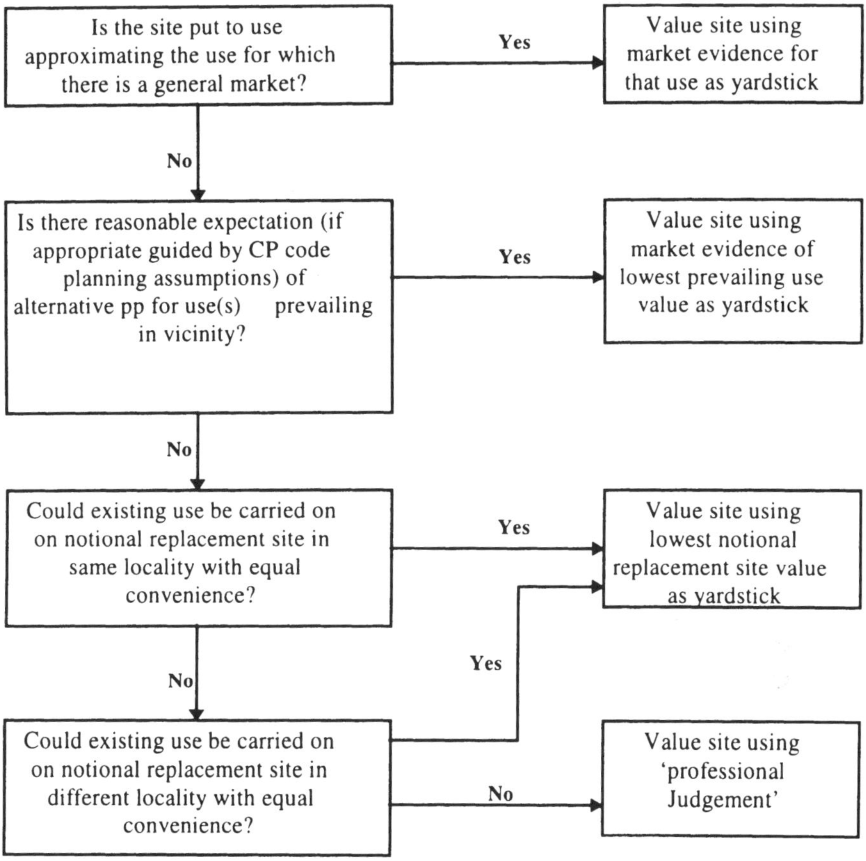

Figure 7.2 Choosing a Yardstick Site Value

Gross Replacement Cost (GRC) of the Building

Algorithm - the classification of buildings can be distilled into a set of decision-based rules as shown in Figure 7.3.

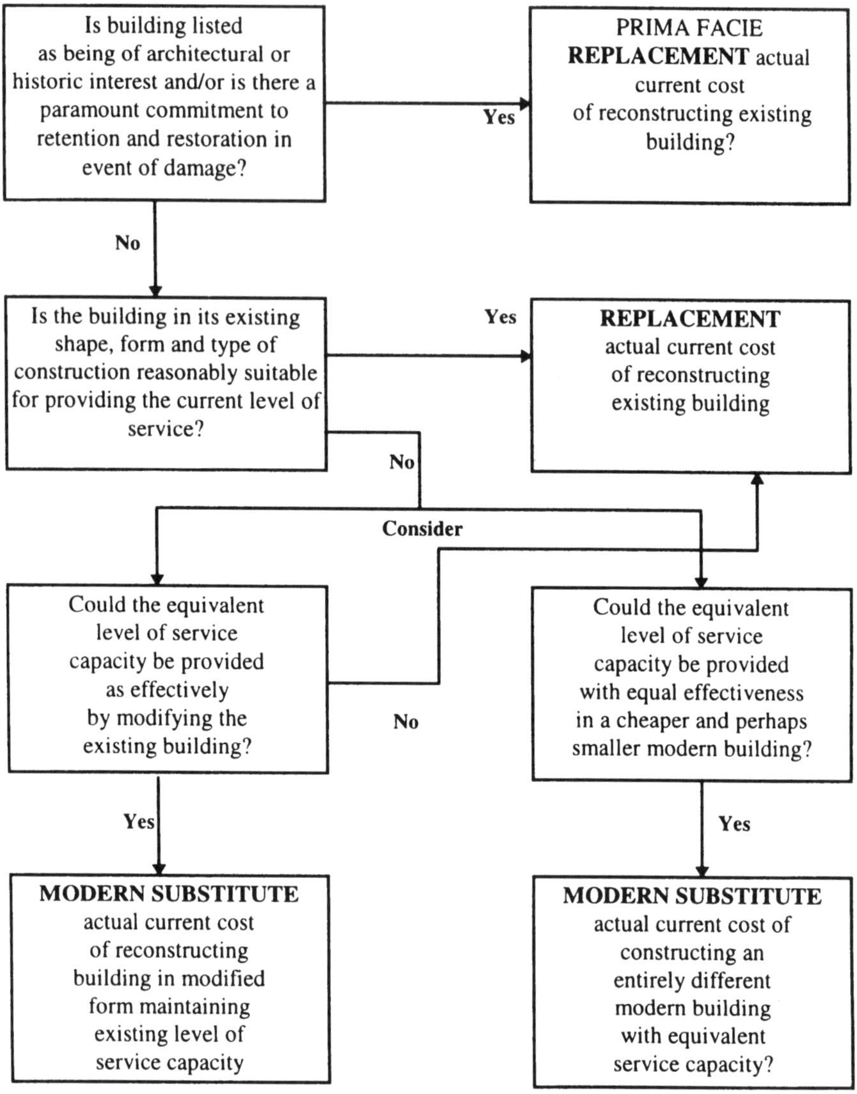

Figure 7.3 Choosing a Yardstick Building

Building costing

PS 4.8.2 states: the cost to be estimated is not to erect a building in the future but that to have the building available for occupation at the valuation date, the work having commenced at the appropriate time. There has been some discussion on whether this provision is intended only to obviate difficulties which would arise from allowing a lengthy construction period or if it also had an effect on the appropriate level of cost.

It is interesting, and perhaps relevant, to compare the Red Book provisions with the following quotation from another RICS publication *The Contractor's Basis of Valuation for Rating Purposes*. The contractor's basis requires an assumption to be made that construction is of the property as a whole based on competitive rates prevailing on the valuation date. Therefore, any actual cost information will need to be adjusted to correspond with that basis.

Other costs

There are various references to costs other than the cost of the building work throughout the Red Book and the majority are manifestly those which any valuer would take into account in preparing this type of valuation. It is clear from PS 4.8.8(a) that these costs should take into consideration everything that is necessary to complete the construction from a new green field site to provide buildings as they are at the time of valuation. The typical cost items are listed below:

- finance carrying charges;
- grants;
- VAT - but the inclusion of irrecoverable VAT may depend on the accounting policy of the undertaking;
- developer's or entrepreneurial profit - but in the vast majority of cases, local authority assets would be created, actually or notionally, without a developer's profit being incurred.
- plant and machinery;
- site improvements;
- depreciation (principles).

The gross replacement cost (GRC) of the building having been calculated, the valuer must address the problem of reducing that gross figure to a net figure which will represent the value of the building at the date of valuation. That deduction is the amount appropriate for all causes of depreciation. There is a tendency to use the expressions 'depreciation' and 'obsolescence' interchangeably. Confusion is avoided if obsolescence is regarded as the cause and depreciation as the effect.

The Red Book addresses depreciation in PS 4.8.8(e) which states:-

> In considering deductions from gross replacement cost, the Valuer must be guided by what is there and this must be considered in assessing the depreciation factor. In assessing deductions the Valuer must have regard to the relative decline in value of buildings of similar age and type for which there is a market when economic obsolescence - the age and condition of the existing building and the probable cost of future maintenance as compared with that of a modern building; functional obsolescence - suitability for the present use and the prospect of its continuance, or use for some other purpose by the undertaking. For example, a building constructed or adapted for specialised uses, including particular industrial processes, may have an apparent useful life for a different purpose (by the undertaking in occupation) longer than contemplated for the actual operation carried on. The Valuer must always consult with the Client to ascertain his future plans; and environmental factors - existing use must be considered in relation to the surrounding area and to local and national planning and environmental policies.

The valuation process requires that, where a building is being normally maintained in relation to its normally expected useful life, a definite provision for the main cause of depreciation must be made, except where the life is indefinite.

Allowing for depreciation

The main form of depreciation is age-related depreciation, that is to say, the wearing away of value over a period of time. This wearing away is not confined to the purely physical effects of time on building components but embraces all of the other functional, economic and environmental changes which happen over time. If a modified 'modern substitute' is used instead of exactly reproducing the actual building, the modifications will have notionally eliminated some of the causes of depreciation and no further allowance should be made for those items. Methods of assessing the depreciation allowance are not addressed in the Red Book but are considered in the following section.

Quantifying depreciation

There are two basic methods of quantifying depreciation within cost-based valuations. The first is that based on the well-established contractor's basis in rating where the equivalent of GRC is reduced by making percentage deductions justified by custom and precedent, and which is termed the estimated percentage depreciation (EPD) method. The second is the straight-line depreciation (SLD) method which makes the assumption that there is an even wearing away of value over the life of an asset. This is the method used by the CIPFA in examples of valuations of specialised operational properties in CIPFA's *Guide to Valuation* (1994) and by the Valuation Office Agency for its original valuation of the NHS estate. These two methods are considered in detail subsequently, as are two other methods of quantifying methods.

EPD, SLD, DAR and S Curve are all cost-based methods and require information on age and unexpired useful life and identification of forms of obsolescence. The major difference lies in how the basic allowance for ageing is quantified and made. The building classifications, 'Replacement' and 'Modern Substitute' can be applied to all four methods but slightly different classifications were originally advocated for DAR.

The following issues also have to be considered in relation to the quantifying of depreciation:

Unexpired useful life

GN 11.11.11 states:

> Local authorities will be looking to the Valuer to provide an estimate of 'unexpired useful life' of operational assets, as this will determine the level of any provision for depreciation. This will in turn influence the capital charges made for the use and occupation of fixed assets. The Valuer's estimates should assume prudent continuing maintenance. 'Useful life' is defined in GN 11 Annex A as the period over which the local authority will derive benefits from the use of a fixed asset.

Deferred maintenance

Despite the requirement to assume prudent continuing maintenance in GN 11.11.11 for the purpose of estimating future life, there may, however, be an accumulation of past maintenance and the cost of remedying this will be a deduction from GRC. It is important to remember that this deduction must be made after allowance has been made for age-related depreciation.

Curable depreciation

Some forms of obsolescence may be capable of being cured by expenditure. Whether or not such a cause of depreciation is capable of being remedied at economic cost must, in the absence of a market test, be a matter of judgement for the valuer.

Algorithm - these instructions can be distilled into a set of decision-based rules as shown in Figure 7.4 but note that they do not necessarily apply to listed, historic and otherwise protected buildings where there would be a paramount commitment to retention or restoration in the event of damage.

Asset rents and capital charges

GN 11.5 states that the purposes of valuations are '...for inclusion in the financial statements ... and to provide a basis for the assessment of capital charges for the use and consumption of the assets'. From GN 11.11.10 it is clear with regard to capital charges, CIPFA has established the principle that service revenue accounts should be charged with a capital charge for all fixed assets used in the provision of the service. As a minimum, such charges should cover the annual provision for depreciation, where appropriate, plus a capital financing charge determined by applying a specified notional rate of interest to the net amount at which the asset is included in the balance sheet (i.e. the valuer's valuation).

The production of the capital figure is clearly the responsibility of the valuer but the production of the annual figure (the capital charge),

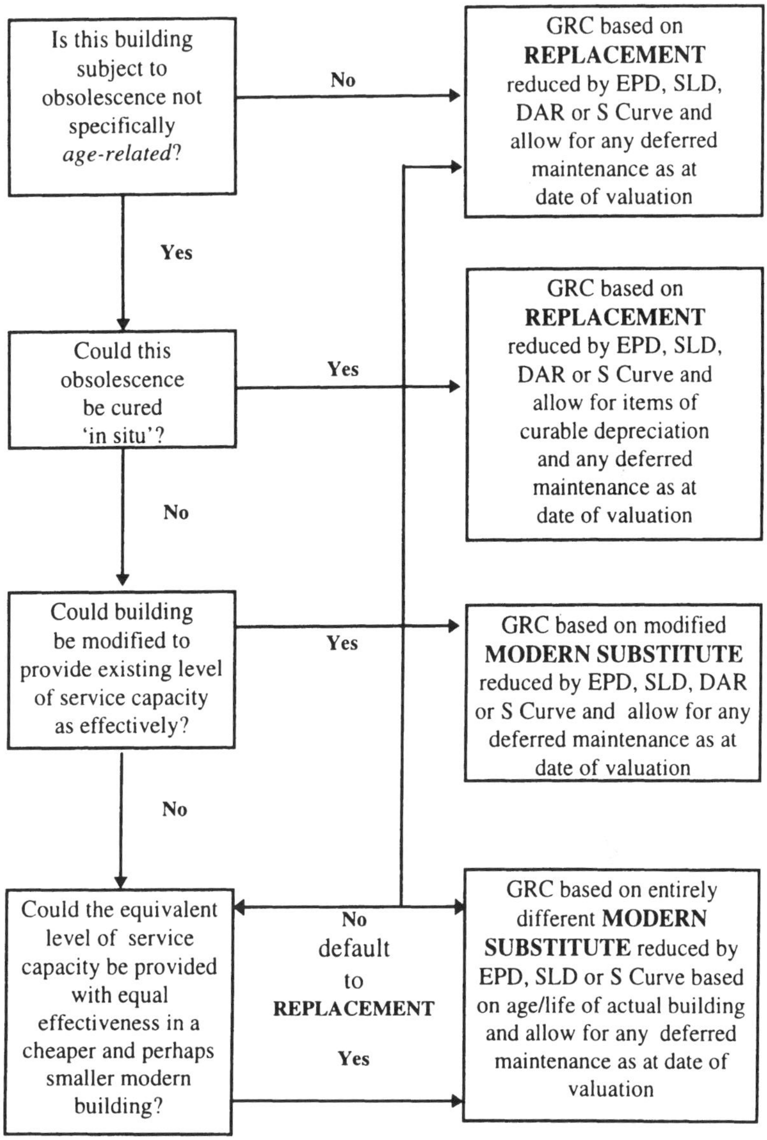

Figure 7.4 Treatment of Obsolescence

although based on the valuer's capital figure, appears to be regarded as a purely accounting function and, therefore, the responsibility of the financial officer. In many valuations, for example in the investment method, the capital value is derived from the annual value and this paper follows the valuation approach, that the production of an asset rent, which should equate with a capital charge, is an integral part of the valuation process.

An asset rent, is like any other rent but explicitly, contains two elements, a charge for the use of capital and, if that capital is wasting, a charge for depreciation. The discussion so far has centred on capital valuations but it is now necessary to consider also the determination of annual figures, in particular, the role conflict in the production of the capital charge and the asset rent and the assumption made in this paper that the valuer, as part of the valuation process, must produce an asset rent. The need in local authorities for liaison between the Valuer and the Chief Finance Officer to ensure consistency has also been noted previously. It should be added that whilst it must be expected that at this stage the capital charge will not necessarily be the same as the asset rent, if the system is to operate fairly in the long term, the two must come together. This was issue which was relevant to a joint research project conducted by Kingston Polytechnic and Surrey County Council (1989) into the *Economic, Efficient and Effective Management of Public Authority Landed Estates.*

Methods for DRC Valuation (see the Appendix for comparative results)

Straight-line depreciation (SLD) method

SLD is a technique for reflecting the wearing out of an asset until it has a negligible value and was used by CIPFA in its DRC valuation examples and adopted by the Valuation Office Agency for the depreciation of hospital assets in its first valuation of the NHS estate (recent revaluations adopted an S shape configuration rather than a straight-line).

At its simplest the SLD method assumes that an asset depreciates at a constant rate from new to the end of its life. Thus an asset with a total life of 40 years is assumed to wear out at a constant annual rate of 2.5 percent from its cost or value at the beginning of its life to nil at the end. The main criticism of this method is the very simplistic assumption of the even wearing away of the asset over its total life. The assumption is clearly correct at two points in the life, the beginning and the end - it would be entirely fortuitous if it were right at any intermediate point.

Discounted asset rent (DAR) method

This method was first introduced by Britton, Connellan and Crofts (1991) and later developed by Connellan (1994). The discounted asset rents (DAR) method is essentially a spread-sheet approach to analyzing the descending asset rents and depreciated capital values over the life of an asset.

The fixed inputs required for the spread-sheet are:

- the required rate of return on the invested capital (IRR - internal rate of return);
- the opening capital cost/value at Year 0 (the beginning of the asset life);
- the closing capital cost/value at the end of the asset life;
- the closing asset rent at the end of the asset life;
- the age and estimated future life of the asset;
- the pattern of descending asset rents over the life of the asset.

The 'S' curve rental method

This is a new rental method of reflecting depreciation and obsolescence in a building by relating estimated economic life to total design life. The 'S' curve method approaches the problem in terms of depreciating the rental value over the life of the building and capitalising that rent at the valuation date by an appropriate investment yield (or cap rate) for the remaining economic life: a capitalising process well beloved of valuers.

The opening rental value is derived from the build-up of the cost components, rather like a developer's balance sheet at the end of the initial development period. This totalled cost of a building is turned into an annual equivalent by dividing it by the years' purchase for the total design life of the building at an appropriate investment yield (or cap rate). This process then gives the opening rental (termed 100 percent good) for a new building.

Theoretically and practically this 100 percent good figure falls away and, assuming constant prices for this valuation exercise, will approach zero when it reaches the end of its economic life. But like Salway (1986) and Baum (1991), in order to quantify depreciation in numerical ratios, it is really necessary to recruit expert opinion. Consequently this 'S' curve exercise involved research conducted and reported by Connellan in 1993/4 in the UK, when valuers were asked to record their perceptions on the falling away of value over time. The example adopted was a specialised building with a total design life of 60 years and each valuer recorded a 'percentage good' rental value at every 5th year interval. In all, 389 valuers took part in the project and their results were data sorted and measures of central tendency for each 5th year interval were also calculated in terms of the mean, median and mode. Each of these calculations showed 'S' type patterns but the median was selected as the basis for the method in line with accepted appraisal rationale as endorsed by the IAAO (1990).

Having thus established the 'S' type pattern over the life of a 60 year building it is possible to adapt the same pattern mathematically for use with buildings of different lives. Such a pattern can be applied to the opening rental, calculated as described above, and from this anchor point decreasing rental values follow that pattern in a downward 'S' curve (all at constant prices as at the date of valuation). The relevant rental value (for the established age of the building) is then capitalised at the appropriate yield (or cap rate) for the remaining life of the building as at that valuation date and the site value is then added to give the complete NCRC of the property asset.

There is also an argument that not only does the rental value decrease over time but the appropriate yield (or cap rate) should also change to match the increasingly unattractive nature of the property investment over the life of the building. In this valuation method it is possible to introduce a similar 'S' shape into a declining YP multiplier over the life of a building running from an opening yield to a closing yield (both inputted by the valuer). Again reference to Baum (1990) lends support to this argument.

The process of this valuation method is demonstrated in the Appendix, with tables and graphs showing depreciating capital values over the design life of the building; these results are also compared and contrasted with other valuation methods.

Estimated percentage depreciation (EPD) method

Britton and Connellan (1994) referred to this technique in the following terms:

> The EPD method, as distinguished from the SLD and DAR methods ... relies purely on the Valuer's experience of previous cases and makes no attempt at logical justification nor expressly revealed methodology ... we attempt to demonstrate the method in the valuation examples in but, perforce, use percentages for which we can provide no rational justification save that the answers do not offend common-sense, being rather a case of post hoc, ergo propter hoc.

In the Appendix the EDP figures in valuation examples are shown merely as averages of the other calculated values.

Stand back and look

However valuers should be well aware that, whichever method of valuation they use, it is always necessary to look critically at the calculated result and ask if it makes sense in the contexts both of other properties being valued and the valuer's own experience. Whilst the author does not subscribe to the rating practice of 'stand back and look' and then possibly change the answer arbitrarily to fit preconceptions, he strongly advocates re-examining a dubious answer to find out where the calculation went wrong and taking appropriate corrective action.

Conclusions

The cost approach is a sound and approved approach for specialised assets and arguably can be related to investment properties. The latest research data on depreciation shows compatibility with previous research findings. The perceptions of 389 valuers as to the decline of rental values over time is undoubtedly a useful amplification and addition to the paucity of existing empirical data. The results achievable through the new 'S' Curve Method fall into line with the precepts on acceptable valuations propounded by Britton et al (1991). Furthermore the new valuation method is readily adaptable to computer use as instanced by the CPD Pack and Demo Disk available from the University of Glamorgan and the 'user and valuer friendly' program available from Quatrosystem Limited.

References

Baum, A. (1991), *Property Investment Depreciation and Obsolescence*, Routledge, London.

Britton, W. and Connellan, O. (1994), *Depreciated Replacement Cost*, College of Estate Management, Reading.

Britton, W. and Connellan, O. (1997), *The Valuation of Public Sector Properties: A Valuation Manual*, University of Glamorgan, Pontypridd.

Britton, W., Connellan, O. and Crofts, M. (1989), *The Economic, Efficient and Effective Management of Public Authority Landed Estates*, Surrey County Council and Kingston Polytechnic, Kingston.

Britton, W., Connellan, O. and Crofts, M. (1991), *The Cost Approach to Valuation*, RICS and Kingston Polytechnic, Kingston.

Chartered Institute of Public Finance and Accountancy (1994a), *Guide to Valuation*, CIPFA, London.

Chartered Institute of Public Finance and Accountancy (1994b), *Specification for Commissioning Valuation Services*, CIPFA, London.

Chartered Institute of Public Finance and Accountancy and the Local Authority (Scotland) Accounts Advisory Committee (1993), *Code of Practice on Local Authority Accounting in Great Britain*, CIPFA *and* LASAAC, London.

Connellan, O. (1994), 'Discounted Asset Rent (DAR) - a new methodology for cost appraisals', *Journal of Property Valuation and Investment*, vol.12 (4): 39-57.

International Association of Assessing Officers (1990), *Standard on Ratio Studies*, Chicago, IAAO. Chicago.

Royal Institution of Chartered Surveyors (1995), *The Contractor's Basis of Valuation for Rating Purposes*, The Joint Professional Institutions Rating Valuation Forum, RICS, London.

Royal Institution of Chartered Surveyors (1995), *Appraisal and Valuation Manual*, RICS, London.

Salway, F. (1986), *Depreciation of Commercial Property*, CALUS, Reading.

Appendix

Note: This valuation example is for illustrative purposes only - the figures are useful only for demonstrating the valuation methods and have no intrinsic significance.

Valuation Example

PROPERTY: Day Nursery
Construction: timber framed and clad walls, flat felt roof
Condition: reasonably well maintained
Site: 0.5 acres - yardstick residential @ £100,000 per acre

Initial cost/value if replaced at current prices:

Building cost 400 sq m GIA @ £450	£180,000
Professional fees @ 10.00%	£18,000
	£198,000
Allow: VAT @ 0%	£0
	£198,000
Interim finance @ 9.00% (9 months rebuild period)	£6,834
	£204,834
Profit @ 0.00%	£0
GRC - Building	£204,834
- Site Improvements	£20,000
GRC - Building etc.	£224,834

Valuation Example continued

Site value 0.5 acres @ £100,000	£50,000
Total	£274,834
Assumptions adopted for depreciation	
- total useful life	40 years
- remaining useful life	23 years
- valuation at	17th year
Assumptions adopted in S Curve method	
- opening ARY/Cap Rate	7.00%
- closing ARY/Cap Rate	9.00%

Summary of Depreciation Methods

	S Curve	DAR	SLD	EPD
Initial Rental(Bldg etc.)	£16,865	£24,058	£19,111	
Rental Value (at valuation date)	£8,481	£11,111	£13,378	
YP 23 yrs @ 7.87%	10.48			
Capital Value(Bldg etc.)	£88,895	£80,400	£129,280	99,525
Allow: defd. maintenance	£0	£0	£0	£0
NCRC(Bldg etc.)	£88,895	£80,400	£129,280	£99,525
Site	£50,000	£50,000	£50,000	£50,000
DRC	£138,895	£130,400	£179,280	149,525
Allow: Grants	£0	£0	£0	£0

Summary of Depreciation Methods continued

DRC	£138,895	£130,400	£179,280	149,525
Equivalent Asset Rent (at valuation date)	£11,981	£14,111	£16,378	£14,156

NOTE: This example introduces varying cap rates and a higher opening cap rate than the standard 6 percent. A table and set of graphs follow to facilitate comparison with the standard approach.

S Curve Valuation Table over Total Useful Life of Building (at constant prices)

	Buildings Etc.					Buildings etc. plus site	
years	ERV bldg etc.	GRC bldg etc.	S shaped YP perp	equiv. ARY %	Capital Value	ERV	Capital Value
0	£16,865	£224,834	14.286	7.00	£224,834	£20,365	£274,834
1	£16,745		14.263	7.01	£221,841	£20,245	£271,841
2	£16,581		14.232	7.03	£218,109	£20,081	£268,109
3	£16,365		14.192	7.05	£213,552	£19,865	£263,522
4	£16,094		14.141	7.07	£208,129	£19,594	£258,129
5	£15,764		14.079	7.10	£201,842	£19,264	£251,842
6	£15,377		14.006	7.14	£194,722	£18,877	£244,722
7	£14,933		13.922	7.18	£186,832	£18,433	£236,832
8	£14,436		13.829	7.23	£178,256	£17,936	£228,256
9	£13,890		13.726	7.29	£169,096	£17,390	£219,096
10	£13,299		13.615	7.35	£159,466	£16,799	£209,466
11	£12,670		13.496	7.41	£149,484	£16,170	£199,484
12	£12,010		13.372	7.48	£139,276	£15,510	£189,276
13	£11,325		13.243	7.55	£128,963	£14,825	£178,963
14	£10,622		13.111	7.63	£118,662	£14,122	£168,662
15	£9,909		12.976	7.71	£108,485	£13,409	£158,485
16	£9,193		12.842	7.79	£98,532	£12,693	£148,532
17	£8,481		12.708	7.87	£88,895	£11,981	£138,895
18	£7,779		12.575	7.95	£79,651	£11,279	£129,651

S Curve Valuation Table over Total Useful Life of Building (at constant prices) continued

	Buildings Etc.					Buildings etc. plus site	
years	ERV bldg etc.	GRC bldg etc.	S shaped YP perp	equiv. ARY %	Capital Value	ERV	Capital Value
19	£7,094		12.446	8.03	£70,868	£10,594	£120,868
20	£6,431		12.322	8.12	£62,599	£9,931	£112,599
21	£5,795		12.202	8.20	£54,884	£9,295	£104,884
22	£5,192		12.088	8.27	£47,750	£8,692	£97,750
23	£4,623		11.981	8.35	£41,216	£8,123	£91,216
24	£4,093		11.882	8.42	£35,284	£7,593	£85,284
25	£3,603		11.789	8.48	£29,949	£7,103	£79,949
26	£3,153		11.705	8.54	£25,196	£6,653	£75,196
27	£2,745		11.628	8.60	£21,000	£6,245	£71,000
28	£2,378		11.559	8.65	£17,329	£5,878	£67,329
29	£2,049		11.497	8.70	£14,146	£5,549	£64,146
30	£1,757		11.442	8.74	£11,406	£5,257	£61,406
31	£1,498		11.393	8.78	£9,063	£4,998	£59,063
32	£1,268		11.350	8.81	£7,069	£4,768	£57,069
33	£1,063		11.311	8.84	£5,378	£4,563	£55,378
34	£877		11.276	8.87	£3,948	£4,377	£53,948
35	£703		11.244	8.89	£2,744	£4,203	£52,744
36	£537		11.212	8.92	£1,743	£4,037	£51,743
37	£370		11.181	8.94	£938	£3,870	£50,938
38	£197		11.148	8.97	£346	£3,697	£50,346
39	£9		11.113	9.00	£8	£3,509	£50,008
40	£0		11.073	9.03	£0	£3,500	£50,000

Valuation Example (cont). Graphs

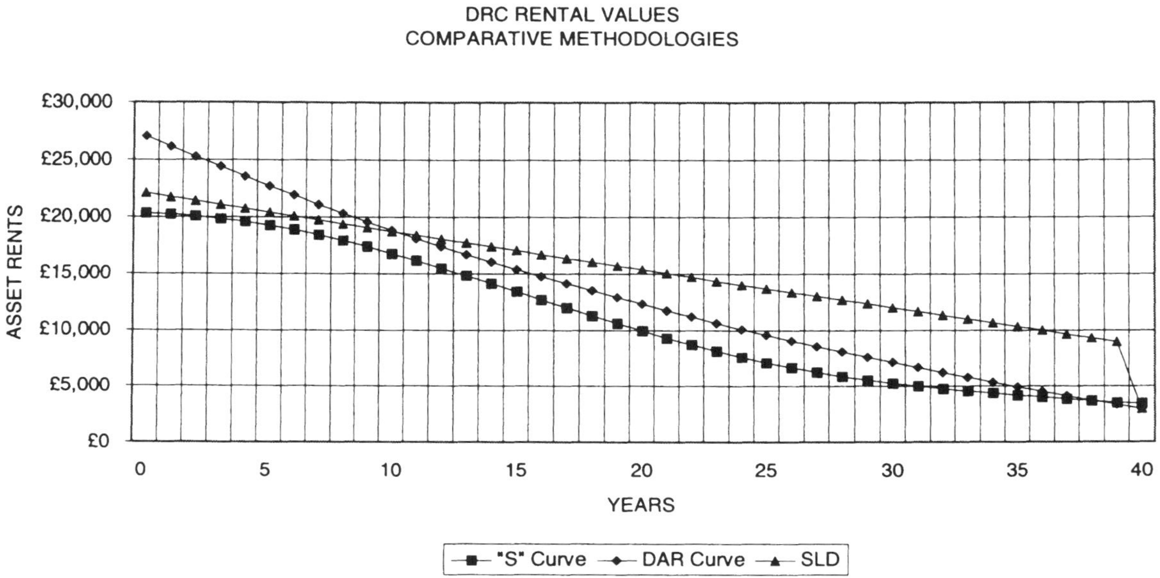

Valuation Example (cont). Graphs

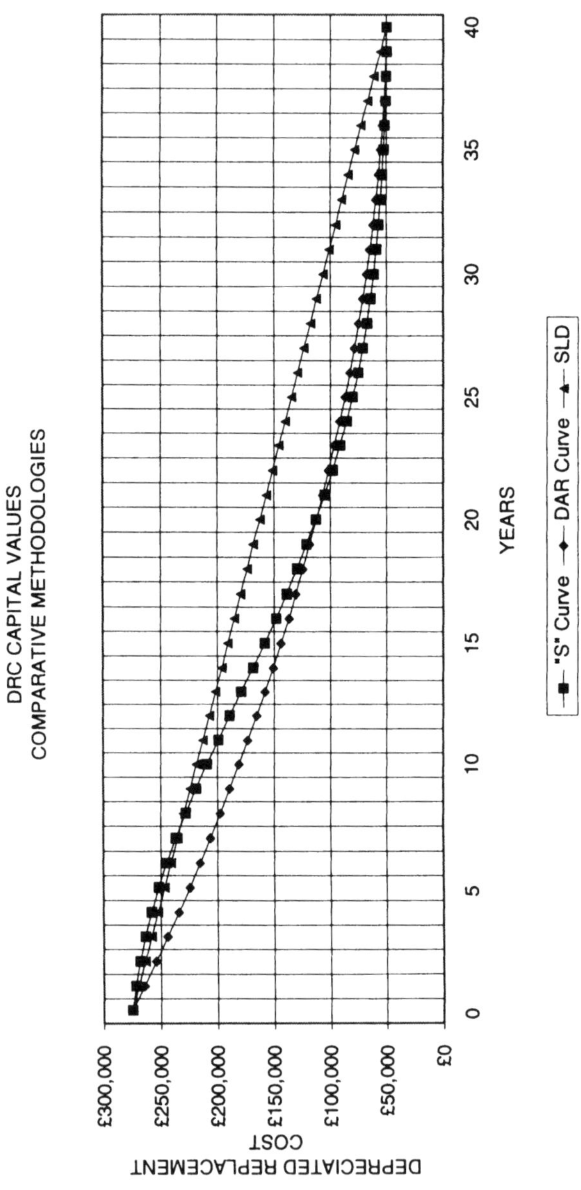

8 The Development of Computer-based Information Systems for Local Authority Property Management

Mark Deakin, Department of Building and Surveying, Napier University

Introduction

The idea that property management needs to embrace the possibilities of the computer and apply information technology in the management of property is a matter which has attracted a considerable amount of attention over the past few years. The reason for this no doubt lies in the fact recent reports by the Audit Commission, Chartered Institute of Public Finance and Accountancy (CIPFA) and Association of District Councils (ADC), all draw attention to the potential computer-based information systems have to improve standards of property management. Yet despite the attention such reports have drawn to the development of computer-based information systems, there is a tendency for studies of this kind to do little more than provide a list of how the application of IT can improve the management of property held by local authorities. As yet relatively little is still known about the application of IT in the development of computer-based information systems, or how they bring about an improvement in the standards of local authority property management.

In the interests of focusing attention on the application of IT and development of computer-based information systems for local authority property management, the paper will first of all set out the issues in question. It will then go on to look at the theory and method of local authority property management. Attention will then turn to the application of such knowledge and the technology of computer-based information systems. Here attention will focus on the information requirements, IT needs and how information systems of this kind bring about an improvement in the management of property held by local authorities. It will then go on to examine the prospects such a system of asset registration, property valuation and performance measurement (referred to collectively as property management) hold for the appraisal of land and buildings.

The paper will provide a case-study of how a local authority has sought to develop a computer-based information system for the management of property. The local authority in question is a District Council: a democratically-elected body that became a unified authority following the recent re-organisation of local government and which is responsible for the management of property employed in the provision of public services to a community of half a million people. The case-study will provide an example of how a property management division has sought to adopt the recommendations of the Audit Commission (1988 a, b, c,) and CIPFA's (1989, 1991a, 1991b, 1992a, 1993 and 1994) reports on local authority property management and measures the democratically-elected body has taken via its central committee, executive and directorate, to apply IT in the development of a computer-based information for the registration of assets, valuation of property and measurement of performance. As such, it seeks to fill the gap that currently exists in our understanding of such matters and draw upon the case-study to provide examples of best practice in the application of IT and development of computer-based information systems for local authority property management.

In seeking to fill this gap, the paper also seeks to demonstrate the relationship between the development of computer-based information systems and an improvement in the standards of property management is not a simple one. What is hopes to demonstrate is that: if a clear relationship between the development of computer-based information systems and improvement in the standards of property management is to emerge; it is necessary to move away from the old professional divisions which can be found in the 'departmentalism' of the Maud and Bains reports, for unlike these reports the post-Audit Commission form of local authority property management does not centre responsibility for the management of property in any one department, but draws instead upon the qualities of enterprise and competition to decentre the process of decision making in local authorities and make property management more accountable in corporate terms. More accountable in the sense the management of property in local authorities is grounded in the technology of computer-based information systems, whose corporate strategy and financial instruments make up a network of communications to not only register assets, but also adopt independent standards of property valuation and performance measurement.

In taking this form, the paper seeks to reflect some of the financial, audit, review and management issues currently being debated in the public sector. Issues such as the over-throw of professionalism, demise of departmentalism, and rise of the 'new managerialism', with generic skills and inter-disciplinary expertise (Dobson and Rosemary, 1988; Chandler, 1991; Common, Flynn and Mellon, 1993). The new form of manageralism that is quality-minded, pro-enterprise, competitive and which decentres power through the delegation of decision making and introduction of greater accountability over the finance, auditing, review and budgeting of expenditure on public services. This is mentioned as the developments the case-study seeks to throw light on are not peculiar to any one, or series of local authorities in England, Wales or Scotland. Indeed in many respects the case-study can be seen to reflect a number of wider developments currently taking place within Europe and North America (see, for example; Banner, 1988; Kooiman, 1988; Young, 1995; Deakin, 1995 and 1996).

Issues

Contrary to the positive image of local authority property management put forward by the Audit Commission and CIPFA, there is evidence to suggest the vision of property management in local authorities as competitive, decentred, accountable and corporate, is fraught with problems and difficult to sustain. Evidence is emerging to suggest the IT needed to develop the computer-based information systems capable of bringing about such a form of property management does not exist and the absence of such technology is tending to cast some doubt on the ability of local authorities to meet the standards of property management set out by the Audit Commission and CIPFA. The evidence in question tends to suggest the problems and difficulties being encountered in the application of IT and development of computer-based information systems for the management of property held by local authorities are as follows and lie in:

- the lack of data available on the development of computer-based information systems (Spicer, 1979; Kirkwood, 1984);
- the low level of IT-related skills in the management of property (RICS, 1984; MAC, 1985; Avis, Gibson and Watts, 1989);
- the absence of suitable guidance on the application of IT for the development of computer-based information systems (Dixon, 1985);
- concern over the design of data-bases as information systems for the management of property (Jenkins and Gronow, 1989);
- questions about the relationship between such information systems and the asset register (Webster, Gronow and Jenkins, 1995);
- unease about the bases of property valuation put forward by the Audit Commission and CIPFA (Dent and Bond, 1993; Young, 1995);
- reservations about the application of income and cost conventions to the valuation and pricing of property under the management of local authorities (Britton, Connellan and Crofts, 1989, 1991; Martindale, 1994; Deakin, 1994);
- worries over the lack of any clear standards for the measurement of property performance (Crofts, 1989; Gammans, 1990; French, 1994);
- the noticeable absence of any information in terms of the corporate strategy or financial instruments required to improve the standards of property management in local authorities (Gibson, 1985, 1994; Kirkwood and Padden, 1988).

As Spicer (1979) and Kirkwood's (1984) observations go some way to show, prior to the Audit Commission's reports on local authority property management, questions about the application of IT and development of computer-based information systems attracted little attention. As both Spicer (1979) and Kirkwood (1984) point out, the origins of IT applications in the development of computer-based information systems lie in the Gazetter and Local Authority Management Information Systems (LAMIS). Data-bases that Kirkwood (1984) notes, have been designed not so much with the question of property in mind as for the management of information having a bearing on the financial planning, budgeting and development of expenditures on public services. Designed, that is, not so much with the property manager as information officer in mind.

This is an unfortunate situation the RICS (1984) and MAC (1985) also draw attention to and see as directly responsible for the low level of IT skills available to assist local authorities in the management of property. It is a view also supported to a large degree by Dixon (1989) and Avis, Gibson and Watts' (1989) discussions about the problems and difficulties being experienced over the lack of suitable guidance on the development of computer-based information systems, design of data-bases and adoption of software for the registration of assets, valuation of property and measurement of performance (see also, for example; Jenkins and Gronow 1989; Martindale, 1994 and French, 1994 on the respective issues).

As a number of separate issues, the problem and difficulties listed give obvious cause for concern. The lack of data, low level of IT skills and absence of suitable guidance, all tend work against any attempts to apply IT in the development computer-based information systems. Perhaps most noticeable of all is the extent and nature of the problems and difficulties property management divisions in local authorities face in attempting to apply IT in the development of such information systems. For in looking at the list of concerns, questions, general level of unease, reservations and worries in question, it is evident the problems and difficulties are not self contained, or isolated to any one issue; for example: the application of IT, development of computer-based information systems, registration of assets, valuation of property, or measurement of performance, but are inter-related to one another. This is most noticeable in the absence of guidance, concern over the design of data-bases and questions about the relationship between such information systems and the registration of assets. For not only does this represent a problem in its own right, but one that also causes difficulties in the form of unease, reservations and worries about the valuation of property and measurement of performance.

Looked at together, it is also evident that such an array of problems and difficulties signal something more significant and tends to indicate the cause for concern does not lie with any one issue, but with the structure of local authority property management as a whole. That is with the theory and method of property management which local authorities have adopted to guide them in the application of IT and development of computer-based information systems. If this is correct it ought to be seen as a matter of particular concern, for it tends to suggest there is a fault line running through the structure of local authority property management and this is placing a considerable strain on the attempts made by local authorities to adopt the theory and method of property management set out by the Audit Commission and CIPFA.

To test this hypothesis, it will of course be necessary to examine the structure of local authority property management and assess how well the theory and method of property management assists local authorities in the application of IT and development of computer-based information systems. The paper will start to carry out such an examination under the next sub-heading. It should identify that a number of practical problems have been experienced by local authorities in adopting the theory and method of property management set out by the Audit Commission and CIPFA. In particular it shall demonstrate that local authorities have experienced problems in translating the theory and method of a quality-minded, pro-enterprise, competitive, decentred and accountable property management into a corporate strategy and set of financial instruments detailed enough to recognise both the information requirements and IT needs of a local authority and how it is the application of the latter in the development of a computer-based information system can lead to an improvement in the management of property held by local authorities.

As should become clear from the review of the developments that have already taken place, if anything there has been a tendency for computer-based information systems to take on the status of asset registers, rather than tools for the valuation of property and measurement of performance. Something the paper suggests is unfortunate and needs to be overcome if the limits it places on the valuation of property and measurement of performance are to be overcome. If, that is, the application of IT in the development of computer-based information systems is to improve the standards of property management in local authorities along the lines which have been set out by the Audit Commission and CIPFA.

The structure of local authority property management

There are perhaps four main variables in the quality-minded, pro-enterprise theory of local authority property management and few constants. The variables are competition, decentralisation, accountability and corporatisation. It is the ideas about the virtues of competition and decentralisation which have to a large degree, brought about a restructuring of local government finance and marked increase in the level of concern that institutions like the Audit Commission and CIPFA show towards the question of accountability and corporatisation of management in local authorities. What the theory of local authority property management can perhaps best be seen to represent, is an attempt by such institutions to reform the structure of local government finance by introducing a competitive, decentralist, more accountable and corporate minded attitude towards the management of property (Henkle, 1991). As an attempt, that is, to break with the monopolistic, centralist, unaccountable and bureaucratic forms of property management, which were ushered in as part of the previous re-organisation of local government and setting up of authorities along the lines laid down by Bains (1972) and Maud (1969).

In theory the introduction of new metaphors like competition, decentralisation and accountability into the language of local government finance appears quite uncontroversial. As does the emergence of terms like 'value for money' and the 'economic, efficient and effective' management of property. But the question of method is more problematic and difficult to resolve because it demands we are more exact in the use of such terms. In view of this and given the more theoretical questions to do with the financial restructuring of local government, emergence of competition, decentralisation, accountability and corporisation of authorities is already well documented by Byrne (1992), Elcock (1994), Stewart and Stoker (1995), this paper does not propose to dwell on the issue. Instead it wishes to focus on the question of method. This will be done by breaking the question down into three parts. The first concentrating on what action needs to be taken if local authority property management is to become competitive, decentralist, accountable and corporate. The second drawing upon this terms of reference to provide a more detailed framework for property management in local authorities. The third drawing attention to the steps that need to be taken if such a form of property management is to develop. The third point should bring us back to the questions about the technology of computer-based information systems.

Table 8.1 Property Management and Local Authorities

Variables	Property Management	Local Authorities
Competitive	market criteria	contracting out, market testing and introduction of internal markets
Decentred	autonomous trading units, non-hierarchical, with flat, broad structures of decision-making, service-based with customer orientation	centre-periphery and community forms of service delivery, with emphasis on quality of service through standards of measure-ment provided by independent bodies.
Accountable	audit of cost centres, with measurement of income and outgoings expenditure - be it revenue or capital based	financial control over budgets and regulation of expenditure to meet pre-determined targets
Corporate	divisional control over budgeting of some services, with executive body and directorate based on the distinction between strategic management and routine operations	small number of core staff responsible for policy and strategic issues, who network with larger numbers of project-based and task centred experts employed on service delivery to customers.

Table 8.1 shows the variables in question and the relationship they have to property management in local authorities. Here, competition is seen to surface through the introduction of market criteria into local authority property management. This being secured through the process of contracting-out and market-testing and to some extent by the trading of services via the introduction of internal markets (i.e. in the form of service

level agreements). Decentralisation goes on to develop this theme by introducing autonomous trading units, with non-hierarchical, or, flat, broad structures of decision making. This takes the form of either centre-peripheral forms of service delivery, or forms of service delivery that transfer decision making power from the centre to the periphery and on to the community.

The accountability variable comes into play via the introduction of tighter financial controls over the budgeting of expenditure. Such control is seen to rest with the executive and directorate responsible for the management of property in local authorities. The former having particular responsibility for managing the uncertainty and risk that surround the formation of a corporate strategy towards the acquisition, use, development and disposal of property (see Leach, Stewart and Walsh, 1994; Walsh, 1995). The executive and directorate together having responsibility for the financial planning, budgeting and control of expenditure on the management of property.

Drawing upon this characterisation of local authority property management, it is possible to develop a more detailed framework for the management of property held by local authorities. This is set out in Table 8.2. As can be seen, it inverts the form of presentation adopted in the previous table by turning it upside down and starting with the corporate variable. It also draws attention to the relationship that exists between property and the management of land and buildings held by local authorities.

Table 8.2 attempts to highlight how the four principles referred to so far as variables, become part of property management in local authorities. How, that is, the principles become 'incorporated' into the management of property and way in which they take on a particular form. The table shows that it is the formation of a central committee which makes it possible to transfer authority for the management of such resources to an executive. It also illustrates that it is the setting up of financial controls and budgetary planning mechanisms to standards set by independent bodies which allows the value for money test to be taken into account and establish whether service delivery benefits from economic, efficient and effective management.

Table 8.2 Property Management in Local Authorities

Property	Management
Corporate	central committee responsible for policy formation and strategy for the management of property through an executive and directorate
Accountability	financial controls over budgets to meet pre-determined targets and standards set by independent bodies (AC and CIPFA)
Decentralisation	delegation of decision making power via network of communications to and from autonomous trading units and made possible by the development of computer-based information systems linking the centre to peripheral activities
Competition	through the adoption of market testing, contracting out and financial criteria for the registration on assets, valuation of property and measurement of performance by unit comparison of income, outgoings and rates of return from the independent sector

Here decentralisation takes place via the break-up of departments into a network of autonomous trading units. An event made possible by the development of information systems linking the centre to the periphery through the authority the committee gives an executive to develop a corporate strategy towards the ownership, use, acquisition, disposal and development of property and it in turn gives the directorate to manage routine operations. The execution, direction, financial planning and budgeting of such a strategy also seen to take place in a competitive environment due to the adoption of market testing and contracting out.

Fortunately it is possible to see how this method is applied in practice by reference to a number of studies undertaken to monitor the development of local authority property management. It should be noted that the studies are limited to the asset registration stage of development. For the purpose of this paper the fact that the information available is limited to the initial stages of the development is not something which raises problems for as should become clear, it serves to pin-point a problem of particular concern.

As already pointed out, the development of information systems for the registration of assets held by local authorities is an aspect of property management the Audit Commission (1988 a, b and c; CIPFA, 1991a and b, 1992a, b and c, 1993 and 1994) have drawn particular attention to. As a general rule neither institution has sought to be prescriptive in laying down the type of system local authorities should adopt and have simply suggested it ought to develop 'fitness for purpose' in terms of fulfilling this particular function. In the first attempt to monitor the development of such information systems, the ADC (1990) found that while many local authorities have introduced IT into the management of property, some have been successful in this venture but others have failed.

In a subsequent exercise aimed at surveying the types of information systems in place, Erdman Lewis (1993) found that 75 percent of local authorities had introduced computer-based information systems for the management of property. Out of this, 39 percent were found to take the form of mainframe data-bases, 36 percent micro-processor, or personal-computer based. The survey also highlighted that a great many local authorities perceive the value of the information systems to lie in the ability data-bases have to act as an electronic filing cabinet, holding information about property in the form of data on ownership, tenure, use, value and the cost of outgoings. In effect in the ability computer-based information systems of this kind have to act as a register of assets. One that not only provides data in the form of an asset register, but information valuable for the next stage of the management process i.e. the valuation of property and measurement of performance.

It is the perception of computer-based property information systems as little more than electronic filing cabinets, capable of speeding up the access to data held on assets which this paper seeks to avoid. Indeed it is hoped that the discussions which have taken place so far have already gone some way in achieving this. In contrast, it seeks to adopt a wider definition and one that places emphasis, not so much on the capacity for systems of this kind to operate as a data-bank, but on the information they provide for the next stage of the management process. It also adopts such a definition in an attempt to transcend the rather narrow view of information systems as data-banks for the registration of assets and in the aim of drawing particular attention to the data and information required for the valuation of property and measurement of performance. It is also adopted because such a tripartite definition of property management provides the key to recognising the significance of property as a corporate resource in the financing of local government expenditure on public services and to understanding the pivotal role computer-based information systems play in the strategic and routine operation of management functions.

The technology of computer-based information systems

So far attention has focused on a number of problems and difficulties associated with the development of local authority property management and how the theory and method of the aforesaid tends to result in computer-based information systems being seen as little more than data-banks: a perception the paper argues is far too narrow and fails to address the questions of property valuation, or performance measurement - the other two dimensions of the management function.

Here the discussion will move beyond the consideration of theory and method and shall consider the technology of computer-based information systems. To do this it will draw upon the case-study forming the central theme of the paper. In focusing on the technology of computer-based information systems, it aims to show what measures can be taken to overcome the difficulties and problems in the theory and method of local authority property management outlined so far. In meeting this objective the discussion will divide into three parts: the information requirements, the IT needs, system design and operation.

Information requirements

As all discussions on the application of IT to the management of property tend to point out, before considering the technology of computer-based information systems, it is first necessary to specify what information is required. Keeping this maxim firmly in mind, the development in question identified the following requirements:

- a central committee, who in conjunction with an executive and directorate would be responsible for the local authority's corporate strategy;
- an executive with responsibility for corporate strategy towards the acquisition, use, development and disposal of property held by the local authority and direction of more routine operations concerning the management of property;
- a computer-based information system capable of providing a greater amount of financial control over the budgeting of expenditure on property - be they operational, investment, or assets held surplus to requirements on the trading account;
- data for the registration of assets on the computer-based information system, manipulation of data and processing of information for the valuation of property and measurement of performance;
- a network of communications to link the property management division to the user of assets held by local authorities.

As Figure 8.1 shows, it is the formation of a central committee that makes it possible to develop a strategy on the acquisition, use, development and disposal of property and management of such holdings. This being done through the division of responsibilities between the executive and directorate. The former having responsibilities for the strategic aspects of property in terms of use, development and disposal, the latter directing the more routine management operations. It also illustrates the question about whether property passes the 'value for money test', or if the management of holdings is economic, efficient and effective, are answered through the introduction of financial controls over the budgeting of expenditure in line with the standards laid down by independent bodies.

What it also illustrates is that decentralisation takes place through the delegation of decision-making power into what can be best referred to as a 'network of communications' to and from autonomous trading units.

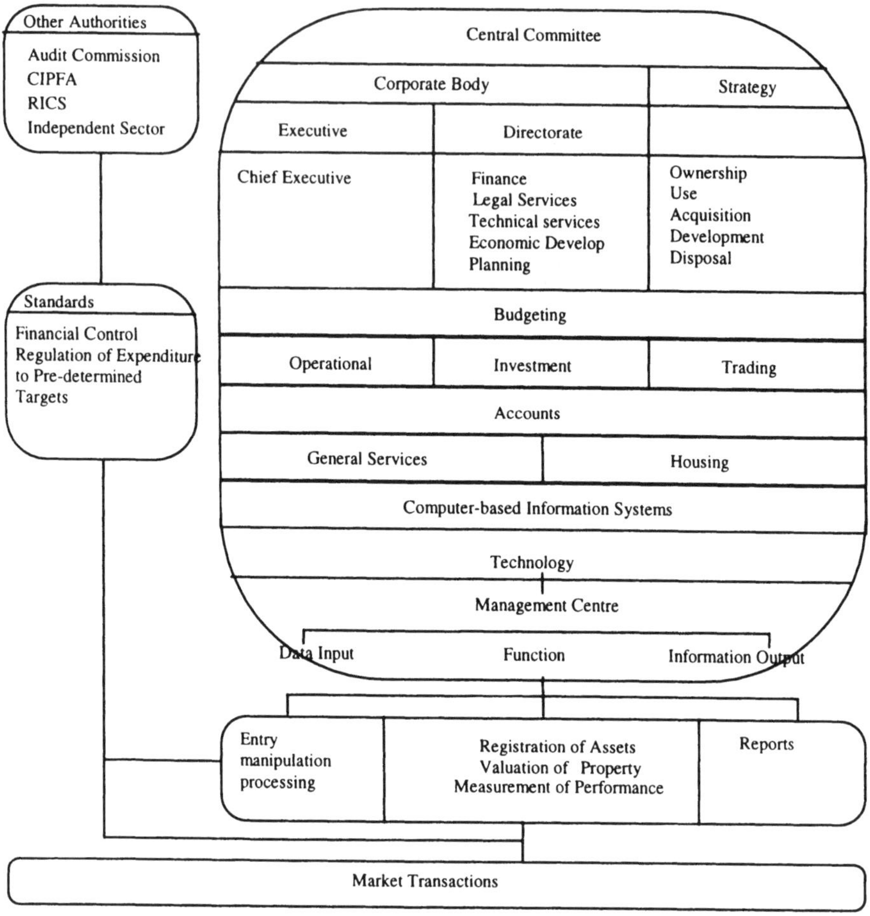

Figure 8.1 Information Requirements

Communications made possible by the development of computer-based information systems linking the centre i.e. central committee, to the executive, directorate and client-customer 'interface', via the circulation of information also required for the valuation of property and measurement of performance. The diagram also attempts to highlight how the four principles referred to so far as 'variables' become part of local authority property management. How, that is, they become incorporated into a strategy for the management of property held by local authorities and way in which the notions of accountability, decentralisation and competition take on a particular form. For as can be seen, at the centre of the development there is the committee, with a corporate body, directorate and assigned strategy towards the financial control and budgeting of expenditure on the operational, investment and trading accounts. In this instance, commercial, industrial and residential categories of property, held on the general services (recreation and environment health) and housing account. Below this is the computer-based information system linking property to the technology required to fulfil the so-called management function.

While the diagram goes some way to show the pivotal role the computer-based information system takes in the management of property under such a structure, it also identifies the points of contact where it 'incorporates' the variables referred to earlier under the theory and method of local authority property management. As can be seen, it is the relationship between the type of information draw upon in the management function and the structure of local authority property management that is critical to meeting the competitive criteria. The fact, that is, it draws upon data from market transactions, which is then made use of as information for the valuation of property and measurement of performance. Such a situation being made possible due to the process of decentralisation that takes place under such a structure of local authority property management: the process of decentralisation which transfers authority (executive and directorate) away from the departments responsible for the direct provision of services (recreation, environmental health and housing; for example), to a central committee - a situation that in effect vests the ownership and control of property in a central committee which allocates responsibility for both the strategic and routine aspects of the management function to an executive and directorate. An undertaking seen as more accountable due to the fact it has become integrated into the democratic body of local government, with an executive and directorate who are responsible for the financial control and budgeting of expenditure on the management of property held by local authorities.

In the process of becoming competitive, decentralised and accountable, the management of property is also see to be more corporate in the sense the delegation of decision making required to support such a structure of property management does not make property the sole concern of the central committee, but the executive, directorate and managers of the information system, - be they responsible for the strategic, or 'other' issues referred to as more routine operations.

Experience suggests it is best to simplify the information requirements by dividing them into the following categories:-

- information regarding legal status, ownership, use, holding purpose etc., from existing, usually card index and manual-based property records;
- plan drawings, site, floor areas from land survey, along with engineering, construction, building design, repair and maintenance details supplied by technical services;
- tenure details regarding the allocation of property rights to service departments from legal services, with class of asset, category, holding purpose i.e. operational, investment or on the trading account held surplus to requirements, along with rents, market yields and transfer prices;
- data from intermediate and service departments on outgoings including energy, cleansing, repair and maintenance, insurance, local tax and management costs.

Having obtained the data, consideration has to be given to the form it should take to represent the material suitable for input into a computer-based information system. In doing this it is considered best not to focus on the IT upon which the computer is based, but on the information system that is required to move the management process from one stage to another. In view of this, it is perhaps best to organise the information in such a way that it allows the exercise to progress through the following stages:

- survey (data collection) as specified above;
- the registration, entry of the specified data to input the physical, legal and financial attributes of assets;
- manipulation and processing of data for the valuation of property;
- further processing of data to provide information for the measurement of performance, including, audit, review and rationalisation of holdings;
- reporting on the management of property held by the local authority.

IT needs

The application of IT in the design of the information system in question has taken place on the assumption it should be geared towards meeting user needs. In this instance, the property management division's needs regarding the development of a computer-based information system for the registration of assets, valuation of property and measurement of performance (see Hsia and Bryne, 1989). Taking into account the comments made earlier about the absence of IT expertise in the field of property management, it is perhaps best to try and meet the users' requirements through the adoption of what is commonly referred to as the 'toolbox' approach to systems design. That is not by the commissioning of a 'bespoke', or 'tailor made' information system, but through the design, operation and maintenance of a computer-based information system which makes use of a micro-processor and data-base with auxiliary software.

The advantages of taking such an approach to the system design are numerous and include the following:

- the relatively low level of skill they require for the design, operation and use of information systems;
- the fact that personal computers are relatively cheap and readily available;
- the software is also readily available and inexpensive;
- it is possible to 'customise' the data-base files and structure of records to function as a information system for the management of property held by a local authority;
- the information system is flexible and can be modified to meet changing circumstances;
- it is also relatively user-friendly, with easy to follow menus, screen layouts, data retrieval commands and report writing;
- auxiliary software allows more complex tasks to be undertaken.

As Kirkwood (1984) points out, the use of micro-processors as the computational basis of an information system has the distinct advantage of allowing the mass storage of data and making it possible to quickly process information - it is also seen to provide users with a high quality output that is both reliable and accurate (also see, Hsia, 1989). As Dixon, Hargitay and Bevan (1991) point out, micro-computers of this kind i.e. with a data-base and software package, have the district advantage of providing data-base management systems capable of mirroring LAMIS, but without the considerable cost of a bespoke mainframe technology.

Design and operation

Figure 8.2 shows the design of the computer-based information system. It breaks the structure of the system down into columns of: micro-computer, data-base, software and function. The form and content of the system require further explanation.

The design of the files and structure of the screen layout set the parameters for the survey and proformas used to input data. In addition to providing the record, or data on the property in question, it also forms the basis of the asset register through the input of data provided from the survey of each holding. Following on from the question of design and data input, are those of processing and information manipulation for the valuation of property. The processing and information for the valuation of property draws upon two data sources: the register for the assets forming the subject of valuation and the property transaction file. The latter holding information on unit rates in the property and construction sector and evidence of current values from transactions comparable to those in question. In drawing on both data sources the information processing required to complete the valuation of property is carried out through the sorting and search functions. Using these functions data can be sorted through any process of indexation and simple mathematical functions can be undertaken to analyse evidence of transactions, standard units of measurement and carry out the calculations required for the valuation of property.

The calculation function requires particular attention. Here the holdings are classified in terms of the standard criteria set out by CIPFA and RICS. The classification of holdings is made in terms of specialist, non-specialist assets held for operational purposes, investment, or surplus to requirements on the trading account. The standards of property valuation laid down in the '*Appraisal and Valuation Manual*' are applied.

Micro-computer	**Data-base**	**Software**	**Functions**
fileserver, with network on token ring	*design* of files, structure of screen layout and records	*dBase II - V*	*survey* of property using proformas
individual personal computers	*input* of primary data and secondary data on current values from the property and construction sector		*registration* of assets, physical, legal and financial attributes
data-base held on file server where processing takes place before being sent to PC's.	data manipulation, sorting, indexation, calculation *processing*, functions, command and programming facilities, data output in the form of reports	*wordprocessor (with memo fields) spread- sheet applications* (Lotus 1-2-3 for Windows, Microsoft Excel) *statistical packages* (Super Calc 5)	*valuation of property* by classifications, base, category of holding and sector
			performance measurement, in terms of costs of outgoings, yields, risk, growth, obsolescence and depreciation, rate of return over cost, *audit, review and rationalisation of holdings*

Figure 8.2 Design of the Computer-Based Information System

This draws upon information contained in the property transactions file and the analysis of current values, construction costs and notional pricing mechanisms available for the valuation of property. Here again the data processing facilities can be applied to the valuation of property so as to provide notional prices for individual assets, or statements of asset value for groups, sectors, even geographical areas of the territory in question.

It is normally through this means the 'automated' valuation of property, for either individual or a 'mass' of assets is carried out. Such assessments tend to be carried out for groups of similar, or comparable subjects with the same classification, base and method for the valuation of commercial, industrial and housing categories of the property market and goes some way to provide the benchmarks to measure the performance of the holdings in question. Such benchmarks are drawn from the degree of usage, cost of outgoings, yield and level of rental growth. Together they represent standards of performance measurement that make it possible to compare assets forming the portfolio of holdings against property in general. This also provides the information to design a strategy towards the acquisition, utilisation, development and disposal of assets within the portfolio of holdings. This is done by drawing on the results of the measurement and its ranking of performance as good, average or poor. If a subject ranks as average, or poor, the asset in question can be selected for review by either (operational/investment), holding (retail, office, industrial, residential) sector (prime, secondary) or area (within the centre, inner or outer suburbs) and subject to a rationalisation. As such a review and/or rationalisation is contingent upon the performance measurement, customised reports need to be specified for such programmes.

Figure 8.3 attempts to illustrate where such a computer-based information system fits into the budgeting of expenditure, the accounts and departments it serves and how the technology in question is applied to the management function. In extending the logic of the previous diagram, it draws attention to the IT applications that assist the management of property. As can be seen, it draws particular attention to the data input needs for the entry, manipulation and processing of material through the registration of assets, valuation of property and measurement of performance. It also illustrates the information which forms the output of the data entry, manipulation and processing.

Turning to the question of how the computer-based information system designed to fulfil the three main management functions actually operates, it is perhaps best to demonstrate the practicalities of asset registration, property valuation and performance measurement by providing examples of the way it works to improve the standards of property management in local authorities. To do this it is perhaps best to

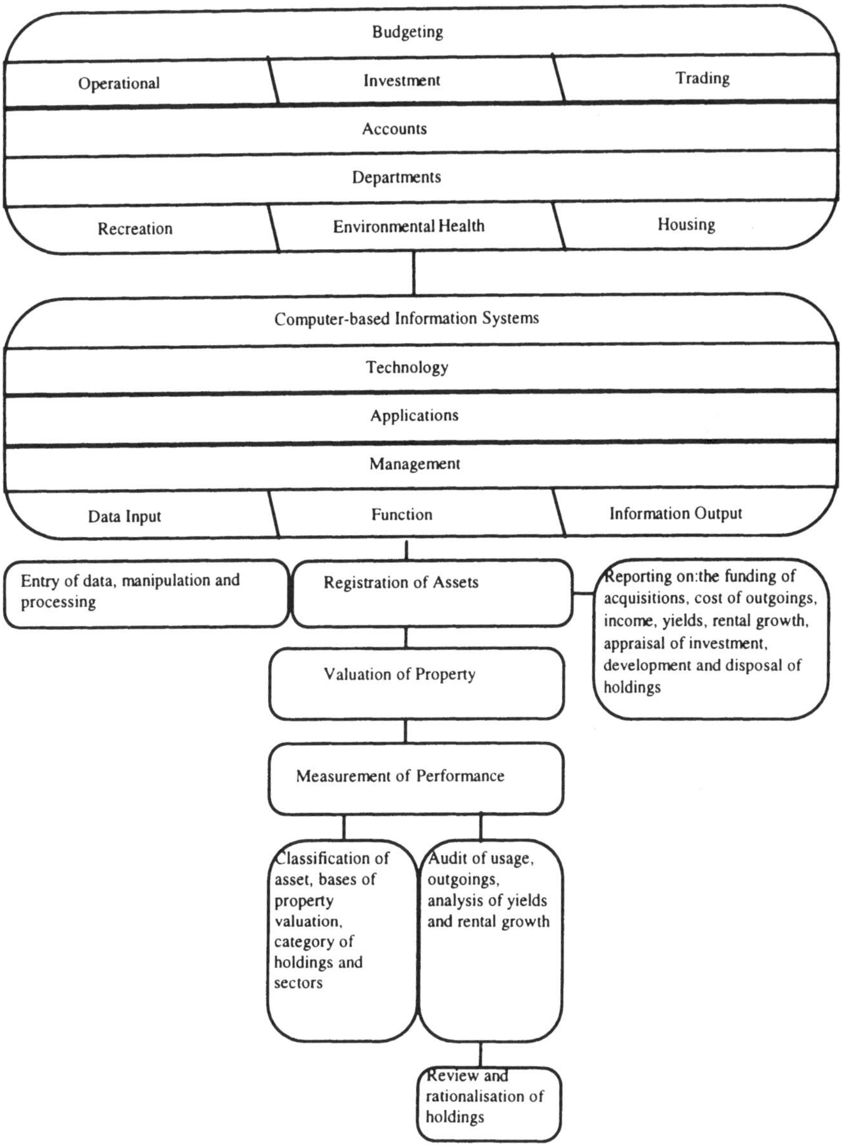

Figure 8.3 The Computer-Based Information System

represent the computer-based information system as a register of asset classifications, set of, bases, methods of property valuation and performance measurement techniques, drawn upon by an 'expert' to model the appraisal process. Or as an expert system that provides a register of assets, valuation of property - be it through a form of an electronic filing cabinet, automated valuation of property and measurement of performance.

Figure 8.4, shows the asset register in terms of 'basic information', central committee, measurement, tenure (lease, rent details, review, termination pattern) market analysis and occupier. Figure 8.5 illustrates the type of information held on each asset for the valuation of property. Information, that is, on asset type, base and method of property valuation, category of holding, sector and techniques in terms of either rental, or capital transfer prices and yield drawn upon as part of the appraisal process. Table 8.3 illustrates the processing and manipulation of such data to sort, index and report on the assets in a form that outputs information on the valuation of property. The report in question is of standard assets, on the OMV base, and investment method of property valuation for prime holdings. It also draws upon the rack-rented and term and reversion techniques of property valuation, along with the all-risks, initial and reversionary yields.

The standard assets are retail units held on the register by ward, street (no. and name), property description, passing/current rent and valuation in terms of transfer price. The illustration draws the data from the register of assets and information held on the valuation of property carried out for each holding on a spreadsheet. What is shows is the rent by asset and valuation of property in terms of the transfer price for each individual holding and as a total.

Asset Register

Basic Information

Use:
Description:
Street number:
Town/city: Name:
Ward: Postcode:
Account: OS Ref No:
Classifications:
Holding purpose (O/I/S to R):
Category (R, B, I* W & D, O*):

Acquisition date: Use class order:
Historic cost: Listed status:
Valuation basis (OMV/DRC):
Valuation: Ratable value:
Date of Valuation ( ):

Central Committee Data

Latest report:
Purpose:
Decision:

Measurement

Analysis (NIA/NEA/GIA/GEA):
Site (acres/hectares):
Floor area (sq.ft/ sq.metres):

Figure 8.4 Asset Register

Tenure

Ownership (F/L):	
Title ref:	Lease start date:
Lease ref:	Termination date:
Rent roll ref:	Frequency (Y/H/Q/M):
Current rent date:	Passing rent:
Rent sq.ft/metre:	Rent review pattern (yrs):

Market Analysis

Current value:
Market yield:

Occupier

User:	
Owner:	
Agents:	Correspondence address:
	....

Figure 8.4 Asset Register continued

File Reference:

Asset classification (S, N-S)
Base (OMV, DRC, AHC)
Method (C, I, R, C*, P)
Category (R, B, I, &, W&D, O*)
Market sector (P*, S*)
Technique

Direct capital comparison:	All-risks yield:
Rack rented:	Initial yield:
Term and revision:	Reversionary yield:
Hardcore/layered:	Equivalent yield:
Site Value:	Equated yield:
Replacement cost:	
Turnover:	
Discounted cash flow:	
Rational:	
Real:	

Figure 8.5 Asset Valuation

Key to Figures 8.4 and 8.5.

O	=	Operational	M	=	Monthly
I	=	Investment	OMV	=	Open market value
S to R	=	Surplus to requirement	DRC	=	Depreciated replacement cost
P*	=	Prime	AHC	=	Amortised historic cost
S*	=	Secondary	C	=	Comparative
NIA	=	Net internal area	C*	=	Contractor's
NEA	=	Net external area	P	=	Profit
GIA	=	Gross internal areas	R	=	Retail
GEA	=	Gross external area	B	=	Business
F	=	Freehold	I	=	Industrial
L	=	Leasehold	W & D	=	Warehouse
Y	=	Yearly	O	=	Other
H	=	Half yearly			
Q	=	Quarterly			

Table 8.3 Rents and the Valuation of Property

Ward	Street		Description	Rent	Valuation
	No.	Name		£	£
41	1,2	....	Shop	10,500	169,000
-	5	....	-	15,000	187,000
-	8,7	....	-	14,000	244,000
-	9,1	....	-	14,000	248,000
-	23	....	-	7,500	121,000
-	26	....	-	6,800	97,000
-	55	....	-	6,800	97,000
-	75	....	-	11,200	168,000
-	77	....	-	9,600	144,000
-	81	....	-	9,600	144,000
				105,000	1,619,000

Table 8.4 Current, Increases and New Rents

Ward	Year	Current	Increase	New Rent
41	1996	-		
	1997	105,000	12,000	117,000
	1998	117,000	6,000	123,000
	1999	123,000	10,200	133,200
	2000	133,200	2,200	135,400
			20,400	

Table 8.4 illustrates the current, increase and new rental incomes that flow from the assets between 1996 - 2000. As can be seen, it projects an increase in rental income of £20,400 over the time-period in question

and demonstrates the significance of the review patterns on the valuation of property held in this category.

Table 8.5 illustrates the current/new level of rent and forecasted figure. It draws upon the contemporary model of property valuation represented in the pricing formula:

$K = RFR + r - g + d;$

Where K is the initial yield, RFR is the risk free rate, r is the risk premium, g is the expected rate of rental growth and d is depreciation. Under the formula RFR and r are taken to make up a required rate of return and g and d are given to represent the net expected growth. Drawing upon this formula, the RFR, is taken to be (11 percent) with a risk premium of 2 percent, this gives an required target, or equated yield of 13 percent. Using the formula $(1+g)^t$, it is possible to calculate the growth rate on a 5 yearly rent review pattern and all-risks yield of 8 percent as 5.8 percent p.a (see Baum and Crosby, 1995). Applying this growth rate in the form of an explicit cash flow, it is possible to forecast the rent for the assets forming the subject of attention. What it shows is that in drawing upon this model of property valuation, rental income is forecast to grow from £105,000 to £146,500 and give an overall increase of £27,280 (see Table 8.5).

Table 8.5 Projected, Forecast and Increase Rent

Ward	Year	Current	Forecast	Increase
41	1996	105,000		
	1997	117,000	118,700	1,700
	1998	123,000	126,860	3,860
	1999	133,200	143,700	10,560
	2000	135,400	146,560	11,160
				£27,280

The significance of such a cash flow model of property valuation lies in the fact it (putting aside the assumption about the equated yield, risk free rate and risk premium) allows the valuation of property to be growth explicit and identify the forecast rent for the period in question. In this respect the usefulness of the model has to be seen to rest not only in the fact it provides an important measurement of performance in the form of rental growth, but in the value it has as an instrument to assist in the financial planning of expenditure on the management of property. To assist, that is, with the budgeting of income in the form of rent and the expenditure of such revenues which take place to cover outgoings - be they to costs associated with the ownership and use of assets, the funding of acquisitions, disposal, or development of property. As such it provides a useful tool for the financial planning and budgeting of both income and outgoing expenditure and can be used as a valuable supplement to the budgeting of capital expenditure and receipts it is more traditional to associate with the management function.

Given the authority forming the subject of the case-study owns in the region of 1,500 commercial holdings and since becoming a unified body this has been increased by a further 75 percent, the potential such a financial planning technique has to assist with the budgeting of expenditure over an annual and five-yearly period should not be under-estimated. Furthermore, as Mollart (1988, 1994) and Bryne's (1995) publications on such matters point out, it also provides the possibility of making the model risk, growth and even depreciation explicit. Projecting, if you like, a range of probable cash flows from the forecast of rental income relative to the valuation and pricing of property. Looking at the cash flow models of the cost approach to property valuation put forward by Britton, Connellan and Crofts (1989, 1991) and Connellan (1994), it is evident the formula for the valuation of property classified as non-standard, or specialist assets is more problematic in the notional rate of interest adopted to represent the initial yield, the lack of consideration it gives to either risk, or growth and the way in which depreciation is taken account of. While it derives rent from the current value of the replacement cost, the initial yield it represents does not appear to combine with risk and growth to form either an expected, target, or equated yield in anything like the growth explicit model of the previous formula. Indeed under the circumstances it might be pertinant to ask how assets of this kind and the valuation of property put forward for such purposes, represents a form of investment? For in its present form the model appears not to give any attention to the question or either risk, or growth. Some of the points are expanded upon in the next section.

In terms of performance measurement, similar spreadsheet applications can be carried out to compute the degree of usage, cost of property-related outgoings and rate of return holdings yield. The outgoing costs include energy, cleansing, insurance, local taxes, or rates and any rental payments. They also include management costs from the appropriate service level agreements. It should perhaps be noted that the use of internal rate of return as a measure of performance is limited to non-specialist, or standard properties which take the form of an investment. It is also limited to a large degree on the level of historical information stored in the data-base. As local authorities have not previously been required to (re)value property, information of this kind may be limited and restrict such a form of analysis. The information for the other forms of performance measurement are not so restricted and should not give any undue problems in this regard (see Table 8.6).

Table 8.6 Performance Measurement

	Asset	Average	Market
Costs			
Energy			
Cleaning			
Rent			
Management			
Local Taxes			
Property Yields			
Rate of Return			
(initial yield)			
(rental growth)			
(equated yield)			

The automated valuation of property and question of mass appraisal

The computer-based information system outlined here provides a form of property management that is comprehensive in the way it facilitates the registration of assets, valuation of property and also makes it possible for such functions (along with the measurement of performance) to be carried out in a manner which cuts across the management of operational, investment and surplus land and buildings held on the trading account awaiting development.

Given the portfolio of asset classes the information system manages is heterogeneous in nature requiring; as it does: bases and methods of property valuation - not to mention performance measurement - suitable for the commercial, industrial and residential categories of holdings in the prime and secondary sectors, the full significance of the development tends to become apparent. Unlike previous studies which tend to focus on the valuation of either the commercial (predominantly office) or residential sectors of the property market, this form of appraisal (the registration of assets, valuation of property and measurement of performance) involves the commercial, industrial and residential categories, prime and secondary sectors, held for operational purposes, as investments and for development opportunities. Related to this is the fact that the valuation of such property cannot reply on the conventions of the income approach, but must also supplement the comparative and investment methods with those of the contractors and residual. This is something that requires the adoption of asset classes and both the open market value (OMV) and depreciated replacement cost (DRC) as bases and methods for the valuation of property, measurement of performance and notional pricing of the holdings in question. The effect of this is to open up the traditional division in the methods of property valuation about the basis of the former to provide good reliable evidence of values and prices assets will exchange for in the market, rather than the more subjective valuation of what a property is worth as a holding under the latter. Given it has also been traditional for local authorities to hold a large amount of specialist assets for operational use relative to investment and development properties, the lack of opportunity to make use of the income approach and requirement to rely on cost, has tended to give a perception of the property management divisions in such organisations as having only a distant relationship to the market. Indeed it is a view that has done much to reproduce the status-quo which existed in local authority property management before the Audit Commission and CIPFA's reports on the matter.

This paper shows that fundamental developments in the subject are taking place which tend to challenge such a view - the adoption of net current replacement as the principle of notional pricing, be it approached on the basis of income or cost - to mention but a few. Moreover, if it can be accepted the income approach concentrates on the investment method and in its present form only covers that category and sector of the market which generates income from standard, non-specialist property (predominantly in the independent sector), the extent of the developments taking place can be brought into focus. Put in as few words as possible, it is perhaps best seen as the development of an emergent pro-corporate, accountable, decentralised and competitive form of property valuation in the public sector which cuts across the specialist, non-specialist, or standard classification and incorporates the logic of the income form in an attempt to price the full cost of holding land and buildings.

When this cannot be done through the application of the income approach (because the assets in question are non-standard, or specialist and not open to the investment method), it is done through the use of the cost approach on the basis of depreciated replacement and the contractor's method. For it is this form of property valuation that generates an income from specialist, non-standard holdings as a return on investment. Given the income it generates represent a rental payment in the form of a capital charge, the return it provides from the structure of yields in the market (to cover notional interest, obsolescence and depreciation) represents the price paid for the right to occupy the asset under a leasehold agreement and with the tenant responsible for the payment of outgoings. But, perhaps most significant of all is the fact what such a development goes to demonstrate is that irrespective of whether the notional pricing exercise is of standard, non-specialist, or specialist assets, of any category, or sector, a form of investment method operates and is drawn upon as the basis of property valuation and performance measurement.

Under these circumstances, perhaps the most pertinent question to ask is what form of investment method and whether-or-not these subtle twists in the theory and method of property valuation bring about an equivalence, or uniform set of standards between the public and independent sector? To answer this question it is perhaps best to begin by looking more closely at the institutional setting of the development and listing the 'pros and cons' of one approach relative to another. That is of the income against the form of valuation which is emerging from the development of local authority property management.

The advocates of the income approach would no doubt want to stress that the emerging form of valuation tends to take the most appropriate elements of its own methodology and augments it with some kind of contractor-based 'capital asset pricing model', the value of which has already come under criticism from advocates of the income approach and pro-investment appraisal lobby - albeit in another, less radical form (see Baum 1989, 1991). One whose rather crude treatment of the income-cost relationship, question of risk, growth, obsolescence and depreciation would no doubt attract considerable criticism for the simple fact it doesn't meet the 'market test'. Because, in essence, there is no evidence of any market transactions taking place on such a basis and due to the nature of the assets forming the subject of property valuation i.e. non-standard and specialist, there perhaps never will be - outside, that is, a more radical shake-up of public sector finance, further re-organisation of local government and reform of authorities, which at this point appears unlikely.

While it would be correct to suggest much work needs to be done on the question of equivalence before it can be given any serious consideration, the outcome of taking such a stance on the matter is unfortunate in that it tends to undermine the value of such an investigation by imposing the standards of the income approach on the one in question. Rather than simply reproducing the status quo, it might perhaps be best to look at the matter as one which places both forms of property valuation under question and represents a position where no particular set of standards should be seen to dominate the other.

Table 8.7 The Income and Emerging Form

	Income	**Emerging form**
Pros	relies on market evidence from analysis of transactions comparable in nature	competitive, decentralist accountable and corporatist

Table 8.7 The Income and Emerging Form continued

Pros	bases the notional prices of property on the investment method of valuation	bases its notional pricing on replacement cost, the valuation of standard, non-specialist and specialist assets in the commercial and industrial categories/sectors and adopts the investment and contractor's method of property valuation along with the comparative method for residential holdings
	is growth, risk and depreciation explicit	the valuation of specialist assets adopts a contractor's form of asset pricing with a rate of return on investment from the structure of yields in the capital market
	draws on independent evidence to compare the relationship between valuation and price	makes use of independent standards of financial control over budgeting for asset registration, property valuation and performance measurement whenever possible
Cons	narrow focus on standard, non-specialist classification of assets and investment method of valuation	as yet the income it generates is not sensitive to risk, growth implicit and problematic in its treatment of obsolescence and depreciation
	does not incorporate a large section of the 'market'	the landlord and tenant type relations of the internal market which underpin such a structure of income are ill-defined

Table 8.7 The Income and Emerging Form continued

	Income	Emerging form
Cons	concentrates on the investment method with some consideration of the residual method for development purposes	legal constraints restrict the circulation of capital into all classifications of assets - be they specialist/non-specialist, the commercial, industrial, or residential categories
	offers no solution to the problem of non-standard, specialist property and is ambivalent about the nature of the relationship between the public and independent sector	the limited circulation of capital and lack of transactional data in the specialist sector make it difficult to obtain independent evidence of the relationship between valuations and price

Looking at the matter in this way, it might be possible to hold on to the possibility of braking the strangle-hold the income approach has over property valuation and opening it up to contemporary developments of the kind outlined in this paper. But this is only half the story, for the development of the computer-based information systems outlined here also mark a radical break with more traditional forms of appraisal. What is perhaps most noticeable is the fact that it adopts a form of appraisal which does not rely on a regression analysis. Examples of such regression based appraisals are provided by Richardson, Vipond and Furbey, (1975); Greaves, (1984); Adair and McGreal (1987). Instead the computer-based information system outlined here draws upon the theory and method of local authority property management to specify the information requirements, IT needs and technology to apply in the registration of assets, valuation of property and measurement of performance. As such it mirrors the expertise of the user (be it the executive, directorate or experts within the property management division i.e. chief executives, finance, legal, estates sections etc.) to input, process and output information and can perhaps best be referred to as an expert system. One that provides an electronic filing cabinet, automated valuation of property and measurement of performance and does so in a format which increases the accuracy, reliability and quality of the management function.

It is a development Czernkowski (1990: 377) has recently drawn attention to in an examination of expert systems. As this particular examination points out, computer-based information systems for registration, valuation and by implication performance measurement are:

> Usually based on regression techniques and hence cannot model the true complexity of the [appraisal] assessment process. Expert Systems (ES) development is one procedure allowing the modelling of complex, non - linear relationships and processes, such as those which exist in the field of [property] valuation.
>
> ES development yields an advantage since it permits discovery of the structure, as well as of the strength of the relationship between value and its predictors. By modelling the decision making process of individuals using ES's, the performance of conventional [appraisal models] may be exceeded since [such] models of the environment invariably contain an imposed structure (the linear regression model) where ES allows users to discover and use the relationship which exists in reality.

As is stated, the use of expert systems, which, it is argued, morphologically model the human decision-making process, can have no counter-part in modelling 'nature', for the true environmental relationships which exist are discoverable only through the models (rule sets) which people build. In building models of the environment, the best that can be done is to impose a structure (e.g. linear regression) and postulate a number of variables which might be relevant, by first of all assuming and then imposing a structure. While under such a formula the strength of the relationship can be determined its form is not necessarily discernible. In contrast expert systems make it possible to model the complexities of the human decision-making process.

Of course, the focus of attention on computer-based information systems as expert models of the appraisal process is not new. There are a number of publications on the matter that pre-date Czernkowski's (1990) statement. Examples include Boyle (1984), Gronow, Scott and Rosser (1989). But putting this aside, what the quote captures is the true value of such systems: the fact they tend to rely less on abstract generalisations and develop a structure that mirrors more closely the realities of the appraisal process in question. The realities property management divisions in local authorities have to face up to and work within as parameters laid down for such a form of appraisal.

Where the appraisal process found in the emerging structure of local authority property management perhaps differs from other such developments, is in the fact the comparative under-development of the subject has made it difficult to mirror those taking place elsewhere. The issues of asset registration, property valuation and performance measurement are perhaps even more complex than those dealt with by existing expert systems, requiring a greater amount of development before the full underlying rational of the exercise can become evident. Perhaps also evident is the fact that in the case of local authority property management, the decision making processes the expert system (i.e. for the valuation of property and measurement of performance) attempts to mirror, is not one which is readily available. For as the discussions that have taken place under the headings of 'systems design and operation' and 'question of mass appraisal' go to show, local authority property management is still in a formative stage, with no hard and fast 'rule sets' to uncover, but rather to discover as part of the model building exercise. It is perhaps a more subjective process that attempts to model the full complexity of decision making in the management of property held by local authorities and one it is impossible to represent the true nature of in a regression analysis.

Summary

This paper has sought to examine the issues that underly the development of computer-based information systems for the management of property held by local authorities. As such it has set out the issues that surround the application of IT to the development in question and has suggested the problems and difficulties currently being experienced in the application of IT, development of computer-based information systems and management of property held by local authorities, lie in the structure of local authority property management and both the theory and method of property management put forward by independent bodies like the Audit Commission and CIPFA.

While it is appreciated that bodies of this kind do not wish to be over-prescriptive in the form of local authority property management they should like to see develop, it is evident the translation of the theory which focuses attention on a competitive, decentred, accountable and corporate form of property management into a method of application (i.e. into a strategy and set of instruments geared towards the adoption of IT and development of computer-based information systems) requires a great deal of further consideration if the exercise is to produce something more valuable than an electronic filing cabinet. If, that is, it is going to improve the standards of property management in local authorities by progressing through this preliminary stage of development and do so in the manner which allows the valuation of property and measurement of performance to take place.

The paper has documented how such a transition from electronic filing cabinet to automated property valuation and performance measurement has been achieved by way of a case-study. It has also drawn attention to how the application of IT and development of such an information system aids the appraisal of land and buildings. In this respect it has sought to show how the development in question represents an emergent form of property valuation which challenges the conventions of the income approach in an attempt to cut across the asset classes, bases and methods of property valuation in pricing the full cost of holding land and buildings. In doing so it has drawn attention to the radical nature of the break this emerging form of property valuation makes with more established conventions. In view of this, it has also sought to qualify the significance of the development and balance the 'pros and cons' of the conventional position against the more radical nature of the emergent form.

While such a representation tends to emphasise the somewhat radical nature of the development, it is important not to mis-represent the situation as a straight forward innovation in the valuation of property, for this should be wrong and would run the considerable risk of trivialising a matter of even greater concern. If anything, it should be seen as representing anything but a straight forward innovation in the valuation of property and ought to be seen as a response to a number of strategic challenges the public sector currently faces in the financial restructuring of local government and attempts made by independent bodies like the Audit Commission and CIPFA to re-organise and reform property management in local authorities. That is improve the standards of local authority property management in a manner which allows the emerging form of property valuation to measure performance and price the full cost of holding land and buildings.

References

Adair, A. and McGreal, S. (1987), 'The application of multiple regression analysis in property valuation', *Journal of Valuation*, vol 6, (1) : 57-67.

Association of District Councils (1990a), *Property Management in District Councils - A Good Practice Guide*, ADC, London.

Association of District Councils (1990b), *Efficiency in Welsh District Councils - Property Management*, ADC, London.

Association of District Councils (1990c), *Property Management in District Councils - A Good Practice Guide*, ADC, London.

Audit Commission (1988a), *Local Authority Property - A Management Overview*, HMSO, London.

Audit Commission (1988b), *Local Authority Property - A Management Handbook*, HMSO, London.

Audit Commission (1988c), *Management Paper No.7*, HMSO, London.

Avis, M., Gibson, V. and Watt, J. (1989), *Managing Operational Property*, University of Reading.

Bains, M. (1972), *The New Local Authorities: Management and Structure*, HMSO, London.

Banner, G. (1988), 'Management development in public administration: how to meet the challenge', in Brovetto, P., Holzer, R. and Kakabadse, A. (eds) *Management Development and the Public Sector A European Perspective*, Gower, Aldershot.

Baum, A. (1989), 'A critical examination of the measurement of property investment risk', *Department of Land Economy, Discussion Paper No 22*, University of Cambridge.

Baum, A. (1991), *Property Investment, Depreciation and Obsolescence*, Routledge, London.

Baum, A. and Crosby, N. (1995), *Property Investment Appraisal*, Routledge, London.

Boyle, C. (1984), 'An expert system of valuation of residential properties', *Journal of Valuation*, vol 2 (3) : 271-286.

Britton, W., Connellan, O. and Crofts, M. (1989), *The Economic, Efficient and Effective Management of Public Authority Landed Estates*, Surrey County Council and Kingston Polytechnic, Kingston.

Britton. W., Connellan, O. and Crofts, M. (1991), *The Cost Aproach to Valuation*, School of Surveying, Kingston Polytechnic and Surrey County Council, Kingston-upon-Thames.

Byrne, T. (1995), *Risk, Uncertainty and Decision Making in Property Development*, E & N Spon, London.

Byrne, P . (1992), *Local Government in Britain*, Penguin, London.

Chambers, D. (1988), 'Learning from markets,' *Public Money and Management*, vol 8 (4) : 47-50.

Chandler, J. (1991), 'Public administration and private management - is there a difference', *Public Administration*, vol 9 (3) : 385-392.

Chartered Institute of Public Finance and Accountancy (1989), *Capital Accounting in Local Authorities - The Way Forward - A Guide to the Proposals*, CIPFA, London.

Chartered Institute of Public Finance and Accountancy (1991a), *CIPFA Statement - Capital Accounting in Local Authorities*, CIPFA, London.

Chartered Institute of Public Finance and Accountancy (1991b), *Asset Registers*, CIPFA, London.

Chartered Institute of Public Finance and Accountancy (1992a), *Capital Accounting by Local Authorities - Report of the Implementation Studies*, CIPFA, London.

Chartered Institute of Public Finance and Accountancy (1992b), *Directory of Asset Management Software*, CIPFA, London.

Chartered Institute of Public Finance and Accountancy (1994), *Asset Registers: An Update*, CIPFA, London.

Clark, S. (1988), 'Local Authority Property Management', in Hillier Parker (ed) *Hillier Parker Occasional Papers*, Hillier Parker, London.

Common, R., Flynn, N. and Mellon, E. (1993), *Managing Public Services*, Butterworth-Heineman, Oxford.

Connellan, O. and Baldwin, M. (1992), 'The cost approach to valuation', *Journal of Property Valuation and Investment*, vol 11 (1) : 50-55.

Crofts, M. (1989), 'Public land management - land audits and asset rents', *Estates Gazette*, 8928 : 66-70.

Czernkowski, R. (1990), 'Expert systems in real estate valuation', *Journal of Valuation*, vol 8 (4) : 376-393.

Deakin, M. (1994), 'Initial considerations on the cost approach', *Cutting Edge*, RICS, London.

Deakin, M. (1995), 'The development of financial services for the property management division of Kiev City', in *Our Common Estates Series*, RICS, London.

Deakin, M. (1996), 'The property management division of Kiev City', *Property Management*, vol 14 (4) : 15-26.

Dent, P. and Bond, S. (1992), 'Public property holdings: evaluating the assets', *Property Management*, vol 11, (4) : 314-318.

Dixon, T., Hargitay, S. and Bevan, O. (1991), *Microcomputers in Property: A Surveyor's Guide to Lotus 1-2-3 and dBase IV*, Spon, London.

Dixon, T. (1985), 'Computer software availability for valuation', *Journal of Valuation,* vol 4 (4): 21-32.

Dixon, T. (1989), *Computerised Information Systems for Surveyors*, Surveyors Publications, London.

Dixon, T. (1995), *Using Microcomputers for Property Valuation and Appraisal*, CEM, Reading.

Dobson, S. and Rosemary, S. (1990), 'Public and private sector management: the case for a wider debate', *Public Money and Management*, vol 10 (1) : 37-40.

Edward Erdman. (1992), *Property Asset Registers - A National Survey of the Local Authority Response to Implementation*, Edward Erdman, London.

Elcock , H. (1994), *Local Government*, Routledge, London.

French, N. (1994), 'Asset registers and asset rents for local authorities: a viable property management tool', *Property Management*, vol 12, (3).

Gammons, J. (1990), 'Property rationalisation - a local authority initiative', *Property Management,* vol 8 (1) : 23-27.

Gibson, V. (1986), 'A management view of valuation in information technology', *Journal of Valuation*, vol 5, (1): 30-40.

Gibson, V. (1994), 'Strategic property management: how can local authorities develop a property strategy?', *Property Management*, vol 12 (3) : 9-15.

Greaves, M. (1984), 'The determinants of residential values', *Journal of Valuation*, vol 3 (1) : 271-286.

Gronow, S., Scott, I. and Rosser, B. (1989), 'The nature and use of uncertainty in property valuation expert systems', *Journal of Valuation*, vol 7 (3) : 218-247.

Harrow, J. and Willcocks, L. (1990), 'Risk and the public service manager', *Public Money and Management*, vol 10 (3) : 61-4.

Henkel, M. (1991), 'The Audit Commission', in Pollitt, C. and Harrison, S. (eds) *Handbook of Public Services Management*, Blackwell, Oxford.

Hsia, M. and Byrne, P. (1989), 'Automated property performance analysis: considerations on the development of a PC based information system prototype', *Working Paper No 2, Land Management Department*, Reading University.

Hsia, M. (1989), 'User-oriented Property Management Systems', *Property Management*, vol 7 (4).

Jenkins, D. and Gronow, S. (1989), 'IT in local government property management', *Estates Gazette,* 8844.

Jenkins, D., Gronow, S. and Prescott, G. (1989), 'Information technology - the changing nature of local government property management', *Property Management*, vol 8 (1).

Kirkwood, J. (1984), *Information Technology and Land Administration*, Estates Gazette, London.

Kirkwood, J. and Padden, J. (1988), 'Property management - what the Audit Commission did not tell us!' , *Estates Gazette*, 8842: 24-28.

Kooiman , J. (1988) 'Public management in Europe', in Brovetto, P., Holzer, R. and Kakabadse, A. (eds) *Management Development and the Public Sector a European Perspective*, Gower, Aldershot.

Leach, S., Stewart, J. and Walsh, K. (1994), *The Changing Organisation and Management of Local Government*, Macmillan, London.

Management Analysis Centre (1985), *Competition and the Chartered Surveyor*, MAC, London.

Maud. (1969), *Report of the Committee on Management of Local Government*, HMSO, London.

Metcalfe, L. (1988), 'Accountable public management: UK concepts and experience', in Brovetto, P., Holzer, R. and Kakabadse, A. (eds) *Management Development and the Public Sector a European Perspective*, Gower, Aldershot.

Mollart, R. (1988), 'Monte-Carlo simulation using LOTUS 1-2-3', *Journal of Property Valuation*, vol 6 (4) : 419-433.

Mollart, R. (1994), 'Using Lotus 1-2-3 for risk analysis', *Journal of Property Valuation and Investment*, vol 12 (3) : 89-96.

Richardson, H., Vipond, J. and Furbey, R. (1975), *Housing and Urban Spatial Structure*, Saxon House, London.

Roberts, B. (1983), 'Property management in a local authority', *Property Management*, vol 1 (3) : 223-228.

Roberts, B. (1984), 'Managing the corporate estate of Leicester City Council', *Property Management,* vol 2 (3) : 198-205.

Royal Institution of Chartered Surveyors (1993), *Valuation Guidance Notes*, RICS, London.

Royal Institution of Chartered Surveyors (1995), *Appraisal and Valuation Manual*, RICS, London.

Spicer, J. (1979), *Property Information Systems for Government*, DOE, London.

Stewart, J. and Stoker, G. (1995), *Local Government in the 1990's*, Macmillan, London.

Walsh, K. (1995), *Public Services and Market Mechanisms*, Macmillan, London.

Young, P. (1994), 'Market valuation with no market', *Journal of Property Valuation and Investment,* vol 12 (3) : 9-27.

9 Local Authority Non-Operational Property - Serviceable or Surplus?

Neil Martindale, Chartered Surveyor

Introduction

This paper concerns non-operational property in use. Rather than employ loaded terms such as 'commercial' or 'investment', it adopts the label 'tenanted non-residential property' - TNRP. It deals with the perceived objectives for which local authorities hold TNRP and the functional, financial and legal setting. It compares category bases for property holdings and in particular examines attitudes to acquisition, management, retention and disposal of TNRP. It notes the confusion between investment and indirect service objectives and the expected returns. It discusses the findings of a survey of councils centering on the characteristics and management of their TNRP holdings.

The paper concludes that both the objectives and management strategy for local authority owned TNRP remain undeveloped. It suggests that the ability to properly manage and develop a real investment portfolio may be ultra vires. In the shorter term, if not ultra vires, it recommends dividing TNRP between those held primarily for indirect service and those held primarily as financial investments. However in the longer term it expects pressures from local service needs and central government will encourage, indeed force the progressive disposal of all non-operational property, including TNRP. Lastly it identifies a new form of TNRP, one within the council. In seeking to clarify and effect the different strategies for operational property between the centralised corporate council landlord and decentralised service tenants, it proposes the creation of 'internal leases'.

Background

In 1994 the London Borough of Croydon sold most of its commercial property holdings to Croydon Land and Estates, for £58 million (Lennox,1994). The purchasers were going to 'transform' the portfolio - one not untypical of those held by other local authorities -'...after years of inactivity under the Council...' (Tyler, 1994). In 1995 the Royal Institution of Chartered Surveyors (RICS) completed research (Warren *et al.*, 1995) designed to '...evaluate the efficacy of county farms in providing ... a low cost route into farming...' and '...the degree to which county farm estates provide other public benefits'. They concluded that these farms generally provided few opportunities for the former and were largely ineffective in offering the latter.

Of the two foregoing accounts, the first concerns non-operational property largely held as an investment, the second, property held primarily for indirect services. In both examples the returns were seen as being far from optimum. They show the continuing need in the 1990s for councils to look more closely at their non-operational property holdings to see where and how objectives have become confused, portfolios neglected and actions contradictory.

How much property is involved ?

It is established that substantial parts of some urban areas are owned by the local authority (e.g. Sheffield and Manchester) (Society of Local Authority Chief Executives, 1986). Figure 9.1 sets out the estimated capital value of the total non-residential property holdings of English and Welsh councils, compared with all UK commercial property and those of other substantial landowners (Currie and Scott, 1991; Audit Commission, 1988a; Debenham Tewson Research, 1989; National Audit Office, 1988a).

Since production of these figures councils should have completed their asset registers and provided at least one year's capital valuations. However the values emerging are sometimes difficult to compare owing to the scope for interpretation allowed within the categorisation and valuation guidelines of the Chartered Institute of Public Finance and Accountancy (CIPFA) and the RICS. Before asset registers, the Association of District Councils (ADC) had 'guestimated' that districts

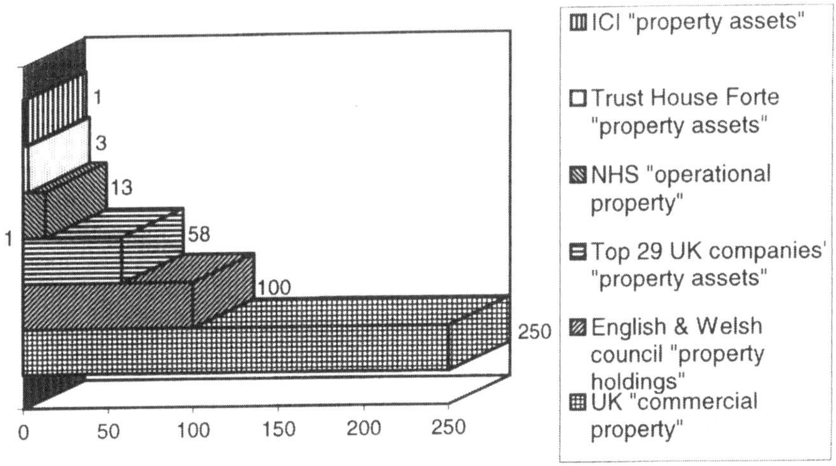

Figure 9.1 Relative Size of Local Authority Holdings

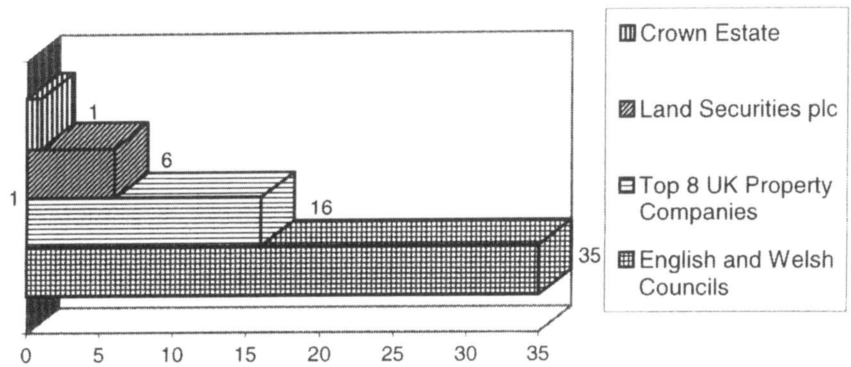

Figure 9.2 Relative Size of Local Authority 'Investment' Property Holdings

held £8bn of 'operational 'and £2-4bn of so-called 'investment' property (Association of District Councils, 1990). 'Investment' could have meant all non-operational property, something akin to all tenanted non-residential property (TNRP), i.e. all tenantable non-operational property, or even actually pure investments. Still, applying these relative measures to the £100bn commonly regarded as the capital value of the holdings of English and Welsh councils in the late 1980s, between £20-35bn would have been 'investment' property. Certainly the value of such property is far from marginal, as Figure 9.2 shows (Martindale, 1994; Debenham Tewson Research, 1989; National Audit Office, 1988b).

Where has the property come from?

A 'rag bag of properties acquired over many moons for a variety of purposes' (Wootten, 1989), TNRP has accumulated in various ways:

- Council functions have changed and with them their operational property needs. When adaptation or redevelopment was insufficient, they purchased more property rather than renting perhaps to match their feeling of permanence. However disposals have generally been much slower particularly where future needs were anticipated or uncertain. Many long-standing 'temporary' lettings have resulted.
- Councils have let property to tenants offering specific services, considered to indirectly assist their functions or the local community.
- Councils have held property as an investment for 'what the *Local Government Act* 1972 calls the "benefit, improvement or development" of their areas ... the ratepayers' inheritance from previous generations' (Roberts, 1983).
- Councils have inherited property from former authorities, but have yet to question their objectives and review these holdings themselves - an important factor with the current local government re-organization.

What are the key constraints on councils?

Government constraints on the functions and finances of councils significantly affect their ability to manage and develop property, and where sought, sustain commercial returns. They were for example a major reason for Croydon's portfolio sale.

Property acquisition powers for service objectives such as education, housing, planning, and highways (by compulsion if Government approved) come from principal service Acts. Councils can also purchase for less specific services 'for the benefit, improvement or development' of the municipality through general powers (HMSO, 1980). However two recent prominent cases concerned failed, but imaginative property schemes, which although decided in favour of Allerdale DC and LB Waltham Forest, emphasised the continuing uncertainty over limits to council powers (Gordon, 1996). Whilst companies adopt self-imposed limits on activity through their 'articles', the Government determines council powers, resulting in '... a lack of enterprise amongst them [councils] and a feeling in many people's minds that they are unimportant and rather dull...' (Bryne, 1992).

Though property can only be bought under a specific statute, it may later be transferred or 'appropriated' to assist another function, and when finally no longer needed for operations, can be let or sold *for* 'the best consideration that can reasonably be obtained' (HMSO, 1972) - money or rights in land. The requirement for prior Department of the Environment consent on disposals for less than best consideration, further controls 'social', 'philanthropic' or other indirect service yields where they may reduce the commercial return from a sale or medium to long term letting (Department of the Environment, 1993). More recently the Government has further reduced the traditional role of councils in providing diverse functions in a concentrated geographical area to one of 'enabler', thus creating more surplus property for re-use or disposal.

Council use of rental income is still relatively unrestricted as are retained and operational property sales receipts which are to be reused for specific property reprovision. However apart from various temporary concessions for certain classes of property (HMSO, 1996b), the Government has increased controls on council finances, so that 50 - 75 percent of other capital receipts from property sales must be 'reserved' to repay loan debt. In the sphere of investment Government further restricts the use of surplus council monies to 'approved investments', essentially short term financial instruments, but not real estate (HMSO, 1990). There is thus limited scope for assembly and subsequent management of TNRP, especially for investment.

How has council property been categorised?

Local authorities should at least begin with a set of objectives, ranked in some sort of order of priority (based on rational criteria such as need or expressed demand). Various ways of achieving those objectives should be considered and the most effective projects (those which maximise benefits) chosen and pursued (Bryne, 1992). The provision of services by local authorities requires the use of ... manpower, goods and material and property (land and buildings) (Audit Commission, 1988a). If property is to serve the authority's objectives, those objectives must be clearly and authoritatively articulated (Society of Local Authority Chief Executives, 1986). All very obvious, but in the absence of extreme financial pressure such expressly stated and defined objectives have been all too often lacking in councils, and for that matter other public and private organisations as well (Avis, Gibson and Watts, 1989).

A first step towards better management is for a categorisation of property. However that employed by councils to date tends to be by current use rather than the more rational basis (albeit harder to define), of the primary council objective that the property is intended to assist. This is because preparation of capital asset registers has been the driving force for such work and the registers (designed by the RICS and CIPFA) adopt categories based on current use. Most recently these defined 'operational assets' as fixed assets held and occupied, used or consumed by the local authority in the direct delivery of those services for which it has either a statutory or discretionary responsibility (The Royal Institution of Chartered Surveyors, 1993).

All else, including 'investment property' is accordingly classed as 'non-operational'. Interestingly whilst 'county farms' as TNRP, started off amongst these (The Royal Institution of Chartered Surveyors, 1992), they ended up with the operational (*ibid*, 1993). Where maximisation of rental or capital return has been accepted by commentators as top priority, then TNRP is described as 'investment property' (Association of District Councils, 1990; Audit Commission, 1988a). However usually categorisation by primary objective has been subverted. In the case of TNRP it led to grouping by management 'style', e.g. 'Commercially Managed Estates', held primarily 'to maximise the financial return consistent with proper regard for the interests of tenants, adjoining owners, employees and others directly concerned with the estate' (Thorncroft, 1965).

How has council TNRP been viewed ?

Whilst it is accepted that TNRP forms a minority (though a substantial one) of council property holdings, there have been few published examinations of it. No other private or public bodies hold anything approaching the same amount. Of the top 1000 UK non-property companies for example, when non-operational space was identified, 80 percent sold it. Unlike councils, retention of non-operational space, including TNRP, had not become an end in itself and whilst 65 percent let some, it was genuinely an interim measure before operational re-use or sale (Debenham Tewson Research, 1989). Commentators' views and council practices differ. Some have concluded that TNRP is unnecessary and should be sold - property exists only to enable public authorities to perform their principal duties and attain their principal objectives '... property should very rarely be held for its own sake' (Britton, Connellan and Crofts, 1989). A council should occupy the minimum possible amount of landed property which it needs to perform its duties and attain its objectives. Nevertheless there might be some important exceptions, including the corporate estates of old City authorities. Whilst accepting 'that different landed property holdings may have different sorts of functions within the authority', some have expressed doubt over the validity of retaining commercial property investments (The Royal Institution of Chartered Surveyors, 1987). Similarly whilst '...the commitment and skill with which many local authorities have for many years managed their investment holdings and other rent producing properties...', have been praised, (Society of Local Authority Chief Executives, 1986), the reality of an investment objective has been denied.

A local authority is not like the kind of property company which exists solely to provide a financial return on its investment '... the uses to which the estate is put must at all times reflect the enduring nature of the public interest' (*ibid*). TNRP has been identified both with temporary lettings (generating income or reducing costs) and 'investment'. The latter was equated with 'the benefit, improvement or development' of municipalities, to be 'prudently husbanded' (Roberts, 1983), presumably something less exploitative than active management. Though noting members accept that the prime function is to produce income and capital growth on behalf of the community, the manager has to accept that the portfolio remains part of the local authority and cannot be used in a way which conflicts with other policies. This can be illustrated by a council estates committee's lack of planning appeal rights.

The RICS identified farming (county farms), planning, economic development, future operations, increasing development value; or increasing rent returns, all as valid reasons for council's to retain 'non operational' property and most would be TNRP. They noted however that '...actual returns from a property may be influenced ... by policy decisions in which commercial considerations are secondary...', adding that though '...the private sector developer would not normally allow...(politics).. to influence its letting or disposal policy' (The Royal Institution of Chartered surveyors, 1987), they implied that a council might. Primacy of an investment objective even for 'joint schemes', was not envisaged.

The local authority valuer is 'the agent for ensuring that the council has the land and buildings necessary to provide its services and secondly...[with] ...a direct responsibility for the management of the corporate...' (commercial) 'estate' (Searle, 1987). That writer recognised that the second, if not a council objective, was an activity and added that 'many authorities have made conscious decisions to retain this...[non-operational]...property which may then be let on the commercial market thus producing a valuable income' (Audit Commission, 1988a). Justification for retention (though not purchase) of TNRP as non-operational property was either on 'straightforward financial' grounds, or 'in furtherance of the wider policy objectives of the Council'. Of the TNRP retained and used for 'commercial' ends, '... management of property for its own sake as an investment for the ratepayers, is more controversial' (*ibid*).

Local authorities are not property companies and do not have the same objectives. That however is no reason to discount some commercial practices. The portfolio must be managed effectively and the manager, must be accountable (*ibid*). However, managed to what end? How proactive is its management allowed to be? Could or should investment be the primary objective for any identifiable council TNRP?

Despite the above, both the Audit Commission (AC) and the Association of District Councils (ADC) whilst accepting that councils, unlike property companies, do not exist to provide a financial return on all of their estate, clearly identified and promoted a new separate 'investment' objective. This 'investment property' should '...not be subject to the same (service and political) pressures...'. However this was clouded in that '...such property is an investment for present and future ratepayers' and should be managed accordingly', and could be used to stimulate 'regeneration' or influence the 'quality and attractiveness of urban life' (Audit Commission, 1988a).

In summary, though some commentators deny the legitimacy of holding TNRP - as non-operational it is 'therefore' surplus and should be sold - many accept its retention in assisting services with a financial return, though in unspecified ways. By contrast the AC and ADC have tried to develop the value of TNRP as a significant and acceptable part of an overall portfolio, by further identifying 'investment' property where financial returns come before service. Indeed 'investment property' is now a sub-category of non-operational for council asset registers.

What are the problems in the management of TNRP?

The AC's 1988 reports on local authority property management showed that the diversity of budgets, geographic spread, number and type of statutory functions largely determined total holdings. Metropolitan boroughs and urban districts held the most TNRP. They also identified many problems affecting TNRP:

- inadequate management information;
- lack of incentives to users;
- absence of property reviews;
- ignorance of opportunity costs of property;
- confused property objectives;
- failure to generate capital receipts;
- excessive retention of vacant property;
- unknown costs of service provision through tenanted property;
- poor performance of investment portfolio.

Confused property objectives

Whilst general written objectives are relatively common in the public sector, they are often poorly conveyed, unprioritised and uncoordinated, serving only to fuel conflict between service and corporate interests about the priority of differing returns. Even identifying who may set objectives and monitor attainment is often unclear. Generally corporate property managers are concerned first to enhance property value, whilst property managers acting for the council service, seek operational efficiency.

Lack of clear, prioritised objectives for property, allowing 'inadequate strategy', poor service and financial returns were particularly common and allowed the 'corporate aspects of property portfolio management' to be ignored (Audit Commission, 1988b). However, given the AC's view that investment might be a primary objective for TNRP, there is justification for two 'corporate' approaches. One strategy for all council service resources (including indirect and direct service property) and another for all council investments (investment TNRP besides general fund monies).

The AC identified that few councils distinguished clearly or at all between categories of property objective - service, investment, or none. This was true '...especially in the case of property which is not being used directly for the provision of services' (Audit Commission1988a) (TNRP). With no prime objective, performance measurement is impossible. The fact that there is a different rationale for ownership of different types of property is never made explicit to those who should be making decisions about them; they tend to remain in the authority's ownership with very few changes in their use, even when circumstances around them have changed dramatically (Britton, Connellan and Crofts, 1989).

More generally local authority managers have been blamed as poor entrepreneurs (Kooiman and Eliassen, 1988) and with specific reference to local authority property management, '[do]...the right entrepreneurial spirits, well qualified, really want to work for long in the stultifying environment of some politically dominated councils...?' (Anon, 1988). Comments made of the public sector in general are readily applicable to a council's TNRP, in that the '...public which seeks value for money and quality enterprise from its public servants also want protection from failure' (Harrow and Willcocks, 1990). However problems centre on the absence of clear prioritised objectives from members and chief officers and their promotion amongst staff. Often managers are left to 'be' rather than 'do', to administer not lead, responsible but without power, failures punished but successes unrewarded.

Confusion in the identity and primacy of objectives and their subsequent implementation is illustrated by council industrial estates. From 1972 to 1986 driven by the rapid expansion of local economic development initiatives the number of councils with small factory schemes increased dramatically (Cook, 1989). Estates were intended to offer business: a wider range of space (by size, quality, design and tenure); reduced rents (by oversupply or subsidy); and increased 'vacancy chains' (easing movement). However the council's original service objectives were often modified depending on which 'professional traditions' took management control. Individual officer perceptions of the lead department were found often to be more important than prior market research or an analysis of past and other results and experiences. Both initially and subsequently, planners saw the estates primarily as indirectly supporting the planning and economic development service, promoting employment creation and business start ups. Council valuers however, often shared the view of private landlords and promoted an investment objective through 'efficient' management, in for example rejecting new unproved business tenants as too risky (Fothergill, 1987). Likewise, Leicester City and several London Boroughs; for example, had lease clauses requiring tenants to be 'good employers'. However as 'there did not appear to have been any particular emphasis by the valuer's staff ... at the time of letting', they were rarely enforced (Mason, 1986). Again, GLC planners looking for particular tenants, sought restricted marketing and tightly drawn leases, but the GLC valuers objected because of damage to the investment value (*ibid*). Thus property managers (usually valuers) whilst supposedly seeking to maximise both financial and service returns, in the reality of a strategic void they actually tended to rely on their 'professional traditions'. Moreover even if management had gone the planner's 'way', it is not clear what proposed or practical measures of indirect service return existed, if any.

Poor performance of investment portfolio

The AC concluded that most councils owned some investment property - 'no different from that held by a private sector property company' (Audit Commission 1988b). Yet many councils failed to distinguish it from other TNRP. For example at Leicester City council: for historical reasons, the portfolio does not represent a balanced selection of different kinds of investment properties; there are many inferior properties which have only found their way into the estate because they were surplus to some other committee's requirements (Roberts, 1984).

The AC found a widespread absence of capital values prevented the measure of growth or return and hence identification of poor performers, but then the AC also failed to widen discussion to include other council investments. Only Wootten has suggested that investment TNRP sale receipts might be re-invested in other forms, rather than services - '...authorities might ...decide that funds not needed for new capital investment or to reduce debt should be invested in other markets' (Wootten, 1989). By comparison a typical scenario in the same council's finance department for the investment of a London Borough Council's surplus General Funds was described thus: '...strategy ...is discussed and agreed between the Director of Finance and the Divisional [finance] Head... at six weekly intervals... [and it] ...seeks to maximise the return on deposits with the minimum of risk [though] the return is constrained by the need to maintain adequate liquidity for short term cash requirements' (Knight, 1991). Strategy for long term investment in property has, apart from the need to pay 50 percent 'tax' (central government loan repayment set aside) on capital receipts from trading, been largely ignored.

A survey of council tenanted non-residential property

Much of the background to the above comes from work carried out in the late 1980s. To review subsequent changes and to investigate the position for TNRP in more detail, the property managers of a representative sample numbering some 50 English and Welsh councils were surveyed in 1993 (Martindale, 1994).

The results revealed that four years on though some had not considered either, both the AC and ADC reports had reached most councils. Independent findings confirmed that nearly 90 percent of councils '...felt that their authority had sufficient information on the main Audit Commission recommendations' (Fuller Peiser, 1993). Though some were ahead of the AC and the ADC, most had still changed practices as a result and had found them beneficial, a finding also supported elsewhere (Edward Erdman, 1992). Nevertheless whilst some identified that good practices for overall property management were followed, few changes had been made specifically for TNRP. This suggested councils had given priority to improving management of direct service property (DS - also loosely termed 'operational') in support of 'front line' services. Other surveys of the progress by councils in preparing asset registers also confirmed a concentration on direct service provision (Richardson, 1993).

Overall property objectives

Most respondents agreed the relevance and need for property categorisation to identify prime objectives for different parts of the estate. They also generally accepted the AC category definitions of direct and indirect service (DS & IS), vacant (VAC) and investment (INV). Some felt however that VAC confusingly included short let property and empty but service controlled amenity land, where DS and IS (or possibly a 'transition' category - where alternative objectives are examined) should apply respectively. Similarly the distinction between IS and INV was regarded by some respondents as artificial, as both should be let at full value, albeit reflecting the terms of restrictive leases for the former.

For management purposes the property category really should define the primary but not necessarily exclusive objective. The primary objective supported by a particular property will depend on the strength and clarity of overall service and investment objectives. Where there is no real investment objective, or where attainment of specified investment returns does not need property, then strategy and practice for IS and INV holdings will tend to merge, as became very evident later in the survey responses.

Property information

Capital and revenue budgets, total numbers of properties and TNRP rent rolls varied widely between councils, even on the same tier. Generally counties had the smallest rent rolls but largest service budgets implying TNRP was less significant to them - confirming the AC's findings (Audit Commission, 1988a). The extent of non-response to questions on these issues suggested a paucity of readily accessible information for the property manager. Facts about the extent and nature of the estate were almost universally unavailable. There was surprisingly little concern (as confirmed elsewhere) (Edward Erdman, 1992), considering their effect on value and sales potential, about the unavailability or need for information on values, planning, or alternative uses. Nearly all managers considered basic lease records for day-to-day estate management as essential and had them available. The survey revealed that council property information facilities and aspirations were significantly inferior to those identified for major non-property companies (Debenham Tewson Research, 1989).

Property committees

TNRP used for indirect service was held by the relevant service committee, but when considered an investment or lacking an objective, was held by 'policy and resources' or a derivative sub-committee. Besides few 'property' committees there was no mention of an 'investment' committee. Rents went to the holding committees. Service committees used income for services, but 'policy' committees passed it to general funds not reserving it for property investment.

Property departments

Officers considered themselves generally clear about property objectives, their role and commitment in devising and effecting management to suit. Though substantial time was apparently spent devising IS and INV TNRP strategies - more from service chiefs for the former, more from treasurers for the latter - these statements were not supported in answers to later questions. Meaningful property strategies were lacking. It was also clear that though most councils with TNRP retained significant in-house staffing, it was consistently directed towards day-to-day, rather than strategic management. Moreover such staff were predominantly arranged by profession not function.

Indirect service TNRP

Responses showed a wide variety of TNRP in many sectors, but as apparently few had been valued, measurement was by number. Most held a mix of what each regarded as IS and INV property with different councils regarding property in the same sectors as serving different primary objectives. Amongst INV TNRP, whilst many councils had substantial proportions of shops and industrial units, most also had significant numbers of 'other', specialised TNRP. Most TNRP were regarded as of secondary or tertiary 'investment' quality, unlike those of the typical institutional property investor but in fact very like surplus (former DS or IS) and some respondents confirmed these origins.

Property review

Though the survey did not specifically investigate TNRP reviews, it is doubtful whether they could take place in the absence, for most respondents, of meaningful criteria and information to enable rationale decisions to improve or sell property. Since neither overall objective nor the individual property performance required had been clearly defined, reviews of INV TNRP on grounds of financial performance were impossible. Such 'reviews' as occurred were designed to generate capital receipts for use in services from the sale of property not immediately required for operations. In many cases as most of the recently redundant DS had already gone, TNRP was now being sold. Nearly all TNRP (IS and INV) was freehold.

Investment TNRP

The survey concentrated at a detailed level on INV TNRP, rather than IS. Virtually all council property was located within respective municipalities, suggesting (at least historically), that a restricted view had been taken towards acquisition of property for investment. Alternatively as DS or IS property would generally be found there, this also suggested that most INV TNRP had been formerly DS or IS and just 'become' INV TNRP.

A majority felt (without reason) that INV TNRP had to be inside the municipality. Indeed for purely investment returns such a policy could be counter-productive. Policies designed to yield maximum financial returns from a property to the owner often impose burdens on neighbours, including the local authority. For example the swift forfeiture of a manufacturing company's lease to allow re-letting to a storage and distribution company, whilst ensuring continued even increased rental income to the landlord, could also create redundancies and provide fewer, less well paid, low skilled jobs, a move probably against the council's economic development plan. The council landlord will only know how best to act in respect of that property if it is clear whether investment or economic development (service) is the primary reason for its retention. Such burdens generally exceed the benefits that a council's services can legally offer to specifically favour its own property investments. Logically therefore councils should have sought investment property anywhere but inside their own municipalities, or at least sought a geographic spread both inside and out.

Normal investment criteria were notably absent. Very few councils had: set any financial objectives; used performance indicators; measured returns; considered indices; decided acceptable risk; or planned an 'ideal' portfolio shape. None even had opted for a complete diversification within property investments or between property and other investments, to minimise risk, albeit offering lower overall returns.

Almost three-quarters of TNRP portfolios were contracting and most councils had disposal policies to generate capital for service expenditure, not property re-investment. By contrast virtually none had policies for acquisition of INV TNRP, and money was rarely available anyway. At the day-to-day level, many managers felt that their council could take a commercial approach towards property. Nearly all felt they should, but many felt that in practice they did not. Respondents hinted at member concern over short term service rather than financial returns. There was considerable confusion over the primary objective of INV TNRP, be it annual returns or capital growth with many insisting that service concerns - job creation and new firm promotion - were still more important.

As councils pay little 'tax' (loan set off) on rents, but a large amount on capital 'gains' and as it is generally to their advantage to delay repayments, they might have sought high yielding property, but with little capital growth and avoided trading. Perhaps more by luck than judgement councils seem to specialise in such 'tertiary' property, making the retention of local (often in-house) expertise appropriate for the more intensive management required.

In setting future performance measures, mainstream rent and capital indices would be of limited use, leaving scope for indices based on secondary property auctions or the creation of bespoke indices suited to their holdings as the Crown Estate has done in conjunction with Investment Property Databank. The AC encouraged councils to model themselves on property companies and seek investment returns from what were mostly originally service properties, the reverse of the situation for the Council staff pension fund trustees. However the question of legality is unresolved. Aside from the special Local Act of Leicester City and the common law authority of the City of London with its Bridge estates, this remains an important question for all other statutory authorities with aspirations to seriously acquire or trade property primarily for investment return. The already weak proposition used by some, that property may be acquired for investment under their powers from *Local Government Act* 1972, would be unlikely to be sustained for *acquisitions* outside their municipalities.

Solutions to the problems in the management of TNRP ?

The survey results indicate how little tangible progress has been made by the chief officers and members of councils in addressing the common property management problems identified by the AC for TNRP. Indeed the generation of capital receipts for re-use in direct service provision (now increasingly TNRP sales) was the only significant exception. It may be that short-term political expediency too often comes before long-term service or investment planning through property, and that of resolving objectives and strategy for the management of TNRP. It may be that non-operational property is generally considered dull and irrelevant to providing electors with 'front-line' services. It may also be that attempts by officers to address these problems are unwelcome and seen by some members as a challenge and part of a hidden agenda.

The AC's solutions (Audit Commission, 1988a), especially those relevant for the TNRP portfolio, are set out below. Apart from improvements to no.2 below (a result it is suggested largely from the compulsion to produce asset registers to comply with new capital accounting regulations), few of the solutions appear to have been widely effected by councils for their TNRP. The following remain to be implemented:

1. setting overall property objectives
2. preparing comprehensive property information systems
3. creating property committees
4. basing property departments on function not profession
5. establishing service costs and returns from IS TNRP
6. measuring investment risks and returns from INV TNRP

7. starting systematic reviews of property holdings

The future for TNRP

Preliminary results from ongoing research into the value of assets for capital accounts suggests that overall the value of 'non-operational' property (including TNRP) may now be smaller at perhaps £15-20bn, but for property held largely without clear purpose this still remains a huge amount.

To date councils seem to have concentrated their response to the AC's reports and more recently the need to assemble data for the new asset registers, on the higher profile operational property. Day-to-day management of council TNRP continues largely without established strategies for each part of the portfolios. The author's current research into non-operational property holdings scheduled in asset registers, regrettably still confirms this.

The AC requires all English and Welsh local authorities to provide specific information on their performance under the Citizens Charter. Despite the value of the holdings, service or financial investment returns do not figure. Presumably they are not sufficiently interesting to the public or helpful to councils deciding how to improve value for money and quality in service (Audit Commission, 1993). The omission of such performance measures is quite unlike the sophisticated processes employed by most property companies (as the AC suggested). The same is true of those adopted by the trustees of property and other investments held by the pension funds, currently aggregating to £50bn (Duck and Gray, 1996). Indeed those trustees, having satisfied the legal minimum of providing for future pensions, are now increasingly seeking secondary 'indirect service' returns. Though they lack specific powers, they are doing so through a rapid growth in corporate governance towards ethical and often environmental matters.

Nevertheless even for council pension funds, serious dilemmas arise between investment and indirect service arise. In Belgium for example to relieve Antwerp City Council's personnel costs (of which staff pensions formed over 40 percent) a fund worth £600m was to be created from existing TNRP holdings. However this would have then meant adopting 'more commercial management' resulting in the loss of many existing tenants already providing indirect service returns (albeit largely unspecified and not measurable) from the same TNRP (Gasson, 1992).

The current position of county farms in the asset register guidelines demonstrates a similar indirect service tension. Tenanted farms do not meet the definition of operational property and started in the non-operational group. However they are currently amongst 'operational' presumably because they provide services, albeit indirectly. Why therefore are not the tenanted industrial estates, leisure centres, and residential care homes operational too ? Do they not also provide services indirectly ? Even so whether operational or not, the returns available from county farms remain unclear as the RICS have concluded and the rationale for their retention questionable. What is clear was the Government's encouragement for their sale (from 1 April, 1996) in requiring only 10 percent rather than 50 percent of the receipt to be set aside (HMSO, 1996a).

It may seem that at present the discussion over property categories is unimportant. It is however significant to note that the categories of the new residuary bodies for England and Wales, due to receive assets of abolished councils, show only (HMSO, 1995) 'operational' and 'surplus' (not 'non-operational'). The 'residual' (or as suggested above, 'transition') is effectively the 'pending' category. The existing rights of those users currently providing or receiving indirect services through holdings may expect to have them recorded and protected in some way. All 'surplus' property will then be programmed for disposal. Linked to these changes are the former Land Registers which, sparingly utilised over the last 15 years, are now abolished. However this was not before the DoE had secured powers to order disposal of any council property which it considered was underused. In this context 'underused' means where they are less than 70 percent used for 'operational purposes' (HMSO, 1980). Indeed the basis upon which the percentage is determined could potentially include most council TNRP which currently falls within the 'non-operational' category of the council's asset register. As an eminent consultant to the new English Local Government Residuary Body was reported commenting on one defunct authority '..there are some funnies as well ... Humberside owns agricultural smallholdings, which will be surplus... [and] ...There is a view that unitary authorities will not be allowed to own investment properties at all' (Jacoby,1995).

With TNRP looking generally set to decline, one scope for its future growth might be in a form of 'internal' leases for operational property. Whilst the creation of asset rents has been a key improvement in its management, the problems faced, particularly in 'multi-let' property could be significantly eased where all of the other main terms of occupation are clearly set out, for both service tenant and corporate landlord.

Conclusion

In conclusion, the AC suggested that TNRP holdings (portfolio and individual) be categorised and managed by principal council objective, be it service or investment. By contrast CIPFA's mandatory asset register categories, designed for valuation and not management purposes, are concerned with the current use of property, be it operational or non-operational. Within councils it is therefore very likely that this latter classification will progressively overtake all others. This in combination with continuing pressure from Government on capital resources, strategic property management of TNRP even if it clearly exists, is unlikely to be driven by long term service or investment objectives, but rather by a need for short term capital receipts. The classification of TNRP in the register as 'non-operational' now, will tend to confirm the general assumption that that it is not serviceable, but instead surplus, and in turn, ease its continuing programmed disposal.

Postscript

In the light of the May 1997 election result, it would appear that direct measures from the new central government administration, for the disposal of local government property assets, have weakened. Emphasis has instead, apparently moved to the Private Finance Initiative. Nonetheless this, coupled with the continuing needs of direct council services for additional capital resources, will maintain pressure for disposals. Publication of the first set of statistics on English local authority assets, in the autumn of 1997, has now provided considerable detail of the operational and non-operational property asset base of many councils (Chartered Institute of Public Finance and Accountancy, 1997). The author is now engaged in further research in this field.

Note

Neil Martindale is Principal Valuer with the Property Department of the London Borough of Waltham Forest UK. The views expressed here are not those of that Council.

References

Anon. (1988), 'Sadly underused assets', *Estates Gazette*, 8806.

Association of District Councils (ADC) (1990), *Property Management in District Councils - A Good Practice Guide*, ADC, London.

Audit Commission (1988a), *Local Authority Property Management Handbook,* HMSO, London.

Audit Commission (1988b), *Local Authority Property - A Management Overview,* HMSO, London.

Avis, M., Gibson, V. and Watt, J. (1989), *Managing Operational Property Assets,* University of Reading, Reading.

Britton, W., Connellan, O. and Crofts, M. (1989), *The Economic, Efficient and Effective Management of Public Authority Landed Estates*, Surrey County Council and Kingston Polytechnic, Kingston.

Bryne, T. (1992), *Local Government in Britain*, Penguin, London.

Chartered Institute of Public Finance and Accountancy (1997), *Local Authority Assets Statistics,* CIPFA, London.

Cook, G. (1989), 'Local authorities and industrial property markets', *Property Management,* vol. 1 (7), 3-12.

Currie, D. and Scott, A. (1991), *The Place of Property in the UK Economy,* London Business School, London.

Debenham Tewson Research (DTR) (1989), *The Role of property - Managing the Cost and Releasing the Value*, DTR, London.

Department of the Environment (1993), *Disposal of Land for Less than Best Consideration that can Reasonably be Obtained - Guidance for Authorities* circ.6/93, HMSO, London.

Duck, C. and Gray, M. (1996), 'Pension funds and their influence', *Public Finance*, vol 24: 15-17.

Erdman, E. (1992), *Property Asset Registers - A National Survey of the Local Authority Response to Implementation.* Edward Erdman, London.

Fothergill, S. (1987), *Property and Industrial Development,* Hutchinson, London.

Fuller Peiser (1993), Councils 'drag heels' over asset registers'. *Estates Times,* February, p.2.

Gasson, C. (1992), 'Tomorrow's just another pay day', *Local Government Chronicle Supplement,* vol 6 November, pp.3-4.

Gordon, R. (1996), 'Local Authority Powers after Allerdale', *Local Authority Law*, vol. 5 19 June, pp.6-8.

Harrow, J. and Willcocks, L (1990), 'Risk and the public service manager'. *Public Money and Management*, vol 10 (3): 61-64.

HMSO (1972), Local Government Act, 1972, ss.123 and 127, as amended by Local Government Planning and Land Act, 1980, HMSO, London.

HMSO (1980a), Local Government Act, 1972, ss.120 and 137, as amended by Local Government Planning and Land Act, 1980, HMSO, London.

HMSO (1980b), Local Government Planning and Land Act 1980, s.95 as amended by the Leasehold Reform Housing and Urban Development Act 1993, s.176, HMSO, London.

HMSO (1990), Local Authorities (Capital Finance) (Approved Investments) Regulations, SI 1990:426 and Local Authorities (Capital Finance) Regulations, SI 1990:432, and Local Government and Housing Act 1989, HMSO, London.

HMSO (1995), Local Government Changes for England (Property Transfer and Transitional Payments) Regulations, SI 1995:402, HMSO, London.

HMSO (1996a), Local Authorities (Capital Finance and Approving Investments) (Amendments) Regulations 1996, SI 1996:568, HMSO, London.

HMSO (1996b), Local Authorities (Capital Finance and Approved Investments) (Amendment) Regulations, SI 1996:568, Local Authorities (Capital Finance) (Amendment No.2) Regulations, SI 1996:2121, HMSO, London.

Jacoby, C. (1995), 'Local authority re-organisation - seizing the moment', *Estates Gazette:* 112-113.

Knight, T. (1991), 'Treasury management - investing within a framework', *Public Finance and Accountancy*, 13 December, pp.13-14.

Kooiman, J. and Eliasson, K. (1988), 'Public management in Europe', in Brovetto, P., Holzer, P. and Kakabadse, A. (eds), *Management Development and the Public Sector: A European Perspective*, Gower, Aldershot.

Lennox, K. (1994), 'Croydon pioneers', *Estates Gazette,* 9426.

Martindale, N. (1994), *Local Authorities as Landlords of Tenanted Non-Residential, Property*, University of East London, London.

Mason, A. (1986), 'Industrial property letting lessons from the GLC's policies and experiences', *Local Economy,* vol 1 (3) : 61-69.

National Audit Office (1988a), *Estates Management in the National Health Service,* HMSO, London.

National Audit Office (1988b), *The Crown Estate*, HMSO, London.

Richardson, G. (1993), 'Asset shortcomings', *Local Government Chronicle Supplement*, 11 June, p.34.

Roberts, B. (1983), 'Property management in a local authority', *Property Management*, vol 1 (3).

Roberts, B. (1984), 'Managing the corporate estate of Leicester City Council', *Property Management*, vol 2 (3) :198-205.

Searle, B.(1987), *Valuation and Estates Management - Valuing your Assets, Proceedings - The Effective Management of Land and Resources*, RICS, London.

Society of Local Authority Chief Executives (SOLACE) (1986), *Our Heritage - Property Management in a Local Authority*, SOLACE, London.

The Royal Institution of Chartered Surveyors (1987), *Property Management in Local Authorities: Evidence to the Audit Commission*, RICS, London.

The Royal Institution of Chartered Surveyors (1992), *Manual of Valuation Guidance Notes*, VGN8A, RICS, Coventry.

The Royal Institution of Chartered Surveyors (RICS) (1993), *Manual of Valuation Guidance Notes*, VGN8A, RICS, Coventry.

Thorncroft, M. (1965), *The Principles of Estate Management,* The College of Estate Management, London.

Tyler, G. (1994), 'Landbank due for overhaul', *Estates Times*, 8 July, p.22.

Warren, M., Whitehead, I., Selton, T., Brunt, P. and The Royal Institution of Chartered Surveyors (1995), *County Farms: Past, Present and Future*, the Royal Institution of Chartered Surveyors, London.

Wootten, B. (1989), 'Portfolio management of council property', *Municipal Journal*, 22 February, p.22.

10 Property Services: The Private Sector Response to Competitive Tendering

Gaye Pottinger, College of Estate Management, Reading

Introduction

Formal tendering for 'white collar' professional services has become particularly associated with compulsory competitive tendering (CCT) in local government, brought in by the *Local Government Acts* of 1988 and 1992. However, prior to April 1996, central government was the dominant public sector player. Estates and facilities management were amongst the most common white collar projects brought into contracting out and market testing within the government's Competing for Quality (CfQ) programme since 1992-1993 (Efficiency Unit Policy Review, 1996) and represented some 16 percent or £423M of the total programme. Private sector organisations are also making more use of bid procedures and 'beauty parades', but public sector tendering is especially significant because of the scale and timetable of the exercise.

In 1995, the College of Estate Management (CEM) therefore identified a need for research into the impact of this major change in public sector procurement practices. The research starts from the premise that irrespective of whether services are externalised or retained in-house, it is in the public interest that the vast public sector estate is managed well. The CEM research has concentrated on the tendering of work undertaken by general practice surveyors, because they are seen as the central advisers on issues of property ownership, development and management, which have strategic and resource implications for the delivery of services by public sector clients. General practice surveyors also tend to have less experience of formal tendering as a procurement method, as against say building surveyors or quantity surveyors. However, the research findings have relevance to all surveying specialists, not least because many public sector tenders involve more than one professional discipline.

This chapter concentrates on the research findings of particular relevance to local government, within the context of competitive tendering across the public sector as a whole. Property consultants see more similarities than differences in the tendering procedures adopted by public sector bodies, although the process and culture behind tendering in central government and local government are nevertheless distinctly different and have a bearing on the response of private sector firms.

The research approach

The first stage of the CEM research (1995) concentrated on the attitudes surrounding preparations for an enormously significant competition round, when London Boroughs and Metropolitan Districts, as well as Central Government Departments, were all working towards implementing property services contracts by 1 April 1996. The first study sought to identify the main issues facing firms and their clients, in order to be able to suggest best practice approaches geared to achieving the clients objectives via competitive tendering.

Public sector organisations are major occupiers of property and some new style contracts were not only large in terms of value, but combine work covering several disciplines not commonly offered by many individual surveying firms. The change in scale, nature and duration of instructions might therefore be expected to challenge not only established client/consultant relationships, but to impact on the size and structure of firms able to support the new style contracts.

A second stage of the CEM research is being conducted to examine the new environment post April 1996, and looks forward to the future of competitive tendering as a procurement tool for property services. The overall aim of the research is to recommend 'best-practice' approaches to developing beneficial client/consultant relationships within the competitive tendering framework. The second stage of the research is partly funded by the Education Trust of the RICS, and will particularly consider:

- the differences between procurement practices in central and local government, their relative success and the way they are impacting on the market for surveying services;

- the relationship between the size / type of firm and success in securing work and delivering a service to public sector clients;
- the role of the surveying profession in actively shaping procurement practices for property services through developing strategies, targeting guidance information and influencing policy.

The first study used a qualitative approach as the best method to gain co-operation from key individuals in the public and private sector, due to the commercial sensitivity surrounding the topic. The findings were based on 49 face-to-face interviews, case studies and an attitudinal questionnaire completed by interviewees. The second study involves major questionnaire surveys to add quantitative weight to the findings. Postal questionnaires have been sent to over 700 firms and 600 public sector bodies. A series of 20 follow-up face-to-face interviews are being conducted.

Competitive tendering pre-April 1996

During the late 1980s and early 1990s, central government was not only enacting legislation to introduce competitive tendering into local government, but was bringing about major changes in the way its own property is managed. The aim of the changes was 'to promote fair and open competition so that Departments and Agencies can achieve best value for money for the customer and the tax payer' and the creation of 'an explicit customer/supplier relationship' was identified as a key advantage of market testing (Efficiency Unit, 1993). The concept of implementing a client/contractor split internally, prior to inviting competitive bids for services, will be thoroughly familiar to local authorities. In central government the first stage of the client/contractor split was brought about when the Property Services Agency (PSA) was split into Property Holdings, taking the landlord or client role, and five trading units which were market tested and transferred to private sector companies. The role of Property Holdings was reviewed (Efficiency Unit, 1994) after three years of operation, and the decision taken that the government's estate would best be served by fully devolving responsibility for property down the line to the occupying departments. As from 1 April 1996, departments therefore acquired full responsibility for managing the property they occupy within their own budgets, and PACE (Property

Advisors to the Civil Estate) was created to play a central co-ordinating role. Many government departments were therefore gearing up to let contracts for property consultancy services at the same time as those local authorities affected by the first round of 'white-collar' CCT.

During the period that government was devolving responsibility to departments and market testing the property function, research conducted by Reading University and Oxford Brookes University (1995) found that almost half of the 155 major occupiers surveyed had centralised their property management in the past five years. The trend towards centralisation was more pronounced in the private sector, and was accompanied by a marked advance in the importance of in-house property professionals. Most organisations (92 percent) still used external consultants for at least some property work. However, there had been a change in emphasis in selecting consultants, in that specialist knowledge had gained in importance over market knowledge.

This is the background against which the first CEM study was conducted and the study came to the following main conclusions:

- *the 'intelligent client'* (or 'informed' client) is central to the success of the competitive tendering, of property services;
- *the factors which motivate private sector firms* and the matters important to public sector bodies warrant greater consideration and understanding. Cultural differences of approach exist between the public and private sector, but the two show signs of coming closer together;
- *price and quality* are the issues respondents felt most separated the basis on which public and private sector organisations select consultants or contractors. Defining quality for a professional service was proving especially difficult, and was of particular concern to managers in government departments;
- *the transfer of staff* in accordance with the *TUPE* regulations, was not necessarily a barrier to firms bidding for public sector contracts;
- *size and structure of firms* was an issue in successfully competing for contracts. A perception existed amongst property consultants that public sector bodies viewed larger firms as 'safe' and better able to offer economies of scale in relation to larger contracts. However, the majority of surveying firms are small and 78 percent of UK offices have five partners or less;

- *developing a sense of partnership* between client and consultant is an important ingredient for success;
- *skills relevant to competitive tendering* need to be acquired by professionals and managers taking the client role and the contractor role.

The first study also found that *best practice guidance* would be welcomed. Many professionals in firms and in client organisations interviewed for the study expressed a degree of 'isolation' in devising a response to competition for property services. The basis for each of these conclusions is now discussed with particular reference to local government.

The 'intelligent client'

Property consultants interviewed for the research recognised the importance of the 'client role' and expressed greater job satisfaction working for a client who was strong, challenging and adequately resourced. Respondents took the view that professional qualification was less important for the in-house manager than:

- good contract management and procurement skills;
- access to the decision making level in the public sector body; and,
- a knowledge of property.

One consultant also commented:

> on jobs where there is a single focal point with the client we have a better chance to build up a good working relationship.

Interviewees identified a different start point for the client base in central and local government. In central government, following the devolution of responsibility to departments, the client representative will generally be from a managerial background. In local government, on the other hand, the client representative will more often be a qualified property professional. Private practitioners had concerns about extremes in both cases. Firstly, a management oriented client who took a 'text book' or 'householder' approach to property matters could be difficult to advise and communicate with, in that '*the client is very often confused as to whether his portfolio is an asset or a liability*'. On the other hand, a professionally qualified client could be too controlling.

A main cause for concern in local government is that the deminimus level for CCT of property services has been set too low to enable the maintenance of an intelligent client capability across all the affected professional disciplines. This issue is discussed later in the report, in relation to developments post April, 1996. For managers in central government, on the other hand, responsibility for the client function has been devolved without additional resources to support it. Despite the expectation that government departments would manage procurement in-house or buy client support centrally from PACE (Efficiency Unit Scrutiny, 1994) a number of departments were appointing consultants to the role of the client's strategic adviser, including giving advice on commissioning work from professionals in other firms. This development reflects findings from research by Reading University (1995) which identified a role for surveyors as management consultants.

The factors which motivate private sector firms

Prospect of success in winning the tender was highly important to surveying firms, owing to the cost of mounting a bid. As one interviewee explained:

> If we're in a situation where we know that the world and his wife is going to be invited then we will normally take the decision not to tender. We know from experience what it takes to actually put together a sensible tender and we will take a commercial view of whether we consider that is an appropriate investment or speculation of time.

Clarity of the clients specification, selection criteria and tender valuation procedures are therefore very important in helping firms assess their own prospect of success at an early stage, and so avoid bidding for contracts they are clearly not qualified to fulfil.

The type or mix of work in the contract and certainty of work volume were the two most important factors in the decision to bid. Several multi-disciplinary and facilities management firms had won contracts involving general practice work. Some had taken general practice surveyors into their organisation, while others sub-contracted this element which they viewed as ancillary to their main business. Recent research by Ernst & Young (1995) on the private sector response to CCT identified a growth in the market towards facilities management, but expressed doubt that 'the market is sufficiently developed to provide facilities management arrangements to the smaller contracts, for example, those let by some district councils'. Several interviewees mentioned having to justify the benefits of public sector contracts to other professionals in the firm's hierarchy who were less familiar with the opportunities available, and less enthusiastic about the low profit margins. The arguments deployed in favour of public sector work included such issues as a secure and regular income flow, despite low profit margins; the opportunity to pick up spin-off consultancy work; and, a higher profile for the firm, which can be helpful when pitching for other business. Many public sector property professionals face a parallel situation and were having to 'sell' or justify the benefits of their input to the employing organisation in conjunction with implementing competition.

Price and quality

In relation to tender selection criteria, both public and private sector interviewees identified price and quality as the issues they felt most separated the basis on which public and private sector organisations select consultants or contractors. A number of interviewees shared the view that:

> public sector clients have got their eyes over their shoulder for the auditor and they tend to go for the lowest price.

However, government managers interviewed later in the study expressed concern at the level of fee-cutting taking place in the market and said that they were prepared to justify why the lowest price should not be accepted if they felt quality could be compromised.

Quality was identified as being particularly difficult to judge for a service which involves the giving of professional advice rather than having a physical outcome which can be visually inspected. A local authority manager took the view that registration under BS5750 would not:

> mean that I'm going to be satisfied with what they do, because in essence I'm going to strike a relationship with a group of people and we, as a team, are going to try and achieve something.

Several government departments were exploring methods to measure quality during the contract, for example through the use of benchmarking and auditing the work of surveyors. Performance based contracts could also provide more scope for the consultant or contractor to exhibit flair and creativity, but prescriptive contracts were used by some government departments as a 'manual' to guide their own in-house managers through unfamiliar territory.

The transfer of staff and TUPE

A number of local authorities exposed all or part of their property function to market competition in advance of CCT, because they perceived advantages for the organisation and staff in entering the market early on a voluntary basis. Five council managers and three of their consultants, who had been party to voluntary competitive tenders (VCT), were interviewed for the first study. They all felt that willingness on the part of the Council and its staff were key to building a relationship of trust within which the contract could be made to operate. Firms and former public sector employees cited motivation deriving from establishing clear objectives and encouragement to succeed as a benefit for staff moving to the private sector.

Throughout 1994/95 the government continued to fight strenuously to exclude CCT from the European TUPE regulations, which confer employment protection, in the belief that higher than average pay rates in local government would discourage firms from bidding for contracts. However, several public and private sector interviewees shared the view expressed by a local authority manager that the two main areas of concern from firms at the point of submitting a bid were:

> the level of guaranteed income and does it cover the staff, followed by did they think that they were taking over a business or did they think they were taking over a dispirit group of people.

Private sector interviewees viewed the prolonged uncertainty about whether or not TUPE would apply as more problematic than deciding that they did. Firms taking on large new contracts generally need additional staff to service them and terms of employment can be varied subsequently for internal reasons unconnected with the transfer. TUPE was therefore not necessarily a barrier to bidding.

The size and structure of firms

The perception from the interviewees was that the way in which work is commissioned from the private sector has been affected by two factors which gives cause for concern. Firstly, the regime governing Market Testing and CCT and secondly, the introduction of European Union (EU) procurement rules. In the late 1980s, several interviewees from smaller and lesser known firms had received a direct approach from procurers and were invited to tender for both central and local government contracts. This experience had allowed them to establish a track record which they felt gave them an advantage. In 1993, the European Union Services Directive 92/50 brought about a significant change, in that firms which are new to public sector tendering must rely on responding to publicly placed advertisements in order to reach the list of selected tenderers. They can no longer apply at any time to be considered for work.

A perception was also developing amongst private sector professionals, particularly those in the small and medium sized firms, that public sector organisations view larger firms as 'safe' and able to cope with larger contract packages because they have an infrastructure and synergy which offers a perceived prospect of economies of scale. Larger firms therefore appear to be favoured and smaller firms, who perceive their prospect of success to be lower, are less inclined to bid. If the government's objective is to be achieved, and all sections of the private sector are to remain interested in being involved in the bidding process, then firmer guidance is needed on the packaging of contracts.

Facilities management companies in particular are developing to serve the combined management and maintenance needs of major occupiers in both the public and the private sector, although related research suggests that the market is not sufficiently developed to service some of the smaller local authority contracts (Ernst & Young, 1995).

Developing a sense of partnership

Public and private sector professionals and managers were generally uneasy about the possible effects of compulsion in relation to the tendering of property services by local authorities. Private sector firms prefer to bid for work from organisations that are obviously willing clients and had two concerns about Councils which are not willing entrants to the market. Firstly, that any bid by an in-house team will be given an unfair advantage and '*whatever they say, the playing field is not level*'. Secondly, that where part of the service is retained in-house Councils are structuring contracts so as to keep '*for themselves the best of the work, while the dross, if you like, goes out to the externalised contractor*'.

Willingness is important to building long-lasting relationships of trust leading to the delivery of quality professional services. The CCT regime therefore appears to be at odds with other areas of policy which aim to foster partnerships between the public and private sector, for example the Private Finance Initiative and legislative proposals for the construction industry, based on recommendations in the Latham Report (1994). Interviewees identified the development of a sense of partnership between client and consultant as an equally important ingredient for success in contracts for property consultancy services.

CCT, therefore represents a particular challenge to property professionals working in local authorities. Where the Council's management of property services does not replicate the way services are offered by private sector firms, an internal re-organisation may be necessary for the purpose of facilitating competition. Devising an internal 'client-contractor split' and developing the specification can prove particularly difficult where the certain specialisms are vested in a few people whose expertise is needed simultaneously by the client's core group, by the various service departments and by the in-house team which will bid for the contract. If the authority favours its own staff and/or restricts the number of firms eligible to bid, by packaging the work in a particular way, this could give grounds for a charge of anti-competitive behaviour. At interview a number of private sector professionals said they would hesitate to bring such a charge against a local authority which they still viewed as a potential future client. The second study will explore whether this position still holds true following the first round of CCT.

Skills relevant to competitive tendering

Professionals interviewed for the study identified a 'blurring' of the traditional divide between the public and the private sector. However, the greatest cultural change is probably being experienced by professionals and managers responsible for the client functions within public sector organisations. Taking the 'client' role involves commissioning and monitoring work undertaken by others via the contracting process. For individuals who had been previously involved in exercising the full range of professional expertise, or who had a management background and lack property knowledge, their previous training and experience is unlikely to have prepared them for their new role. Looking at the 'contracting' role, some of those who are now required to compete for their jobs have had difficulty in coming to terms with a 'commercial attitude', as opposed to a 'service attitude', which they perceive is now necessary.

There are therefore two main areas to be developed which are complementary to one another and are essential if delivery of a quality service is to be achieved:

- the procurer or client needs to have contract management and procurement skills which provide a formal framework and provide for formal and informal development of the working relationship; and,
- the provider of services or contractor needs skills in tendering, contract management and quality management. Personal communication skills are also highly important to achieve an understanding of the client's objectives and to develop an appreciation of the client's needs which leads to trust.

The tendering of significant volumes of work in a depressed market has undoubtedly challenged surveyors in public bodies and private practices to address new processes and issues of operational efficiency in order to remain competitive. The relationship between client and consultant, whether in-house or external, is shifting from one based solely on professional skills in delivering the required service, to one of commitment to achieving a common objective. A balance of the formal and informal relationship akin to 'a partnership' is therefore what is required and is an important ingredient of success.

Competitive tendering post-April 1996

Since April 1996, the DoE has produced its own review of CCT and several other organisations have produced research documents and guidance information relating to competition in the public sector, including the tendering of property services. This part of the report examines the related research and guidance, which forms the background to ongoing research by CEM. The findings are particularly interesting from the local government viewpoint, because the changes proposed to the basis of property services by CCT appear at odds with government sponsored research.

During 1995, it was apparent that a situation was emerging in the market where tenders for property services were failing to attract the level or quality of response for which the government had hoped. The DoE review of CCT of professional services (May 1996) found that much less work had in practice been subject to competition than had been anticipated. In relation to construction and property services, 9 percent of the estimated total of work in 68 London and Metropolitan authorities had been exposed to competition by the 1 April, 1996 deadline, compared with a competition requirement of 65 percent. For many contracts there was too little competition. The average number of bids, including the in-house bid, for construction and property services was 2, and just 8 contracts were awarded to external suppliers. By value, 98 percent of construction, property and legal services was awarded to in-house teams.

The government's response to these findings has been to propose changes to the basis of CCT for professional services. The Royal Institution of Chartered Surveyors (RICS) responded to the consultation on the basis that the level of work exposed to competition was roughly as expected at this stage and highlighted two areas of particular concern. Firstly, the proposal to abolish the credit for work in progress, thus putting pressure on Councils to include part completed work in external tenders, was viewed as harmful and impractical. Not only would this be likely to result in delays, upsetting local authority strategies, but was more likely to discourage private sector interest due to difficulties with professional indemnity insurance. Secondly, the proposed reduction in the de minimus level from £450,000 pa to £300,000, above which construction and property services must be tendered, was criticised on the basis that it will 'undermine the ability of many authorities to maintain an intelligent client role' across the six affected disciplines, that is architects, engineers, building surveyors, quantity surveyors, structural engineers, estate surveyors and valuers. The RICS therefore felt that: 'these new proposals will confirm the impression prevalent in the private sector that CCT is a mire into which they are unwilling to be drawn. They will, therefore, have precisely the opposite effect to that intended.'

Research into competitive tendering developed apace through 1995. In June 1996 the DoE published preliminary findings from research commissioned to follow developments in the run-up to white-collar CCT, based on case studies with 4 Metropolitan Districts and 5 London Boroughs. Of the nine authorities, only one had awarded a property services related contract to a private firm. However, the study found that nearly 20 percent of construction and property services was already in the private sector, the highest of any of the six services under consideration. The size of the client function tended to be larger for construction and property services, on average 15 percent of the defined activity, whereas for most functions it is less than 5 percent. The research summary reports the view of local authority officers that 'authorities already operate within a mixed economy for professional services, using private sector firms to cope with demands for scale and expertise on a flexible basis.' CCT had acted as a catalyst for developing more robust quality measures, but interest from the private sector in all professional services had eroded as tendering progressed. Few local authorities had investigated the reasons behind this loss of interest, an issue on which the CEM research seeks to shed light. The effectiveness of the governments own CfQ programme since 1992-93 is examined in an Efficiency Unit Policy Review (1996). The CfQ review focused on the competitive element, that is the £1.85 billion worth of activities exposed to competition through market testing or contracting out. Across the whole CfQ programme, net savings of 13-15 percent were achieved. However, net savings varied considerably between projects. For many smaller packages, the cost of implementing competition exceeded savings. The scrutiny team concluded that the competitive tendering of projects with an annual value of under £250,000 was unlikely to be cost effective and should be avoided. Projects with a value of under £500,000 should also be looked at very critically. The current CCT deminimus level of £450,000 for local authority property services is therefore already below the threshold at which it is recommended alternative approaches might provide better value for money.

The CfQ review found that the main source of savings was new working practices. However, there was little difference in the sources of savings between in-house teams and private sector suppliers. It could *not* therefore be said to be a universal truth that the private sector could engineer cost efficiencies which the public sector could not. The research also found that savings could have been greater had there been more imaginative packaging and specification of services. The report recommends that the basis of choice between contracting out, market testing and internal restructuring be based on an assessment of the balance of costs, benefits and risks following reviews of the organisations strategic objectives and the markets capabilities.

Research published by the Chartered Institute of Public Finance and Accountancy (CIPFA, 1996) also recommended consultation with private sector contractors prior to tendering, especially in relation to deciding on contract packaging. The research found that the commitment of senior management is essential to the success of competitive tendering, but is the exception rather than the rule and 'in some sectors considerable amounts of creative energy would seem to be expended on frustrating CCT and devising ways of keeping the service in-house'. The RICS has also been concerned that the services which chartered surveyors can offer, whether they operate in the public or the private sector, should be properly understood and deployed to the best advantage of the client organisation. The RICS '*Guide to Securing the Services of a Chartered Surveyor*' (April, 1996) aims to provide clear guidance to clients seeking to procure surveying services, as well as providing a framework for surveyors responding to invitations to tender. However, if finance officers continue to advance their role in resource management, as the result of the combined effects of CCT and local government re-organisation, then guidance issued by CIPFA (1995) in relation to financial services might be expected to take on greater importance in local government. This is because CIPFA is generally accepted as a 'safe' standard which will be recognised by the District Auditor, and certain aspects of CIPFA's recommendations are of equal relevance across other professional services, including property.

Research Conclusions

The continuing CEM research is therefore taking place against a background where proposed changes to the basis of local authority CCT for property services can be viewed against the governments own procurement experiences. Councils face a particular challenge in individually ensuring that they can maintain a full intelligent client function across all the property disciplines and satisfy the objective to generate net savings. Higher value packages may, as in the government's experience, be more likely to produce savings, but in the context of the individual local authority are more likely to have to include more than one property discipline. The number of surveying firms able to compete is correspondingly limited and failure to generate sufficient competition could leave an authority open to a charge of anti-competitive behaviour. Multi-disciplinary packages also place demands for staff managing the client function to possess a range of skills which their previous role is unlikely to have demanded. Those who fill the 'intelligent client' role within individual local authorities are therefore being squeezed in the middle between the competing demands to improve efficiency and generate competition in accordance with the regulations.

The challenge for local authorities and the surveying profession is therefore to demonstrate alternative ways in which efficient and cost effective property services can be delivered to meet local government's objectives, using a combination of public and private sector expertise and balancing available resources against market capabilities. Unfortunately, the combined effects of implementing CCT and European procurement rules are currently mitigating against the formation of the kind of 'partnership' relationships between public and private sector which are more likely to prove beneficial.

Property professionals who would seek to influence the way in which policy and practices for procurement is structured and implemented need to be close to decision making levels in central and local government. The opportunity for surveyors to develop a role in property resource management has been stressed in research by Reading University (1995), and CEM has recently been commissioned to conduct a study to further examine the role of the 'intelligent client' for property services in central government.

Now that we are in the run up to a general election in 1997, discussions about CCT could become somewhat more academic if a new

Labour government chooses to abolish compulsion and to implement its own ideas about public/private sector partnerships, competition and new model direct service organisations supervised by a standards inspectorate. However, the prospect of further change is all the more reason for property professionals to keep close to the forefront of procurement practices in local government.

References

Avis, M. and Gibson, V. (1995), *Real Estate Resource Management*, Reading University and Oxford Brookes University, GTI Specialist Publishers Ltd.

BMRB International Ltd. (1995), *CCT: The Private Sector View,* Department of the Environment Local Government Research Programme/Department of Employment, London.

Chartered Institute of Public Finance and Accountancy (CIPFA) (1995), *Compulsory Competitive Tendering For Financial Services - The Evaluation of Quality,* CIPFA, London.

Chartered Institute of Public Finance and Accountancy (1995), *Compulsory Competitive Tendering for Financial Services - The Evaluation of Quality,* CIPFA, London.

Chartered Institute of Public Finance and Accountancy (1996), *Achieving Value For Money Through Competition - 27 Case Studies of CCT/Market Testing Experience in Great Britain,* CIPFA and the Chief Executive's Forum, London.

Chartered Institute of Public Finance and Accountancy (1995), *The Selection and Packaging of Financial Services to Meet CCT Requirements,* CIPFA, London.

College of Estate Management (CEM) (1997), Procuring Property Consultancy in an *Age of Change: The Role of the Intelligent Client,* RICS, London.

Department of the Environment (DoE) (1996), *Compulsory Competitive Tendering: Consultation on Proposals for Changes to Framework,* DoE, London.

Efficiency Unit (1996), *Competing for Quality Policy Review*, HMSO, London.

Efficiency Unit (1993), *The Government's Guide to Market Testing*, HMSO, London.

Efficiency Unit (1994), *Review of the Management of the Government's Civil Estate,* DoE, London.

Ernst & Young (1995), *Analysis of Local Authority CCT Markets,* Department of the Environment Local Government Research Programme, London.

Latham, M. (1994), *Constructing the Team*, HMSO, London.

Newchurch and Company (1996), *Research Summary: The Exposure of Professional and White Collar Services to CCT (Phase 1: Preparations of Competition among London Boroughs and Metropolitan Districts).* DoE, London.

Pottinger, G. (1995), *What Am I Bid? - Competitive Tendering of Property Services by the Public Sector*, The College of Estate Management, Reading.

Pottinger, G. and Law, V. (1997), *'Pitching for Public Work: Property Consultancy and Competition'*, The College of Estate Management, Reading.

The Royal Institution of Chartered Surveyors (RICS), (1995) *The Chartered Surveyor* as *Management Consultant - An Emerging Market,* RICS, London.

The Royal Institution of Chartered Surveyors (1995), *Compulsory Competitive Tendering: Consultation on Proposals for Changes to the Framework*, RICS Policy Document PULET (96) / MJC London.

The Royal Institution of Chartered Surveyors (1996), *Securing the Services of a Chartered Surveyor - Valuation, Property and Estate Management*, RICS, London.

PART 3
RE-ORGANISATION AND REFORM

11 Property Management in Local Authorities

Alex Linkston, Chief Executive, West Lothian Council

Introduction

The volume of property owned, leased and occupied by local authorities and its scale, value and importance is often underestimated. This is perhaps partly due to a lack of central information within existing authorities since property on its own is not a service provider rather, in the context of local government, it is simply a tool used by every service providing department. And yet, without the correct type, size and location of property that service would suffer in delivery, quality and cost.

Local authority property management

Very often, the responsibility for managing this portfolio is unclear because it is spread between several officers in a number of different departments, none of them having property as a primary interest, nor the expertise required to manage it effectively. Also, the costs involved in acquiring, maintaining and running properties are often similarly spread throughout various departments, with variable levels of controls and knowledge being applied to its management.

Except for our larger authorities, there will not usually be a property committee which often means that there is a lack of political interest or support for property when it comes to budget setting or some of the more sensitive decisions are required - unless of course you are lucky enough to own a one hundred million pound South Gyle asset and in which case, it will have all the support and attention that is needed. Looked at logically, this is surprising since after meeting our salary bills, the costs associated with properties are usually the largest drain on the budget. Not only are there these revenue costs which must be controlled, there is also an enormous amount of capital tied up in our property that is difficult to release even if good monitoring and decision making processes are in place for it. Changes to either the use or ownership of these assets is a slow and complex matter which must be carefully monitored and planned for. If well managed, property is a very valuable asset providing the means for service delivery, substantial capital receipts when required and constant revenue production. Badly managed it becomes an expensive drain on limited resources. Overall, property is not a very flexible friend and planned management is essential.

The Audit Commission (1988a,b) obviously recognised these factors and the thrust of their reports was directed towards encouraging local authorities to recognise the scale of the problems and to become much more pro-active in the management of their property portfolios. They pointed out that: assets would have to be identified and databases created to allow meaningful management practices to be introduced. They also suggested that local authorities should question the purposes behind holding properties and the performance of the property measured against the reasons for holding it.

In the capacity of chief executive the importance and relevance of many of these factors, most of which have been addressed within my own local authority are recognised. However, despite this it is still common to see 'departmentalism' or 'protectionism' affect property decisions in an unhelpful way. In the current climate of capital and revenue restrictions, it is absolutely essential that a local authority's second largest source of expenditure and the highest cause of capital investment is carefully analysed, monitored and used effectively to meet corporate objectives.

Reflecting upon such matters, it is evident that the solution to the types of problems referred to are not to be found in a single magic answer. The answer will vary between authorities depending upon their own culture and scale of portfolio. The Audit Commission leaned heavily towards a property committee and account being formed to concentrate accountabilities and to ensure adequate support was given to the problem. However, experience suggests this form of corporatisation does not necessarily provide the answer and it may simply result in duplication of services without the required improvement in performance.

Culture

The essential factor in addressing problems associated with property is the need to establish within our organisations the culture and practices leading to the belief that property is an asset of the local authority acting as a corporate body. Service departments will use the property but it is owned by the local authority and both its use and performance must tie in with council objectives. This sounds simple enough but for many local authorities it represents a significant cultural change in departmental attitudes. For instance, many of us will recognise that within our organisations there is an established practice which dictates that schools, simply as an example, although other facilities act in a similar way, are owned by the education department and unless the school is closed and declared surplus to operational requirements then that property has nothing to do with any other department. Most chief executives find this unacceptable. Half filled schools are expensive schools and we must establish monitoring and reporting systems that identify where such situations exist and which ensure alternative uses for the empty rooms are considered.

Two recent external factors present authorities with an excellent opportunity to look afresh at our property portfolios and how they should best be managed. Local government re-organisation offers a unique opportunity to start again without already established practices hindering our decisions. New department structures, new committees and different staff should offer new corporate solutions and opportunities. Also, the introduction of capital accounting to local authorities obliges us all to form asset registers and if done properly, those registers offer property professionals an ideal opportunity to establish good databases for our assets without which, any policy adopted for monitoring the performance of those assets will flounder. While many of us viewed the introduction of asset registers as something of a nuisance, property professionals must surely see the potential in such databases for establishing the value of our property assets and providing the key data against which performance can be analysed and measured. These registers will become very expensive luxuries if neglected. Property professionals should claim ownership of them and ensure that they become key tools for use in the management of property. Information is the key to performance monitoring and asset registers may provide that essential key.

Strategy

The chief executive's role is to give a corporate direction to the management of the portfolio by setting aims and objectives for property used by local authorities both in terms of budget control and front line service delivery. It is property professionals who should devise and deliver the detailed means for achieving those aims and objectives. A chief executive seeks to establish a clear property strategy for a local authority, which sets out the corporate overview, aims and objectives for property ownership and the performance of the portfolio. The overall objective will be to ensure that the portfolio is managed to maximise the benefits to be gained from the portfolio at the minimum cost to the council. We need to see, on a regular basis, that steps are being taken to achieve that objective. This will mean establishing methods of monitoring performance, and reporting mechanisms on actual performance coupled with a regular review of the entire portfolio.

The systems installed must cut across departmental boundaries and to ensure that this happens, the officer responsible for monitoring and reporting must have the full support of the management team of the local authority. That is not always easy to actually achieve since the majority of political support is channelled towards direct service provisions. The direction we see developing for property management under re-organisation and reform can perhaps be best explained by outlining some of the key issues chief executives pay particular attention to in piecing together a corporate strategy for the management of local authority property.

Databases

As already pointed out, the asset registers provide the perfect opportunity for gathering all of the required property data together at a single point for use in analysing the performance of the portfolio. It should not stop at just enough for the minimum asset register, but should be formed as a working database gathering enough information to allow analysis of, for instance, the running costs of each property, staff numbers at each location, the level of use made of the asset etc, so that an overall picture can be built up of each property and everything associated with it. This database will be the key to the real point of the exercise - an overall property portfolio review.

Review of the portfolio

The objective of the review is to establish bench marks for the performance of each property to maximise its benefits and minimise its costs. Ideally, a single officer should be made responsible for this work. That should perhaps be a property professional, although he need not carry out all of the work, service departments could be obliged to provide the details as required. It will be important at this stage to ensure that full corporate support is given since it is at this point when 'departmentalism' can get in the way of the free flow of essential information and therefore prevent a meaningful review to take place. For an effective review, this is perhaps the single most critical factor and it will have to be stressed to everyone involved that the important element here is the need to take an overall corporate attitude.

In this review, a chief executive will want to know the fundamentals of why we hold property, whether it is performing financially against what kind of bench marks and whether cost savings can be made. As an example, because of the geographical nature of my local authority, we occupy four major headquarter buildings and a number of smaller satellite offices. As an authority, we have an urgent need to either reduce costs or to increase revenue, or perhaps achieve both and of course, property can uniquely achieve that. If we give up occupation of a property it can then be used instead to produce income. We need to know how these offices perform in relation to one another in terms of cost per person, or per square metre to repair, maintain, heat etc. We want to be advised of relevant occupancy levels. We want to know whether it has scope to move staff around to reduce office space or perhaps to follow the Birmingham example of 'hot desking' or working from home to reduce costs.

After Dunblane, schools are obviously a sensitive issue but the fact remains that if there is spare capacity, even if only on a temporary basis while school rolls fluctuate, we must consider alternative uses for the spare space. For instance, within my own council, one under-utilised primary school is being looked at to allow part of it to continue as a school with the rest being used for the relocation of a library headquarters and an information technology training centre. Another school which had been closed because of falling school rolls, will be used to accommodate a number of local area office functions until housing development planned for the town generates the increase in school rolls required to bring the same school back as an educational establishment. Only a corporate overview revealed the non-educational requirements for any spare accommodation. There will undoubtedly be similar opportunities elsewhere in the portfolio which could be identified via an appropriate property review. We fully understand service department's concerns over this type of situation but frankly, the options must be identified and debated openly by the corporate body rather than be shut up within the service department where corporate views may or may not be practised.

Opportunity costs and rationalisation

Nowadays, very few things remain unchanged or static for very long. Working practices, staff numbers, information technology and other factors are all constantly changing and affecting workplaces and working practices. This affects the quantity and the type of property needed at any one time. Local authorities are very large users of this kind of property and these changing factors must mean that with a regular review of our properties there will be opportunities for rationalisation and realisation of savings in cost and capital. This is an ongoing unstable situation which reinforces the need for regular independent property reviews outwith service departments.

Active reviews and management will realise opportunity costs as well. For instance, in the school/library headquarters situation described earlier, the under utilised school problem is resolved, at the same time, a capital receipt will be created from the disposal of the existing headquarter buildings which the libraries department are vacating. Exactly the same logic applies to a local authority's land banks which most authorities have to some degree. Active management and detailed knowledge of the market and land bank will result in land being released onto the market at the most opportune time to maximise income. Such opportunities and rationalisations do not happen by accident, they must be planned for.

Commercial portfolio performance

Again, most authorities own a commercial/investment portfolio of property usually built up on an ad-hoc basis over many years. Re-organisation has in almost all cases created entirely new portfolios for the new authorities and these are unlikely to be carefully balanced, high performing properties or at least, not in total. These portfolios must be critically assessed and analysed by property professionals to question why they are being held and establish whether they are performing against other bench mark investments. If they are not performing, or are unlikely to then alternatives should be investigated.

Like all other aspects of the whole property portfolio, the service department in this instance, probably the property department itself, should not be the sole judge of the situation. The review process must result in a report mechanism being established for advising chief executives and their management team so as to allow corporate decisions to be taken.

Conclusion

In conclusion, it can be said that because of the scale, value and costs of property in local government, there is a clear strategic requirement to establish, on a corporate basis, the aims and objectives of property management in local authorities; which in turn requires: the creation of accurate up-to-date property databases; the active monitoring, management and review of property by a responsible officer; the introduction of reporting/review mechanisms to the chief executive and his management team, allowing them to assess the performance of the portfolio. If this is achieved there will undoubtedly be major financial benefits in terms of value for money - available to local authorities via improvements in the efficiency, effectiveness and economic management of their property.

References

Audit Commission (1988a), *Local Authority Property : A Management Overview*, HMSO, London.

Audit Commission (1998b), *Local Authority Property: A Management Handbook*, HMSO, London.

12 Heritage Issues in Local Authority Property Management and Funding

Peter Bower, Geoffrey Heath, Jean Morgan,
Peter Reynolds, Beverley Wilson and Joan Wyld,
the Business School, Staffordshire University

Introduction

Many local authorities, particularly those associated with the 'major cities', have responsibility for maintaining a part of the national heritage, which may be in danger of serious depreciation due to inadequacies in the funding process. The generosity of nineteenth century industrial magnates bequeathed many of our finest cities with extensive formal and semi-formal parks, all of which require ongoing maintenance. Similarly, in post-war years, the reclamation of industrial waste land has resulted in much improved 'open spaces'. National and European funding has variously been available to support these capital projects, but rarely to meet the ongoing stream of current costs which are necessarily incurred if such projects are to lead to the long-term benefits intended. Again these environmental improvements place pressure on current budgets for the operational management of the land.

Similarly, the major cities typically played a unique role in Britain's industrial development. As home to the pottery industry, Stoke-on-Trent is one of the clearest examples of this. Such industrial concentration almost inevitably led to the development of a wealth of local heritage. The relevant local authorities have often been reluctant to see this heritage storehouse destroyed - and for sound economic reasons. Again focusing on Stoke-on-Trent; the city has become a tourist centre, resulting from its rich heritage and although the economic benefits accrue to some extent locally, other benefits to the British economy are widespread. For example, the recipients of transatlantic airfares are not residents of North Staffordshire. Yet in common with similar authorities, Stoke-on-Trent City Council pays heavily in terms of the financing of that heritage conservation through the operation of museums and other such services.

Against this background of potential spending on maintenance of the heritage local authorities have to acquire the requisite financial resources. The ability to raise local taxes has been curtailed in recent times leaving funding very much in the hands of central governments and there is more than a hint of a financial resource gap between the demand by local authorities and the supply from central government.

The financial implications of a glorious past

The aim of this paper is to focus attention on two sectors of local authority spending where heritage may be an important determinant of cost and where the resources necessary are possibly restrained by funding arrangements. The sectors concerned are Parks and Public Open Spaces and Museums and Art Galleries. The paper therefore starts with an analysis of the funding system and tests its appropriateness to match locally perceived resource needs with those available from the centre.

Local authority funding

Local authorities obtain funds to carry out their responsibilities from certain specific sources. They are able to:

- charge 'clients' directly for services provided or on the sale of assets;
- charge and collect local taxes, Council Tax for example; and
- receive grants from other agencies.

The last of these forms provides the context for this paper which specifically refers to the situation in England. Fundamentally the system operates in the same manner in Scotland and Wales although the timing and some details are different.

Grants

The vast proportion of the income to local authorities comes from central government grants. Possibly the most important reasoning for grants is an attempt at resource equalisation because authorities with greatest need are not always those with greatest resources. Therefore the gap between a local authority's need to spend, and its capacity to finance the kind and level of services required should be covered in this transfer system. The first grant system which attempted explicitly to take account of these varying needs was introduced by the 1929 *Local Government Act*. Further refinements have been introduced over the years, aimed at improving the match between need and resources. Consequently resource allocation continues to be a live and vital issue requiring some sort of needs assessment for grant disbursement.

The present system stems primarily from the 1998 *Local Government Finance Act*. Prior to that, the main sources were much the same as today and included domestic rates; business rates; government grants; and sales, fees and charges. However, then, over half of the funds came from local sources. This has changed considerably in recent times. In 1988 the Community Charge replaced domestic rates, itself being replaced by the Council Tax three years later. The locally set business rate was replaced by a uniform centrally-set one, the national non-domestic rate (NNDR). Consequently, local authority income from central government grants now amounts to around 70 percent of the total with local tax and charges accounting for around 15 percent and 11 percent respectively. It is now even more important that resource allocation through grants is achieved fairly and is responsive to local and wider needs.

The grant process

The process commences with the Public Expenditure Survey. This is a competitive process where individual public sector departments bid for their resource requirements whilst the overall total fund that can be shared out between them is set by the Cabinet. The total fund may be more determined by macro-economic considerations than need. Also the proportion of total public expenditure likely to go to local authorities is based on central government's assessment of the appropriate level of total local government spending. This is not the summation of each local authority's view of its own needs, but by central government's own assessment of those needs. Of course there is dialogue in the Consultative Council for Local Government Finance relating to the level of spending, grant distribution and policy initiatives, but should there be a divergence of opinion, central government makes the final determination.

The Standard Spending Assessment (SSA) is central government's view of the appropriate expenditure for each local authority in producing a standard level of service. Therefore the SSA is central to the determination of the amount of grant each individual council receives. It consists of assessments for the following seven major service blocks, with sub-blocks for Education and for Personal Social Services:

- Education;
- Personal Social Services;
- Police;
- Fire and Civil Defence;
- Highway Maintenance;
- All other Services;
- Capital Financing.

Although each authority has its own characteristics and types of services it is possible to break them down into sub sets with common characteristics. Of course this is just the same sort of exercise that valuers pursue in segmenting property markets when looking for comparative information. The groupings are the Metropolitan Districts, Major Cities and Other Non-Metropolitan Districts. The latest re-organisation into Unitary authorities will bring further changes but for simplicity has not been introduced here. Similarly precepting by one authority on another is an unnecessary complication and distraction and has been ignored.

The research has concentrated on the Major Cities group and focused specifically on the District Services component of the 'All Other Services' block. This block is built up from about 30 separate services as diverse as 'Homelessness' and 'Planning'. However, it does include both Museums and Art Galleries and Parks and Open Spaces which are of particular interest since spending in these categories is heavily influenced by heritage considerations.

As outlined above, the SSAs are central government estimates of the cost of providing these services. They are determined at a high level of aggregation and derived from formulae that are constructed to take account of the social, economic, demographic and geographic characteristics of the council concerned. This particular allocation is determined almost entirely via a regression equation, as discussed below. Since 1984 the Secretary of State for the Environment has had the power to 'cap' local authorities, that is to set limits on increases in local taxation. This controversial feature has led to local authority overall budgets now matching their SSAs very closely and also controversially the SSAs are used in the capping criteria. With little room for financial manoeuvring, the local authorities are very concerned about the amount of the SSAs and whether they match local needs.

The Standard Spending Assessments

This section aims to outline the SSA approach to the assessment of the 'Other District Services' block and provide a critique of the SSA methodology. The SSA allocation within the ODS block is determined primarily via a regression equation, although an adjustment is made to take account of Sparsity, since the estimated regression coefficient associated with this particular variable did not accord with the DoE's *a priori* expectations. An Area Cost Adjustment is then applied to account for different levels of cost in different parts of the country in exactly the same way as surveyors adjust construction costs. In recent years there have been changes made to the equations. Data sets have changed, such as the utilisation of the 1991 census information, the 'All Ages Social Index' has been replaced by the 'Social Index' and the 'Economic Index' introduced. The calculation of the client group and the enhanced population, has changed; as has the density measure from being ward-based to enumeration district-based.

For this paper, the detail of the calculations is not important but the complexity of them is worthy of note. The Department of the Environment's estimated equation for 1994/5 is set out as Equation 1 below:

Equation 1

District Services = 83.2303 + 2.1616 Econ + 3.5209 Soc + 0.2820 Den

Where:

District Services:	is the expenditure per head of enhanced population in 1990/91 on district services divided by the Area Cost Adjustment.
Econ:	is the Economic Index
Soc:	is the Social Index
Den:	is the density of population

Full definitions of the variables used are available from the Department of the Environment.

Criticism of the system may relate to the system *per se* or to the application of it in the ODS block in particular. The Audit Commission undertook a fairly comprehensive assessment of the system, using the criteria of economy, efficiency and effectiveness and reference is made to some of the main points below.

In principle the system should allow different councils to set a similar level of local taxation and provide a 'standard level of service' regardless of revenue raising potential and cost of providing services. However, there is no definition of what is a 'standard level of service' and therefore the performance of the SSAs cannot be determined. Clearly the SSAs are used to apportion the funds available rather than to determine total local authority spending. By this means they appear to be control mechanisms rather than need/resource matchers. With capping taking away the flexibility for decision making at the margin, locally raised finance is negated somewhat ironically by the SSAs utilised in the process. Another aim of the system is to promote stability yet, despite changing definitions of indicators and 'fine tuning' this has not been brought about.

The SSAs are broken down into the seven major sub blocks. This is appropriate where the expenditure drivers are different between the sub blocks but reasonably the same within them. If the drivers within each sub block are not the same the SSA will not reflect true expenditure needs. If the drivers are the same across some blocks any error in the calculation of one block is likely to be duplicated in the others. For example, a fault in the determination of the Social Index will cause errors in the calculation of SSAs in 'All other Services' as well as the 'Personal Social Services' block which utilises the same index. The fact that the National Non-Domestic Rate (NNDR), having been collected by local authorities and paid to central government, is distributed as a common per capita sum gives another cause for concern. This assumes industry and commerce do not impose costs, or that they are accounted for, in the areas they are located. Another problem is that the assessments relate to the running costs and take no account of capital held by the authorities.

The simplification of the Grant Related Expenditure system into SSAs in 1990 has meant the loss of a number of important indicators. Despite recent changes to the equations, they continue to exclude any measure of low income or social class which should influence spending decisions. No account is taken of district councils' environmental responsibilities or their maintenance of the national heritage. These factors are particularly important for the 'major cities'. Often there is the responsibility for maintaining reclaimed land at high recurrent cost not covered by reclamation grants. Where industries are, or historically have been, heavily localised it often falls on an individual city to maintain the store of cultural heritage through such media as museums etc. Charges may help but as the benefits ensue for generations 'market forces' might be expected to lead to substantial under-provision. It is also possible that industry does not pay the full cost of local authority services or the externalities caused are not accounted for fully.

Empirical results

The empirical work reported below is part of a larger research programme being undertaken at Staffordshire University Business School. Initial motivation for the project derived from conversations with officials at Stoke-on-Trent City Council, who were concerned that Stoke-on-Trent, along with other 'Major Cities', were not receiving an appropriate grant allocation as a result of the SSA system.

Reasons, at that stage were not entirely clear but it was suspected that some sort of 'Major Cities Effect' possibly resulting from the cities' role as a sub-regional centre may be at work. Hence the initial work was largely directed at exploring whether or not such an effect existed and what, if anything, lay behind it. The early work was conducted at three levels:

- disaggregate analysis of spending patterns;
- interviews and questionnaires;
- regression analysis.

Disaggregate analysis of spending patterns

This entailed an analysis of local authority expenditure by category, so as to identify any obvious pattern or significant difference between spending by Stoke-on-Trent, the Major Cities as a group and 'All English Non-Metropolitan Districts' (AENMDs). The results are reported in full for the 'Other District Services' at Appendix 1, whilst Tables 12.1 and 12.2 below provide a synopsis for the two particular blocks concerned.

Of significant note is that whereas AENMDs devote 1.89% of their per capita expenditure to Museums and Art Galleries, the equivalent figure for Major Cities is 4.59%. Stoke-on-Trent devotes 7.54% towards this and 17.2% of its spending to Parks and Open Spaces compared to 10.64% for the Major Cities as a whole and only 8.99% for AENMDs. Thus, taken as a whole, the Major Cities spend 20% more, per head of their enhanced population, on Parks and Open Spaces.

It was also noted that the Major Cities devoted 2.4% of per capita spending to Economic Development compared to the AENMDs' figure of 1.02%, though the comparable figure for Stoke-on-Trent was 0.53%. Acknowledging that these figures may be strongly affected by local differences in accounting procedures, part of the agenda is to attempt to derive a cleaner set of data. Nevertheless, data shortcomings not withstanding, those categories of expenditure which *prime facie* might be expected to be strongly influenced by industrial heritage are at least suggestive of the fact that major cities incur costs to a significantly greater extent than AEs.

Table 12.1 Spending on Museums and Art Galleries

	% of service expenditure	£000s service expenditure	£/ head service expenditure	% of per head
AENMDs	53,168	1.89	1.83	1.75
Major Cities	13,754	4.59	4.35	n/a
STOKE-ON-TRENT	1,876	7.54	7.36	7.5
Bristol	2,641	5.74	5.39	6.77
Derby	4.86	1.104	4.86	
Hull	2,189	6.71	6.59	8.14
Leicester	0	0	0	0
Nottingham	2,082	5.07	4.74	7.37
Plymouth	709	2.70	2.49	2.74
Portsmouth	1,323	4.45	4.32	7.17
Southampton	1,830	7.86	7.17	8.93

Table 12.2 Spending on Parks and Open Spaces

	£000s service expenditure	% of service expenditure	£/head service expenditure	% of per head
AENMDs	253,403	8.74	8.34	8.99
Major Cities	32,455	10.26	n/a	10.64
STOKE-ON-TRENT	4,275	16.77	17.1	17.20
Bristol	5,795	11.83	14.86	12.00
Derby	2,703	11.89	11.9	12.09
Hull	1,889	5.69	7.02	5.79
Leicester	5,443	9.49	19.07	9.57
Nottingham	3,998	9.1	14.15	9.73
Plymouth	2,764	9.69	10.69	10.52
Portsmouth	2,215	10.82	17.97	11.16
Southampton	2,273	8.91	11.09	9.76

Interviews and questionnaires

Local Officials, with responsibility for Spending Departments, were identified. Structured interviews were carried out and a questionnaire issued in order to ascertain how the Stoke-on-Trent City Council, a 'Major City' and the case study area, works under the SSA system. It also aimed to establish how people within the council view its expenditure determinants. The intention was to find out whether these answers would provide a 'better' way of describing the council's expenditure than the SSA method. The questionnaires were utilised to gather some empirical evidence that would facilitate statistical analysis in order to identify cost drivers. The main drivers of costs indicated in the interviews were history and possibly the city's sub-regional role. The results of the questionnaire suggest that the SSA factors in general are not regarded as good indicators of spending requirements whilst historical spending patterns were. This result also came out of the interviews. Other indicators such as the type of employment and industry, local income levels and industrial deterioration were indicated as also being important.

Regression analysis

Having replicated the DoE's regression equation for District Services, the equation was re-estimated for various sub-groups of expenditure. The statistical analysis showed that although the DoE's equation was moderately well defined for the aggregate, it was poor when applied to subgroups of expenditure. The particular sub-blocks highlighted are Museums and Art Galleries and a composite 'block' comprising 'Parks and Open Spaces' and 'Economic Development'. Economic Development was included because many of the Major Cities have an old industrial structure, with the consequent problems. The results for both categories are given in Table 12.3, with the aggregate equation (Equation 1) repeated for ease of comparison.

The DoE's convention of dropping variables which are statistically insignificant or 'wrongly signed' has been followed. In this case the Social Indicator and Density are insignificant for Museums and Art Galleries and the Social Indicator for Parks and Open Spaces.

Table 12.3 Other District Services: Regression Equations

	Constant	Econ	Soc	Den	ADjR^2
1. Aggregate equation	(β_0	$+\beta_1$Econ	$+\beta_2$Soc	$+ \beta_3$Den)	
	83.23	2.16	3.52	0.28	0.67
2. Museums and Art Galleries					
	2.11	0.15	-0.05	0	0.04
	4.8	*4.88*	*-0.94*	*-0.53*	
Social indicator and	1.89	0.11			0.04
density removed	*19.07*	*4.97*			
3. Parks and Recreation and Economic Development					
	7.64	0.35	-0.55	0.12	0.23
	6.06	*4.13*	*-3.9*	*4.91*	
Social indicator	11.45	0.39		0.45	0.20
removed	*14.14*	*4.53*		*2.93*	

Note: t-ratios given in italics

Of particular note are the differences in coefficients as between the aggregate equation and the sub-blocks; and the differences in adjusted R^2, particularly between the aggregate equation and the sub-blocks for Museums and Art Galleries. Although the DoE's equation is moderately well defined for the aggregate, it is poor when applied to sub-groups of expenditure. Furthermore, the considerable differences between the equations for the sub-groups suggests that this particular methodology is not well suited to an aggregate comprising such diverse spending categories. Despite replicating the DoE's equation, there is some mystery about the apparently good fit of the aggregate equation, when the same equation exhibits such a poor fit when applied to sub-categories. The finding that the lack of importance of the Social Index for these categories of expenditure mirrors that found in the questionnaire responses. Some factors of particular importance to Major Cities may be missing from these equations. As a preliminary test for such an effect, a 'Major City Dummy Variable' was introduced into the equations. For both sub-categories of expenditure the dummies turned out to be statistically significant at the 1 percent level, although the nature of such a 'Major Cities Effect' still requires further investigation. These results are not reported here but are available on request.

Interpretation and further research

The results so far lend general support to the view that the industrial heritage of the major cities places particular pressure on the District authorities' budgets. This would help explain the continued higher maintenance costs experienced by these authorities for Parks and Open Spaces and Museums and Art Galleries relative to other authorities. The initial hypothesis is that the costs flow from the maintenance of the physical legacies of former industrial magnates who provided them, or the initial funding for them. This would include, in part, the open spaces formed by the reclamation of the former industrial and Mining and Mineral sites which were not covered by modern planning conditions and statutory environmental controls.

Coal mining was a major contributor to despoiled land for decades despite restoration of open-cast coal and ironstone sites being enforceable by law. Deep mining produced much waste and in the early 1970s, the National Coal Board was disposing of 65 percent of its 'land-dumped' wastes on tips not subject to planning control, and the industry has fully exploited a freedom which has resulted in thousand(s) of acres of untidy and rubbish-strewn landscapes. Spoil heaps are possibly the most common form of dereliction. It is interesting to note that Stoke-on-Trent and its environs was a major coal mining and mineral extraction area. The 'Major Cities' group includes Nottingham and Leicester, both high spenders on Parks and Open Spaces and localities formerly associated with coal mining.

The extent of the pervasiveness of the link between previous land reclamation expenditures and expenditure on initial park provision on the one hand and recurrent maintenance expenditures for Parks and Open Spaces on the other, is deserving of further study. It is one of the areas which is currently being investigating. For many years local authorities have had the power to bring derelict land back into use and improve the appearance of neglected land. Grants have been available at various levels depending on the category of land and the economic status of the area. It is recognised that at the micro level, the use to which the land will be put, and the habitat created, will affect both capital and recurrent costs. Spending priorities of the authorities concerned will come into play. The decision will invariably involve a political element since the local authority will be wholly or partially responsible for the implementation of the scheme. It may be that the ultimate decision rests on the availability of grants and the conditions to be satisfied to obtain them. The differential spending patterns show that the nature and extent of local recreation provision varies from authority to authority. For some their statutory powers enabling provision of recreation facilities are seen as opportunities to be taken whilst others downplay such provision and escape the cost implications.

Yet it is not just in the maintenance of bequeathed parks or reclaimed land that history imprints itself on the need for current provision. Disused docks need redevelopment, redundant waterways require maintaining. Even the tourist industry has its legacies and redundant Victorian piers are a dangerous and unsightly blot on local land and sea-scapes. All these have attendant cost implications for the local authorities concerned. The ultimate outcome of the research would be a single indicator which captured the current cost implications resulting from previous activities of which the current generation of local inhabitants have no control.

A similar methodology is being adopted for the Museums and Art Galleries. Here care has to be taken to differentiate expenditure between the buildings and the artefacts or works of art. Apart from the latter being classed as capital items, recurrent costs on 'maintenance' have to be differentiated. It could be argued that with Parks and Public Open Space the local authority property manager is primarily concerned with maintenance at lowest cost. However this does not reflect the situation found in many authorities where civic pride requires a high standard of provision. Perhaps the management of Museums and Art Galleries is more in the mould of traditional estate management. However, even these show the specialised nature of public sector estates necessary to meet social and public needs.

Conclusions

There is at least a strong suggestion that the disproportionate spending by the Major Cities in certain areas derives to a greater or lesser extent from industrial heritage. Heavy maintenance costs associated with reclaimed land, inherited Victorian parks and other open spaces may indicate environmental costs falling on certain authorities, including in particular the Major Cities group. They may have a greater share of responsibility for maintaining the national heritage from their industrial history.

The current system of grant allocation, based as it is on Equation 1, makes no allowance for these factors. If these can be identified and measured more precisely then there is at least the potential for including them in the 'Other District Services' SSA regression equation. This would increase the explanatory power of the equation (as captured by the adjusted R^2) but more importantly would result in a grant allocation more closely related to authorities' needs and in consequence help to ensure that sufficient resources are available to maintain and enhance a legacy that will benefit generations to come, both locally and elsewhere.

References

Audit Commission (1993), *Passing the Bucks: The Impact of Standard Spending Assessments on Economy, Efficiency and Effectiveness Volume*, HMSO, London.

Chartered Institute of Public Finance and Accountants (June 1994), *Finance and General Statistics 1994/5,* CIPFA, London.

Department of the Environment (1994), *The Local Government Finance Report England) 1994/5 Appendix D,* HMSO, London.

Department of the Environment (1995), *The Local Government Finance Report (England), 1995/6,* HMSO, London.

Harris, J., Birch, P. and Palmer, J. (1996), *Land Restoration and Reclamation: Priniciples and Practice*, Longman, Harlow.

Moss, G. (1981), *Britain's Wasting Acres: Land Use in a Changing Society,* Architectural Press, London.

Seabrooke, W. and Miles, C. (1993), *Recreational Land Management,* Spon, London.

Stapleton, T. (1994), *Estate Management Practice* , Estates Gazette, London.

University of Salford (1992), *Standard Spending Assessments: A Report for Wigan Metropolitan Borough Council* , Salford University, Manchester.

Appendix 1 Other District Services Expenditure by Category

1994/95	STOKE-ON-TRENT				MAJOR CITIES			ALL ENGLISH NON-METROPOLITAN DISTRICTS			
SERVICE	£000 SERVICE EXPEND.	% OF SERVICE EXPEND.	£HEAD SERVICE EXPEND.	% OF PER HEAD EXPEND.	£000 TOTAL SERVICE EXPEND.	% SERVICE EXPEND.	% OF PER HEAD EXPEND.	£000 SERVICE EXPEND.	% SERVICE EXPEND.	£HEAD SERVICE EXPEND.	% OF PER HEAD EXPEND.
Museums and Art Galleries	1876	7.36	7.5	7.54	13754	4.35	4.59	53168	1.83	1.75	1.89
Pools, Sports & Phys.Rec. Centres	1841	7.22	7.36	7.4	29676	9.38	9.85	256871	8.86	8.46	9.12
Parks and Open Spaces	4275	16.77	17.1	17.2	32455	10.26	10.64	253403	8.74	8.34	8.99
Planning	1188	4.66	4.75	4.78	12769	4.04	4.43	271217	9.35	8.93	9.62
Economic Development	132	0.52	0.53	0.53	8283	2.62	2.47	28848	1	0.95	1.02
Waste Collection	2695	10.57	10.78	10.84	21986	6.95	7.21	310533	10.71	10.23	11.02
Street Cleaning & Litter Response	1619	6.35	6.48	6.52	20014	6.33	6.31	170382	5.88	5.61	6.04
Environt & Public Health Services	1524	5.98	6.1	6.14	22615	7.15	7.28	266819	9.2	8.79	9.47
Cemeteries & Crematoria	523	2.05	2.09	2.1	1386	0.44	0.52	19330	0.67	0.64	0.69
Consumer Protection	468	1.84	1.87	1.88	1773	0.56	0.62	12008	0.41	0.4	0.43
Housing Benefit Administration	1170	4.59	2.2	2.21	17663	5.58	4.64	138747	4.79	4.57	4.92
Other Housing	551	2.16	4.68	4.71	14658	4.63	5.82	88309	3.05	2.91	3.14
Homelessness	247	0.97	0.99	1	5379	1.7	1.64	42993	1.48	1.42	1.53
Other Services	4052	15.89	16.21	16.3	47985	15.17	16.2	363908	12.55	11.98	12.91
Cost of All Rate Collection	5	0.02	0.02	0.02	310	0.1	0.09	6980	0.24	0.23	0.25
Net Cost of Residual Com.Ch.Colln	607	2.38	2.43	2.44	8394	2.65	2.87	63684	2.2	2.1	2.26
Council Tax Collection Costs	1907	7.48	7.63	7.67	27594	8.72	8.7	311038	10.73	10.24	11.03
Corporate Management	511	2	2.04	2.05	21002	6.64	7.05	193337	6.67	6.37	6.86
Unallocated Admin & Support Serv.	571	2.24	2.28	2.29	2981	0.94	0.82	33120	1.14	1.09	1.17
Concessionary Fares	638	2.5	****	****	10962	3.47	****	81156	2.8	****	****
Other Highway Services	(906)	(3.55)	(3.62)	(3.64)	(5313)	(1.68)	(1.76)	(66671)	(2.30)	(2.20)	(2.37)
TOTAL	25494	100	99.42	100	316326	100	100	2899180	100	92.81	100

13 Evaluating Property Performance

Elizabeth Carter, Department of Land Management, School of the Built Environment, De Montfort University, Leicester

Introduction

This paper presents the outcomes of a recently completed research project undertaken with the Leisure Services Department of a Local Authority. The overall aim of the research was to explore the development of a procedure for evaluating the performance of operational property and to consider the development of appropriate property measures. Operational property may be regarded as the property required to support the organisation's main activities.

The paper commences by placing the project in context with the findings of the Audit Commission Report into *Local Authority Property Management*. It goes on to discuss the case-study and the application of the procedure for property performance evaluation. The paper concludes that the property performance evaluation procedure is a constructive attempt to compensate for the shortcomings of traditional estate management practice in identifying and assessing the performance of operational property. The procedure offers potential as a new tool for better strategic property management and is directly relevant to the property management functions of local authorities.

The relevance of local authority property management

The Audit Commission surveyed approximately sixty local authorities for the purposes of their above report, which is subsequently referred to as the 1988 Report. Their published findings contains harsh observations about the lack of strategic property management, the absence of criteria and targets, the inadequacy of management information, and the general level of ignorance about property performance. The 1988 Report also contains many highly instructive suggestions for dealing with these and other observed shortcomings. For example, the Report laments the absence of defining reasons and objectives for owning property and states: 'The benefits of continued ownership by the authority, whether to the recipients of direct services or to ratepayers, must be viewed in relation to the value of the property held ... and its running costs.' In order to effectively control property running costs (which most local authorities were not recognised to be doing) the Report recommends that an assessment of whether a property is 'expensive' or 'cheap' to run can only be made by looking at unit costs. The chosen units must be appropriate to the building's use and must enable valid comparisons to be made.

The sentiments and, indeed, some of the specific recommendations contained in the 1988 Report, played a part in the development of this project. This research illustrates how one local authority is attempting to address the shortcomings identified by the 1988 Report in the management of their operational property. The project centres around the development of a practical procedural approach which may be applied for the purposes of improving the performance of any operational property.

The case study

The subject material for the case-study concerns four different swimming pool facilities owned by the Leisure Services Department of Leicester City Council. During the period of this research, from March 1995 to September 1996, the ownership and management of the Council's property assets were not centralised and each service department was responsible for its own property holdings. The operational owner for this project, therefore, was the Leisure Services Department, otherwise referred to as the 'client'. Although there was no formal management structure for a strategic property overview, there was a general acknowledgement within the local authority that property needs more effective monitoring in relation to the contribution it is making. A 1995 internal management report expressed these views succinctly and illustrates the background against which this research was conducted: 'Property is useful to the Council in only two categories. It must *either* provide an appropriate "home" for an element of the City Council Service provision, *or* be held to provide an income to the City Council, either now or in the future, to fund those services which the Council wishes to supply. As such property can be regarded as a support function sharing the objectives of its internal customer.'

As from October 1996, the City Council is changing to a centralised property management structure. The management of all property (except housing) is being transferred to the Property Services Department which reports to the Council's Property Services Committee. A landlord and tenant system will operate in reflection of the relationship between the corporate ownership and tenant user functions.

The project

Traditional estate management techniques were not providing the City Council with the information required for making decisions about the effectiveness or the comparative performance of their operational property. At the time there was a particular need to assess the performance of Council owned leisure facilities. It was decided to select four different swimming pool facilities as case-study material to see if a procedure could be developed to identify and evaluate the performance of these properties.

More precisely, the aims and objectives of the project are as follows:

Aims

- to explore the development of a procedure for evaluating the contribution of operational property performance to organisational effectiveness and to consider the development of appropriate property measures.

Objectives

- to devise a procedural approach for operational property performance evaluation which is transferable to other property owning organisations;
- to facilitate the development of property performance measures which are relevant to the corporate goals and objectives of the owning organisation;

- to facilitate an approach for defining property performance criteria which are capable of relatively easy measurement, analysis, monitoring and reporting by the property owning organisation;
- to promote objectivity and consistency in the assessment and evaluation of operational property performance.

Property performance evaluation: the procedure

The project was tackled in a series of stages. This approach was influenced by the work of S.L. Duckworth presented in his research paper at the 1992 American Real Estate Society meeting. Recent refinements have been influenced by the work of Bernard Williams Associates, particularly the system of 'Building Quality Assessment', and also by the Real Estate Norm Netherlands Foundation.

Stage 1. Determine organisational/business aims and objectives

The aims and objectives of the property owning organisation provide the setting within which the property resource is to perform. Reference was made to a wide range of departmental and corporate documentation. Personal interviews with key personnel, supported by a specifically designed survey form, provided vital information about the nature of the business; the provision and purchase of services; what must be done to survive or to succeed; key issues; and internal/external relationships. The 'familiarisation' process was critical in order to achieve any degree of understanding about the part to be played by the operation's property resource.

Stage 2. Establish the key property user perspectives and identify categories for the measurement of property performance

Every property user has a view about the property they use. Often, different types of users have different sets of requirements. This stage involved close consultation with the client. Firstly, it is necessary to identify the key user perspectives from which the organisation's property performance should be considered. Secondly, property performance is categorised under broad property outcome headings.

This stage results in a framework for identifying property performance expectations as indicated in Table 13.1 The rows represent the range of relevant user perspectives from which property performance should be considered. The columns represent the categories under which property performance should be measured. Each cell of the diagram is used in the following Stage 3 to identify the principal 'Property Issues' for each user perspective under all categories of property outcomes.

Underpinning this stage of the procedure was the use of focus groups which individually represented the various user perspectives. The focus groups comprised approximately five individuals with the researcher as facilitator. Using Table 13.1, each focus group identified the main property issues as perceived from their user perspective. The group then decided how these property issues could be developed into measurable items through the use of performance indicators.

Table 13.1 Property Performance Expectations

User Perspective	Property Outcome Categories			
	Utilisation	**Functionality**	**Condition**	**Costs**
Consumer	Property Issues	Property Issues	Property Issues	Property Issues
Centre Manager				
Real Estate				
Building Services				
Corporate				

Stage 3. Define property issues and develop performance indicators

Defining performance indicators helped to focus attention on the relevant factors affecting property performance which could be measured. Table 13.2 provides an example of the performance indicators identified for three property issues under the broad heading of functionality.

Table 13.2 Property Performance Indicators

Property Issue		Performance Indicators
1.0	Functionality	
1.1	Accessibility	• Number of on-site car parking spaces per NIA m^2 • Public transport services
1.2	Locational Suitability	• % age of catchment population with < 20 mins walking distance • Distance from nearest Leisure Services facility
1.3	Visual Prominence	• Signage • Visual prominence to passers by

Stage 4. Measure, record and evaluate property performance

It is at this stage that the necessary facts and figures are collated and assessed in order to arrive at conclusions and evaluations as to the performance of the property. The approach is centred around an extension to the right of the table in Table 13.2. When placing an assessment on a performance indicator it may be necessary to first provide descriptive levels of the 'performance' which would qualify for each of the assessment ratings cited. In practice some property issues and their respective performance indicators carry a higher priority than others. Various models for weighting assessments were considered. The one illustrated in Table 13.3 was the simplest and clearest to operate and therefore the preferred approach. Table 13.3 provides a hypothetical and summarised illustration of the performance assessment of one Leisure property under the heading of Functionality. Applying the same process under the remaining 'Property Issues' headings would produce a complete evaluation of the property's overall performance.

The role of property performance evaluation in strategic property management

There has only been a limited time in which to apply this property performance evaluation procedure and further testing is needed. However, the early indications are encouraging.

The procedure has been effective as a means of identifying the performance requirements of property as defined by the needs of the owner or user. It has provided a process for specifying what information is needed in order to measure and monitor property performance. It also illustrates an approach for the evaluation of the examined property's performance results. As with any examination results, these figures present opportunities for comparison, for benchmarks, and for monitoring trends in performance over time. The true test of the value of the property performance evaluation procedure lies in the question of whether or not it results in better strategic property management decisions. This test was actually presented midway through the project with a trial property performance evaluation on another Leisure Services property.

The property was a recognised landmark in terms of the City's history, development and culture. Its original function had long since ceased but it continued to provide a public service as a mixed leisure facility despite the obvious unsuitability of the accommodation. A consensus decision about the property's future was proving extremely difficult to achieve. Bearing this in mind, a property evaluation was taken and produced information which clearly highlighted the poor functionality of the property for its current use. Its physical condition was steadily worsening and was linked to increased maintenance costs and a mounting need for substantial capital investment. Utilisation was showing a downward trend from a peak of five years ago. This information and the details contained in the evaluation had a strong bearing on the subsequent strategic decision to investigate the redevelopment opportunities for the site whilst seeking suitable alternative accommodation for the leisure facilities which should not be discontinued.

Table 13.3 Property Performance Evaluation

Property Issue	Performance Indicators	Assessment Rating		
		4 Very satisfactory 3 Fairly satisfactory	2 Fairly dissatisfactory 1 Very dissatisfactory	
		A of major importance	B of average importance	C of minor importance
1.0 Functionality				
1.1 Accessibility	• Number of on site car parking spaces per NIA m^2	2		
	• Public transport services	2		
1.2 Location Suitability	• % age of catchment population within <20 mins walking distance	2		
	• Distance from nearest Leisure Services facility	4		
1.3 Visual Prominence	• Signage		3	
	• Visual prominence to passers by		2	
		Total actual score 10	5	0
		Total poss score 16	8	0
Functionality		Total % score 62.5%	62.5%	

Conclusions

The project provides an actual example of a recent development by a Local Authority to manage its property more effectively, more strategically and on a more accountable fashion. It addresses directly, and in some depth, the exhortations contained in the 1988 Report to view the total benefits of property ownership by a local authority in relation to its total costs.

The property performance evaluation procedure is driven by an over-riding concern that operational property is essentially a resource, or a factor of production, and that this provides the basis for an evaluation of property performance. The property performance evaluation procedure outlined here doubtless requires further testing and refinement. Some of the fact-finding may currently appear cumbersome and the evaluation could be more sophisticated. However, the procedure is deliberately adaptable and all the various parts may be customised to fit the user's own specifications. At this point in the life cycle of the project it seems reasonable to suggest that the property performance evaluation procedure provides a new tool for better strategic property management. It is clearly relevant to the property management functions of a Local Authority and is a strategy which could be usefully employed when facing the changing property management demands from local government re-organisation and reforms such as unitary status or compulsory competitive tendering.

References

Anderson A. (1993), *Real Estate in the Corporation : The Bottom Line from Senior Management*, Arthur Anderson & Co. SC.

Avis, M., Gibson, V. and Watts, J. (1989), *Managing Operational Property Assets*, University of Reading, Reading, UK.

Balch, W. (1994), 'An Integrated Approach to Property and Facilities Management', *Facilities*, vol. 12 (1)

Bernard Williams Associates (1994), *Facilities Economics*, Building Economics Bureau Ltd.

Duckworth, S. (1992), *Best Practice Benchmarking*, Industrial Newsletters Ltd.

Gibson, V. (1994), 'Is Property on the Strategic Agenda?', *Cutting Edge*, RICS, London.

Oxford Brookes University and University of Reading (1993), *Property Management Performance Monitoring*, Oxford Brookes University and GTI, UK.

REN Netherlands Foundation (1992), *Real Estate Norm,* REN Netherlands Foundation.

University of Reading and DTZ Debenham Thorpe (1995), *The Chartered Surveyor as Management Consultant*, RICS, London.

14 What about the Workers? Some Implications of the Private Finance Initiative for Property Professionals

Michael Nevin, Advisor, Scottish Office Private Finance Unit

Introduction

The great Austrian economist Joseph Schumpeter once described the process of development in a market economy as a 'gale of creative destruction', in which new enterprises are continuously emerging to attack old modes of production.

The Private Finance Initiative also has the potential to be a gale of creative destruction for existing methods of delivering public services. It will create opportunities for new concessionaires to emerge, but it will simultaneously threaten to destroy long established delivery systems. It may therefore be perceived by some as representing a threat to their job security and career prospects. But this need not be the case. In any period of rapid and radical change, the winners will be those who recognise that change is happening, think through its full implications, and then position themselves to seize the new opportunities on offer. The object of this chapter is to describe the new market for property professionals which is now developing as a result of the PFI.

The principal factors

The principal factors driving more and more Scottish local authorities towards the PFI is their continuing need for capital investment to meet their service delivery obligations, combined with constraints on conventional public sector borrowing which historically has been the single most important source of funds for new public investment. Figure 14.1 shows the capital allocations to Scottish local authorities during the 1990s. The data are actual allocations for the years between 1990/91 and 1995/96 budgeted allocations for the current 1996/97 financial year, and the Public Expenditure Survey (PES) forecast for the next two financial years.

THE SCOTTISH OFFICE

Private Finance Unit

Figure 14.1 : Capital Allocations to Scottish Local Authorities, 1990-99*

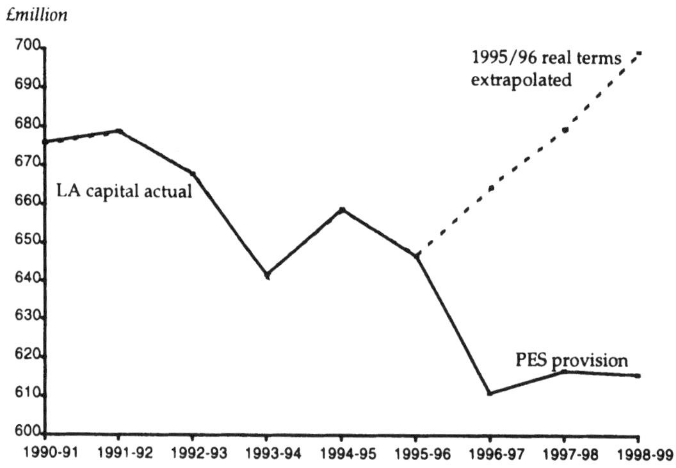

**Excluding provision for water and sewerage and one-off expenditure in 1995-96 for purchase of New Towns' housing stock. 1990-93 provision includes further education colleges which were then under local authority control*

It shows that there has been a decline in the amount of capital allocated under Section 94 to local authorities. During the early 1990s, annual Section 94 capital allocation amounted to some £670m - £680m per annum. This year, and for the next three years, it is forecast to be between £610m and £620m per annum. In nominal terms, this represents a decline of approximately 9 percent over the period. In real terms, after adjusting for inflation, the decline is somewhat greater, as shown by the hatched line on Figure 14.1. This line shows the level of capital allocation to Scottish local authorities which would be required to maintain 1995/96 levels in real terms, allowing for inflation at 2.5 percent over the next three years. It can be seen from this line that the gap between real 1995/96 allocations, and the actual PES provision over the next three years, is likely to widen. And when account is taken of capital commitments that councils have already entered into, it will be appreciated that the amount of discretionary capital finance available for new projects is very constrained.

One strategy which councils might be tempted to adopt is to try and survive the next few months in the hope that more conventional Section 94 funding will become available over the medium term. However, it is increasingly clear that 'wait and see', so far from being a low risk strategy, is in fact an extremely high risk strategy. Under any realistic policy scenario, there is unlikely to be any significant real growth in the funding available to local authorities. Therefore, a 'wait and see' policy will merely defer the time when hard decisions need to be taken, and innovative approaches developed to meet the real needs for new investment in the delivery of council services.

My conclusion is that, rather than waiting, councils throughout Scotland should give serious consideration to mobilising additional capital investment through the Private Finance Initiative. The PFI represents the best, and in many cases the only, realistic option that Scottish local authorities have for implementing essential new projects.

Whereas traditionally local authorities have been both the *clients* for public services and their direct *providers*, the essence of the PFI lies in the separation of these two functions. Under traditional procurement arrangements, a local authority is responsible for the design, construction and operation of property assets required to deliver local authority services. Under the PFI, these functions are transferred to a private sector concessionaire, working to an output specification set out by the local authority as the final client. Figure 14.2 shows how this might work. The local authority would execute a service agreement with a private company established to provide a new facility, such as a leisure centre, a school or a library. The company is responsible for raising the finance necessary to provide the facility, designing it, and executing the contracts required to build and operate it.

In order for such an arrangement to work, it is essential, as for any successful deal in a free market, that there is a willing seller and a willing buyer. So the council has to be willing to buy the services it requires from a new facility owned and operated by the private sector. The terms on which it buys must be sufficiently attractive for a private concessionaire to be willing to sell. So the question is - what conditions must hold for such a transaction to be of benefit to both parties?

For the council, a PFI deal offers the following advantages:

- service provision levels will be assured by the terms of the contract concluded with the concessionaire;
- the council may preserve certain exclusive rights : for example, it may retain nomination rights for a social housing project, or have exclusive use of a school building during term time;
- by mobilising private finance to develop certain essential facilities, the local authority can release scarce Section 94 resources for investment in other service areas;
- the council thereby achieves vital refurbishment and upgrading work which would otherwise have to be deferred.

For the private sector concessionaire, the service agreement offers the following benefits:

- by concluding a 'take-or-pay' type of agreement for at least part of the facility's capacity, it guarantees a minimum level of revenue against which project financing can be secured;
- the concessionaire can augment these minimum guaranteed revenues by sales to third parties, and performance incentives linked to superior service delivery;
- depending on the structure of the deal, if a council divests surplus assets into a PFI scheme, the private concessionaire might have the ability to realise other commercial projects within the framework of a PFI deal.

THE SCOTTISH OFFICE
Private Finance Unit

Figure 14.2 : Basic PFI Project Structure

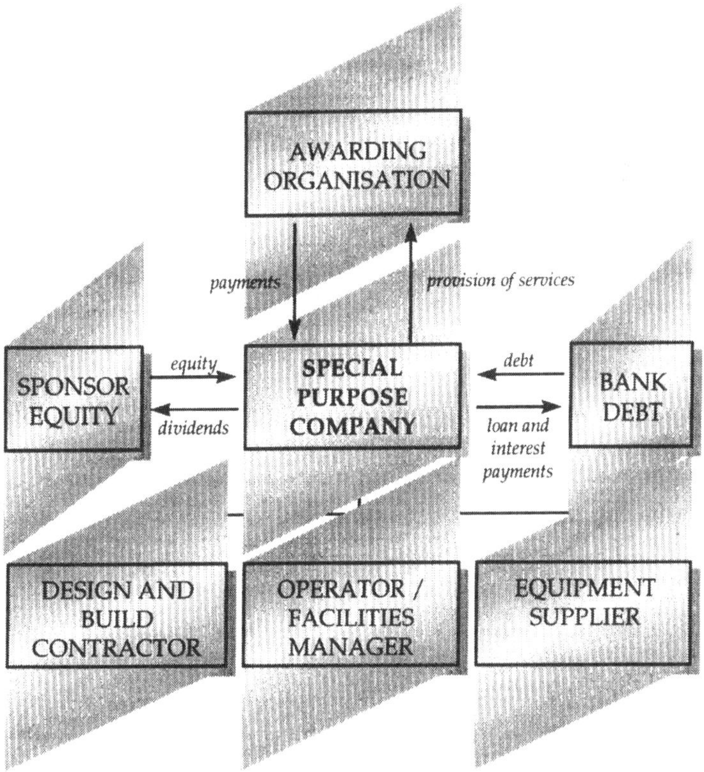

For the clients whom the council and the concessionaire seek to serve, whether they be schoolchildren, library users, road users, or social housing tenants, the PFI deal also offers benefits in the shape of additional investment and superior performance through the introduction of transparent 'arms-length' contractual arrangements in which payments are explicitly linked to service quality.

What about the workers?

But what about the workers? It is evident that if a private concessionaire is responsible for the design of new facilities, large in-house design teams will no longer be required in local authorities. Some local authorities have asked whether it would be possible for a local authority team to undertake the design of a PFI project. Unfortunately, the answer is no. It is an essential requirement of the PFI that the concessionaires undertake the design. It is desirable to have a number of competing designs in order to maximise value for money, by encouraging genuine innovation in the design process. Where only one design team is involved, no matter how good they are, the scope for design innovation is limited. In addition, the exclusion of a formal link between a concessionaire and the council's own design team is necessary to ensure fair competition.

What this implies is that, if the standard method of procuring new projects is through the PFI, the number of design staff directly employed by a local authority will be small. There will still be a need for a core of highly qualified, experienced design personnel within local authorities to enable them to act as 'intelligent clients' in the specification of the services they require, the management of the PFI tender process, and the evaluation of the bids submitted by short listed consortia. But the 'intelligent client' design team will be far smaller than the teams that currently exist in many local authorities, who have a commission to undertake the detailed design of new capital projects.

So what will happen to the local authority staff previously responsible for these functions? An immediate response is to see the PFI as a threat to job security and job prospects. In my view, this is fundamentally misconceived. It is true that, like any radical change, the PFI can pose a threat for those unwilling or unable to respond. But for those who approach it in a positive frame of mind, it offers enormous opportunities. Individuals whose careers were previously circumscribed by local authority pay, conditions and grading structures now have the opportunity to consider an alternative career progression through PFI Special Purpose Companies. These companies could promote and manage a portfolio of projects when the PFI develops as the preferred method of procurement for many local authority projects in Scotland.

In the initial phase of the PFI, Special Purpose Companies were contractor-led. However, as the PFI matures, it is anticipated that more companies will be driven by designers and facilities managers, with contractors taking a back seat. In many cases, this is the appropriate approach, since a significant source of value from the PFI compared to conventional procurement derives from the ways in which it can stimulate design innovation and a life-cycle approach to asset development and maintenance.

This offers exciting opportunities for design professionals and there is already evidence that some design practices are beginning to position themselves to take a lead in PFI service companies. If these trends have fundamental implications for local authority design teams, the possible impact on the architectural and chartered surveying profession could be even more profound.

Towards partnerships

In the past, professional firms have been structured as unlimited partnerships, and have earned their living exclusively from professional fees. If PFI develops in the way that is anticipated, this role will need to evolve. If architects, surveyors and designers are to take a leading role in the new PFI service companies, then they will have to be structured in such a way as to take some of the equity risks in these companies. This indeed is the essence of the PFI : value for money can only be achieved if risks are genuinely transferred from the public sector to the private sector. So designers may have to be prepared to take some of their fee, not as cash or even as a contingent fee, but as an equity stake in the project company. Whereas under traditional procurement, the designers' job is finished when the design is complete and the project built, under the PFI designers will be locked into the Special Purpose Company for the whole lifetime of a service agreement, which in many cases will extend for 20 years or more.

Conclusions

In order to take such a long term position, it is likely that professional firms in the design sector will need to incorporate and have a permanent risk capital base which they can allocate in part to the new service companies. Some of their return will come from the dividend flow from successful projects over a period of years rather than being taken immediately a design is complete in the form of professional fees. These are radical changes. Many firms will be unwilling to go down this route, and will prefer to maintain their traditional role of independent advisers who earn their return exclusively from professional fees payable in cash. There is, of course, nothing to stop them doing this. However, to the extent that other firms are positioning themselves to become shareholders and directors of PFI service companies, the traditional professional firm is likely to lose market share and, over time, see its revenue base erode. Those who will prosper in the new PFI market will be the dynamic and innovative firms prepared to back their professional skills with an equity stake in the projects they design. In the gale of creative destruction which will be brought about by the new procurement methods, those who remain stuck in the past risk being swept away. But those with the intelligence, foresight and daring to seize the new opportunities, whether they are currently in the public sector or the private sector, are likely to emerge as winners, with immense opportunities for personal and professional development.

Note

Mr Nevin's presentation was made while on secondment from Deloitte & Touche to the Scottish Office's Private Finance Unit. He has since returned to Deloitte & Touche in Edinburgh.

15 Property Management in Scottish Enterprise: The Means to an End?

Ewan Hall, Head of Property, Scottish Enterprise

Introduction

Before we deal with the operational system and controls of the Scottish Enterprise property portfolios it would be helpful to summarise the history of industrial accommodation provision in Scotland. From the beginning of the 19th Century until the turn of the 20th Century, Scotland experienced major growth in population, which rose from 1.6 million to 4.5 million. The prime industries of coal and pig iron production spawned the steel, engineering and shipping industries, all of which became major employers. The accommodation needs of these heavy industries as well as the textile and farming industries were provided on a custom built basis and were owner occupied - a true market economy.

Scottish Industrial Estates Corporation

When the traditional and heavy industries waned in the 1930s during the depression, the government introduced an industrial policy for regional economic growth which would encourage and direct new manufacturing industries offering new employment to specific regional areas. As an instrument of this policy Industrial Estate Corporations, were established in England and Scotland, which were empowered on specific direction to acquire land, and, build factories to house the new light industries. New light industries would be encouraged to locate in areas of high unemployment with - as a direct consequence of the Corporation's activities - an availability of modern premises to rent, a plentiful supply of skilled labour and financial assistance (*land, labour and capital!*). In

Scotland the policy was operated through the Scottish Industrial Estates Corporation who were responsible for the development of industrial estates and factories to meet the government's criteria for new industrial companies.

The first industrial estates were at Hillington which was started in the second half of the 1930s and others followed in Greenock, Dundee, Kilmarnock, and Newhouse, Lanarkshire. The factory building programme of the Scottish Industrial Estates Corporation continued for nearly 40 years until the mid-1970s developing factories built to a common design in sizes of between 20,000 sq ft and 60,000 sq ft and predominantly speculatively built. These comprised either advance factories, or in certain circumstances specialised buildings erected to the requirements of a specific user which we refer to as custom built, or bespoke. The development philosophy was 'need' during this period, (indeed potentially in advance of need), and not as now on a financial investment criteria of demand and supply. It is interesting to note that during that same period the lease terms stipulated that:

- the user was manufacturing - no storage, warehouse, transport, etc uses were permitted and the companies had to be new not relocated from other local premises;
- the lease period was 21 years at a fixed rent set by the District Valuer and there were no rent reviews;
- the landlord would be responsible for wind and watertight repairs etc.

With the abolition of owner's rates in the late 1950s and the creation of New Towns during the 1960s, new players entered the industrial development market and a number of changes started to take place to past development and leasing practices.

Scottish Development Agency

The government which periodically changes its regional industrial policy, made a major change in 1975 when it created the Scottish Development Agency with extensive powers for industrial and economic regeneration matters. It also subsumed the Scottish Industrial Estates Corporation. At that time the property portfolio comprised 68 estates, 22 million square feet of factories, 500 tenants and £5 million rental income. The Scottish

Development Agency created a Commercial Estates Department to oversee the assumed Scottish Industrial Estates Corporation function and to set development and management policy. The first changes were to introduce modern commercial leasing terms in terms of:

- the easing of user restrictions;
- widening the scope of tenant selection;
- establishment of 20 year leases with 5 year rent reviews;
- tenant full repairing and ensuring terms;
- rents at market levels negotiated by SDA valuers;
- commercial marketing of vacant property which at that time extended to over 2 million square feet.

It was then necessary to establish the development strategy having regard to the changed demand criteria. Consequently new layouts were introduced for a whole range of business units comprising space standards from a few 100 sq ft to multiples of 5,000 sq ft. Accommodation would be provided within either new buildings, conversions, rehabilitations or modernisations of existing empty stock or modernisations of acquired property such as the Templeton Business Centre. Furthermore business space was designed for erection in rural areas and specialised units were also designed for urban regeneration areas such as GEAR (Glasgow Eastern Area Renewal Scheme), Clydebank, Glengarnock, Dundee, Leith, etc and lastly high-tech accommodation which was identified as requiring special locations. Projects in this regard were provided for by developments such as Digital at South Queensferry and by the introduction of accommodation in various science parks, ie. West of Scotland Science Park. The portfolio was therefore changing quite dramatically and further changes were brought about as a direct consequence of the Agency's activities in urban renewal and regeneration and also in land renewal schemes where other properties had been added to the portfolio, and, of course, a considerable amount of old industrial floor space had been demolished due to the obsolescence of the accommodation.

The pioneering of commercial practices and the rising rentals obtained offered the opportunity, particularly at the end of old 21-year leases, to sell factory premises to the existing occupiers. All of these progressive initiatives had brought about a substantial change to the composition of the property portfolio which by 1980 comprised approximately 25m sq ft of factories rising to 26.8m sq ft by 1985. At this time the Agency began to positively encourage private sector initiatives in the provision of factory accommodation.

The administration, control and monitoring of the property portfolio and its total management had been carried out up to 1985 in-house by the Scottish Development Agency in accordance with the financial guidelines laid down and altered from time to time by the Treasury. In 1985 it was decided that the management of the lettable properties in the portfolio should be carried out by external agents and following public advertisement six chartered surveying practices were engaged, each being given a territorial area to manage on behalf of the SDA. The SDA continued with the employment of regional chartered surveyors managing the portfolio in this way until the creation of Scottish Enterprise in 1991 (following the amalgamation of the SDA and the Training Agency). Prior to the new creation being in place, however, substantial areas of the portfolio were sold in packages to the private sector investment market with the hope that the sale would lead to market adjustment and encourage private sector provision of industrial premises, with limited financial support from the public sector. Approximately 10m sq ft was disposed of in this way to, amongst others, Caledonian Land.

Following the creation of Scottish Enterprise in 1991 the original intention was that individual Local Enterprise Companies, of which there are 13 in the Scottish Enterprise area, would naturally take over the management of former SDA assets in their operational areas. The decision was taken, therefore, to allow the continuation of the existing arrangement with six regional managing practices, until the prospective new arrangements fell into place. At the creation of Scottish Enterprise in 1991, Scottish Enterprise owned just short of 2,000 acres of what was considered strategic land for primarily inward investment spread across the country. This comprised large, single user sites such as Newhouse, Lanarkshire, (now home to Chungwa) and the site of the former steelworks, Hallside, and approximately 3.8m sq ft of buildings again of a strategic nature, or, residual portfolio such as business centres which were considered vital to encourage the start up of new ventures. A sector which at that time the private sector were not active in. At this time the portfolio was valued at circa £35 million. By 1993 the portfolio had risen to approximately four million square feet of mainly industrial accommodation and two and a half thousand acres of land with a value of £80 million.

Enterprise Company Network

In early 1993 it became clear however the fundamental belief that the Enterprise Companies would be able to, or indeed wish to, take over the management of the assets as part of their economic development role was not in keeping with their desires. At this stage we still had six managing agents all of whom ran their own independent property management systems reporting monthly to Scottish Enterprise who maintained a mainframe computer system, part of which analysed the input from these managing agents. With the evolution of IT, it became apparent that the mainframe was not the ultimate answer and the Enterprise Company Network moved to desktop PCs served by local area networks.

As the Enterprise Company Network matured at this stage decisions were taken on the way ahead for issues such as the management of assets. Whilst it is still Scottish Enterprise's strategy not to retain a substantial 'let' portfolio, it has been accepted that in order to facilitate the economic development and regeneration aims of Scottish Enterprise, a portfolio is needed, perhaps contrary to the theory of the late 1980s which resulted in 'land' being removed from the economic equation(!), with Scottish Enterprise originally being expected to concentrate on training and encouraging inward investment, indigenous company expansion and new capital investment.

By early 1994 it had become apparent that having 6 regional surveying practices dealing with the reshaped Scottish Enterprise was not offering either value for money or indeed consistency across the country and it was accordingly decided firstly to de-commission the ancient mainframe and proceed towards the provision of a new single property management system within Scottish Enterprise. In accordance with this proposal a management review was undertaken by external consultants, which highlighted that one agent should be appointed for the entire portfolio with responsibility for maintaining Scottish Enterprise's system in-house, thereby avoiding duplication with one overall management system and ensuring full accountability for Scottish Enterprise together with an asset register.

The option still remains however for the Local Enterprise Companies to manage the portfolio in their area locally - Grampian Enterprise are currently the only Enterprise Company who have taken up this option. Having said this the managing agents for the Grampian area are required to report to Scottish Enterprise's managing agent to ensure full knowledge and accountability as the provider of funding to the Enterprise Companies. As a point of information all properties bought by the Enterprise Companies are either registered in Scottish Enterprise's name or if acquired in the Enterprise Company's name have standard securities granted to Scottish Enterprise.

In late 1994 Messrs J. Trevor Webster were appointed, following a tender, as Scottish Enterprise's managing agents with responsibility for maintaining the in-house property management system so as to allow a strategic overview of the portfolio from within Scottish Enterprise, whilst liaising at a local level with the property directors and executives within the Local Enterprise Companies on a regular basis. Undoubtedly this raises its own tensions, as within any network, however as the Enterprise Company Network has matured and as financial belts have had to be tightened, the provision of central services, such as the management of the Scottish Enterprise portfolio, has evolved to meet the demands of the organisation.

Scottish Enterprise's portfolio as at 31 March 1966 stood at approximately 4,930 acres of land comprising approximately: 3,500 acres of development land; 1,400 acres of derelict/contaminated land and approximately 4.2 million square feet of industrial accommodation/business centres with currently approximately 30 percent of the lettable space void. The value of the holdings is approximately £195 million. The portfolio is not static, it is an evolving portfolio with development land being acquired as necessary, infrastructured as necessary and generally sold to the private sector where the private sector can be encouraged to take over the responsibility for development. Where private sector activity is sparse, Scottish Enterprise through its network of Enterprise Companies or in conjunction with Locate in Scotland; will act to ensure the provision of accommodation to suit the needs of inward investors and indigenous companies, such as in the former new towns where Scottish Enterprise maintains strategic land holdings. Scottish Enterprise's factory building programme has seen production of approximately 1 m sq ft through 100 percent public sector provision over the last 3 years, however close to 8 m sq ft has been provided by the private sector during the same period with support from the Enterprise Company Network in response to demand. As those buildings which are directly built fulfil their economic development uses by attracting new companies, be they indigenous or inward investors, the properties are then disposed of at the appropriate time on the open market.

The one aspect not touched on is the financial aspect of disposal of portfolio properties which is indeed vital to any organisation: as most local authorities will undoubtedly agree and particularly so given the change in receipts legislation which will affect the majority of property management divisions next year. Scottish Enterprise as a body agree annually with the Scottish Office its bid with gross and net figures. This year the difference is circa £30 million of which property is expected to raise circa £25 million to bridge the gap. This we do by disposing of assets when they have fulfilled the economic development use and disposing of land actively.

Conclusion

It is difficult to not conclude that this paper is a fairly long winded way of describing what is a fairly mundane system of property management, however it is a system which has evolved with the evolution of the network and which undoubtedly will alter again before the turn of the century. What will a new Parliament bring in 1997 with regard to regional development policies or indeed development agencies? Whatever comes - portfolio management to Scottish Enterprises is merely the means to an end.

PART 4
THE WAY AHEAD

16 Towards a Research Agenda

Mark Deakin, Department of Building and Surveying, Napier University

Introduction

The aforementioned has gone some way to identify that the development of LAPM marks a transition from the traditions of the estate to contemporary issues surrounding the management of property in local authorities. The discussions have also gone some way to show that the transition to LAPM has started to embed a moral code whose ethic is not transaction-based but process orientated. A moral code and corporate ethic whose philosophy has forced an audit, review and rationalisation of landed estates in an attempt by the state to make public expenditures on the management of property more accountable.

As a development it is one often characterised by the phrase: 'from state to market', or 'marketisation', built upon a process of re-engineering that introduces a quality-minded, pro-enterprise, decentred and competitive structure to property management in local authorities through initiatives in the design of information systems, modelling of data-bases and testing of programmes which drive towards a greater degree of corporatisation. One that in turn provides the informational basis to develop the strategy and financial instruments required for property management to be incorporated into the mission statements and business planning of local authorities. In demonstrating this, the discussions have shown that the information systems acting as the communicative structure of LAPM are abstract in nature requiring the knowledge of both regisrative procedures and evaluative measurement criteria. The discussions have also highlighted the commonly held view that while there are a plethora of initiatives, including those on asset registration, property valuation, audit, review and performance measurement; there is the so-called enigma of strategy. The enigma whose code needs to be deciphered in order to expose how the technology and economics of the initiatives crossover with the culture of corporate strategy, combine with the financial instruments in question and fuse with the informational basis of LAPM to produce the communicative structure of property management in local authorities.

As a research agenda, the enigma in question represents the search for the strategic dimension to property management originally put forward by Gibson (1991, 1994) and reiterated in the article by Gibson and Carter (1996) entitled: 'Is property on the strategic [management] agenda?' It is a question that has also pre-occupied Veale (1990) and Joroff, Lovargand, Lambert and Franklin (1993) and goes some way to suggest the issues surrounding the development of LAPM in the UK and USA share common terms of reference.

However, as has been pointed out, the use of the managerialist thesis to explain the rise of property in general and in the development of LAPM in particular, is not a straight forward exercise and illustrates a number of difficulties. The difficulties in question being as follows: firstly; there are some obvious difficulties over the 'Anglophonic' use of the terms real estate and property: secondly; the research tends to 'downplay' the technical and economic concerns about the informational basis of communicative structures in favour of the cultural question surrounding the corporate strategy and financial instruments: thirdly; as a consequence, the managerialist thesis tends to 'blur' any distinction between values in terms of the technical, economic, cultural, informational and communicative composition of the structures in question: fourthly; all the publications from this school of thought illustrate an ambivalence towards the corporate strategy and financial instruments of the public sector.

The second point is important for the fact those following the enigma of strategy illustrate a tendency to place the technology of initiatives to one side and focus on the culture of corporate strategy. As already pointed out, the difficulty with this line of enquiry is that it tends to split the subject in two - resulting in the search for a technical fix which ends up economistic, or pre-occupied with the culture of corporate strategy in the search for some form of ideal communication. The problem with this being that it encodes the emerging 'technical/economic' (Kingston and Glamorgan) and cultural schools (Reading, Harvard and MIT) with two incommensurate forms of logic rather than one. With two forms of logic, that is, which tend to divide and fragment, rather than make up and unify the subject in question.

Rather than running the risk of putting as much distance as is possible between the two schools and removing the possibility that exists for one to inform and communicate with the other, this research agenda will focus on the idea of bridging the two. It shall draw upon the engineering metaphor seen as central to the developments in question and focus on the 'building of bridges' between the initiatives and strategies making up the structure of LAMP. Before setting out how this is to be done, it is perhaps worthwhile clarifying the position that has been taken for the purposes of the bridge-building exercise. In this respect, it should be realised that the exercise attempts to reflect the nature of the developments taking place: those which place the manager of property at the centre of things. In particular - where, it might be added (s)he belongs! The reasons for this are as follows: firstly; it is the property managers who draw upon the technology and economies of the initiatives in question and develop a less standardised, quality-minded, pro-enterprise, competitive, decentralised and accountable culture for the required corporate strategy: secondly; it is the corporate strategy drawn from the initiatives property managers piece together that gives the authority for executives to set up, organise, take command of and control the direction of property management in local authorities; thirdly; it is this piecing together of the initiatives which allows property to be managed as a strategic resource; fourthly; it is this articulation of the initiatives into a strategy that leads to the design of information systems, modelling of data-bases for the registration of property, testing of programmes for valuation, audit, review and measurement of performance by management; fifthly; it is the development of computer-based information systems, for the storing, processing and circulating of information about the level of value and economies the financial instruments in question produce that acts as the main communicative structure for the management of property in local authorities.

Together the five points outlined here provide compelling evidence to support the view that any research agenda should place the needs of property managers at the centre of things. Given the development of such skills and expertise requires what is termed 'reflexive' knowledge - theoretical, discursive and methodological, the need to place property managers at the centre of thing becomes even more apparent. It is also done to try and represent the novel, experimental and in many respects 'trial and error', iterative logic of the development. The fact that faced with the steep learning curve underlying the transition from estate to property management, it has become necessary for surveyors to dispense with the tried and tested, innovate and become more strategic, enterprising and competitive. If we recognise the driving forces behind this have not been so much technological, economic, or cultural, but political the magnitude of the task becomes clear. This is because it is the 'cutting and reshaping', demand for 'responsiveness' and greater 'democratisation' of public services as a form of governing civil society, that has forced property managers to draw upon the technology and economics of the initiatives in question, develop the quality minded, pro-enterprise, competitive, decentred and accountable culture of the corporate strategy, information systems, data-bases and financial instruments as the main communicative structures servicing the state under post-Fordism.

It is the magnitude and extent of this response which the term 'post-AC LAPM', also attempts to capture in the sense that it indicates the lack of direct involvement government bodies, the professions and institutes: for example the AC, RICS, ISVA and ADC have had in the exercise. The fact, that is, their involvement in the exercise has been to do little more than provide guidance and not direction. The authority to execute, command, control and direct the initiatives, strategies, informational basis and communicative structures coming instead from property managers in local authorities. Put into perspective, the situation may be perhaps best described as the said institutions providing the framework to guide the development in question rather than the machinery to drive it forward. The absence of the latter meaning that it is the property managers who have been forced to engineer the initiatives and strategies which have the power to 'fill in the detail' and 'get on with the job'. Get on, in this instance, with piecing together the technology and economics of initiatives, culture of the emerging corporate strategy and combining them in such a way - via the information systems and data-bases - to produce the financial instruments, that not only structure lines of communication, but which also give property managers in local authorities the means to govern over, re-organise and reform the provision of public services in civil society.

Of course, getting on with the job in all its detail is problematic in itself because it has not only meant undertaking a process of re-engineering, design, modelling and testing, but a transformation of working practices. The transformation referred to as the development of reflexive knowledge, theory and method that challenge normative standards in the experiments which are undertaken to support such design, modelling and testing exercises. The experiments that require a basic knowledge of cybernetics, innovation in analytical techniques, market economics, culture, corporate strategy, financial instruments and informational systems underlying the communicative structures of property management - the object of which is to apply such forms of theoretical knowledge into the method and practice of property management so as to progress the transition from the estate and in so doing, address the problem of running cost control in local authorities. As there is no tradition of such knowledge, this has also meant pooling resources, sharing skills and expertise in group-based activities, multi-dimensional and inter-disciplinary in nature. Resources, skills and expertise, whose horizontal arrangement also demands that property managers possess strong networking skills and the level of expertise required to negotiate partnerships.

However, as always, there is the exception to the rule and while it is true that post-AC LAPM is not so much under the direction, control, command or execution of government bodies; or professions representing property managers, a number of issues exist which can only be addressed by such institutions. As a consequence it is felt appropriate to begin the agenda with reference to these points.

The first is that research is hindered by the lack of basic data on property management employment, occupational status and socio-economic groups. Added to this is the difficulty regarding the value of the resources they work with: the value of fixed capital as a stock of wealth and flow of services undergoing development. Basic information is required to identify the exact number of property managers, operations by professional divisions, skills and expertise as producer services employed in either the public sector - again broken down by authority - or independent sector. It also needs to be added that such information should be made available at the national, sub-regional and local level. This is an important point for a number of reasons: firstly; because in post-AC LAPM, it is not the national structure of property that is critical as it is not organised on such lines: while it is guided at such a level, it is driven at the sub-regional, or local unit of analysis: secondly; as a consequence, the 'response' in question does not take a standard form and is dependent on the initiatives and strategies of property managers in local authorities: thirdly; if this is the case - and there is little doubt it is - it is at this level that examples of best practice and improvements in the standards of property management in local authorities will exist.

The second point relates to the development of the reflexive knowledge required by property managers in local authorities. Here it is important for the institutes mentioned so far to appreciate such knowledge is discursive, requiring a full appreciation of the subject in all its dimensions i.e., technical, economic and cultural - it is also important to recognise the object of such knowledge is the challenging of norms, stimulation of research, experimentation etc. This leads on to the third point: it has also to be recognised that the discursive nature of such challenges means that techniques like VFM and the 3E's need to be based on a critical appreciation of the subject because they tend to be outside the conventions of formal, rule-bound, or more logistical standards. While the comments here relate to VFM and the 3 E's, it should be noted they also apply to other initiatives and strategies underlying the structure of property management in local authorities. In view of this, it is felt perhaps best to proceed with the research agenda by breaking the remaining points down into three component parts: initiatives, strategies and structure.

Initiatives

As has already been pointed out, initiatives tend to be isolated from each other, running in parallel - along a horizontal plane in this instance - and as a consequence, make it difficult to give any collective identity to. The effect of this is, of course, to force a response that deals with each of them on an individual basis - one-by-one, so to speak. However, if a collective noun could be drawn upon to represent the 'plethora' of initiatives it would probably be the term 'marketisation'. The question that follows is what do we mean by this in the context of property management in local authorities. What we mean is the development of property markets for transactions in the ownership, use, occupation and exchange of fixed capital under the command and control of local authorities along with the registration of such assets, valuation and calculation of notional transfer prices for whatever structure of tenure exists. It also means the auditing and reviewing of expenditure on fixed capital goods and services supporting them. Perhaps most importantly of all, it means measuring their performance as either operational, investment or surplus assets. The audit, review and performance measurement of the latter being accompanied with disposal, transfer to the independent sector and rationalisation.

As such the discourse on the marketisation of property under the management of local authorities is all pervasive and is seen to represent the moral code of 'good, high quality stewardship'; managing 'better with less' and the corporate ethics of both enterprise and competition, copied across, it ought to be added, from the private sector. Copied across, not, it should also be added, in any pure form, as such a proposal would be so naive as to be counter-productive, but in a way its initiatives are strategically located so as to simulate the rule governing logic of the market and all the virtues thought to follow from this. The advocates of such a project propose the virtues of the exercise outweigh its vices because it has the advantage of driving the principle of VFM and the 3 E's into the consciousness of property managers, so introducing the initiatives and strategies required to marketise the resource in local authorities. Critics no doubt see the exercise as of only symbolic significance, a sign of the market rather than real evidence of its existence and discipline.

If we are to overcome this scepticism, it will be necessary to identify how property markets work in the management of things i.e. the allocation goods and services as resources. It will be necessary to show how the initiatives are embedded in market transactions, have a long historical tradition as such and have not recently been 'manufactured' to project any such image. It is perhaps here that surveying, the profession and its managers have a major contribution to make. If it is to do this however, it must break with the ideologies of the past. For instance the idea that the public sector in the form of local authorities or any other such institute monopolise transactions. On the contrary, legislation and statute supports the understanding that market provision is the norm and it ought to be these standards which govern its allocation. This is, of course, the point which is made by everyone with an interest in LAPM: the point in question being the management of property in local authorities is not only embedded in the market, but that such transactions provide its foundation.

While this goes someway in adding weight to the argument that the marketisation thesis is of real rather than symbolic significance, it is a field of study which requires further examination if the relationship between markets and property management in local authorities is to be clarified. The irony of the situation lies in the fact that as isolated developments this cannot be done by studying them on their own, but only through an examination of how the technology of initiatives are pieced together with the economics and culture of corporate strategies forming the informational basis and communicative structure for the management of property in local authorities.

Strategies

As pointed out, it is here that the technology and economics of initiatives are pieced together to form the culture of corporate strategy and the point where the horizontal and vertical combine with each other and fuse together to produce the informational and communicative structure of property management in local authorities. The first point to note is that the culture of the strategies in question are corporate and are not departmental-based as in the situation under the logic of estates, but mark the onset of property management which is seen to represent a 'core' issue and set of values, (VFM and the 3E's) lying at the centre of local authorities, under the transition to post-AC forms of LAPM.

For such purposes we have the central property unit with authority over the resource, now referred to as strategic and both in command and control of the execution and direction of its management. Something that requires the design of information systems, modelling of data-bases, testing of programmes for the registration of assets, valuation of property, audit, review and measurement of performance as financial instruments for the strategic management of the resource in local authorities. As the registration stage is quite straight forward, the following will restrict its comments to how technical and economic initiatives in the field of property valuation have been brought together to represent a quality-minded, pro-enterprise, competitive, decentred and accountable culture for the corporate strategy and financial instruments such matters relate to. This is done because in spite of the guidance available on property valuation from CIPFA and the RICS, it is this issue that remains the most contentious to property managers and in many respects, the key issue around which the others turn.

Looking at the discussions on this matter, it is evident their is a great deal of unease about the categories, classes of property and bases of valuation (see, Dent and Bond, 1993; Young 1995 and Deakin 1997a,b). The issue of contention focuses on the 'open market value', and 'depreciated replacement cost' bases of valuation for standard (non-specialist and specialist property). As Baum and Mackmin (1989) and Britton, Connellan and Crofts (1989, 1991) point out, it is a debate over the application of the income and the cost approach to property valuation. Framed in these terms the problem centres on the relationship between non-market property and the cost approach for the valuation of specialist categories and classes. In essence the debate is over the valuation of property for which there is no market, that is for property so specialised few, if any transactions exist and which local authorities hold the vast majority of. The question that results from this debate is how to value property which has no market? Putting aside the particular concerns of both the income and cost approach, it is agreed the approach should be as follows:

- to copy across the logic of the income approach by separating landlord for tenant, central property units from users;
- assess the net current replacement costs of the property;
- assume an income yield to represent the opportunity cost of capital;
- calculate a financial annuity that takes account of notional interest, risk, growth, obsolescence and depreciation by the use of discounted cash flows;
- take the notional interest and depreciation as a capital change forming the scarcity and transfer earning of the property (the economic rent);
- appropriate the economic rent to build a repair and maintenance, replacement and development fund.

Objectors to this suggest that its weakness lies in the fact there is no independent evidence that the valuation represents the 'true' market price of property. The logical extension of this argument being that it is little more than a internal market, manufactured to simulate the real, but only in a symbolic sense. The argument follows the mercantile line of 'no transactions, no market, no prices to verify valuations'. The problem with this, as its counterparts try to demonstrate, is that such an argument is based on an idealisation of the market and does not recognise its limits in the valuation of property. The fact that in copying across the logic of the income approach, it draws upon the indirect capital comparison method, investment and contractor's method of property valuation by route of the capital markets, supporting the corporate sector and 'external' to the authority of any 'locale'.

Irrespective of this, critics will question whether this 'copying across', 'manufacturing' or 'simulation' of markets produces a counterfeit, more symbolic than real. For them the piecing together of the technology and economics of the initiatives, with the culture of both the corporate strategy and financial instruments will be seen as lacking credibility. The counter-arguments are numerous: the often forgotten reply to this argument is that the criticism only relates to the valuation of property based on the depreciated replacement cost, rather than open market value categories and classes. For those falling into the latter, it appears, almost by default to be accepted the transactions for the management of such property are on a market footing. In view of this, perhaps the argument is not whether the management of property in local authorities is on a market footing, but the extent it can be said to be based on such a foundation. Of course, the ultimate, well rehearsed response, irrespective of whether such categories and classes of subjects are held by local authorities, is that in the absence of them being provided, the public services upon which commerce, trade and civil society stands would not exist and by extension neither should the economic values of market transactions.

Perhaps it has to be recognised these arguments can not be easily resolved and to a large extent are the artefacts of the welfare state. The fear from the 'libertarian' camp of the property profession is that the nation-state may take command and control of the capital markets. There is also a reluctance on their part to acknowledge that the economics of such transactions are no longer external to the authority of any locale, or the nation-state for that matter, but are becoming increasingly global under post-Fordism (see Cloakley, 1994). In these circumstances i.e. under the 'globalisation of post-Fordism', there appears to be little chance that either the 'liberty' of property or 'freedom' of the capital markets ought to come into conflict with the state. This is because of the way in which the income approach to property valuation now approximates the global/post-Fordist nature of the capital markets in question and manages to structure the relationship each have to cost in the economics and culture of both the corporate strategy and financial instruments underlying the neo-Schumpeterian workfare state.

This need to clarify the relationship between property and capital markets is important for another reason. It relates to the need for the financial instruments in question to be capable of servicing policies towards either 'cutting and reshaping', 'greater responsiveness' or the demand from the public for a greater degree of democratisation (see

Hambleton, 1989, 1989a, b, 1993). At present this is evident in the valuation of heritage and community classes. With the former it is the legitimacy of the approaches to property valuation that is being questioned under the democratic demand for a stronger management of the environment (see Deakin 1996, 1997a, b and c). Here market, sovereign consumer and citizen, appear to be out-of-step with each other, this having the effect of calls for contingency valuation methodology to provide the financial instruments required to service development projects (also see Altfield and Dell, 1996).

Structure

Turning to the question of structure, there are two component parts: the informational and communicative. With the former we have the initiatives in the informational basis of property management and culture of strategies under the communicative. So far attention has been drawn to the corporate strategy side of communication and the consumption of both the technology and economics of the initiatives in the form of information systems, data-bases and the like. The information systems and data-bases, it has been stressed, which following the stage of system design, data-base modelling and registration, provide the basis to test programmes on property valuation, audit, review and performance measurement. Perhaps, more importantly, it should be added - provide the basis to model and test the financial instruments in question and communicate a knowledge of the technical, economic and cultural (i.e. civic) values (VFM and the 3E's) currently providing the means to govern over any possible cutting or reshaping, improvement in responsiveness or greater degree of democratisation.

As everything else in this exercise appears as a mere means to this end, further information on how these financial instruments act as a basis to not only govern over, but re-organise and reform public services by such measures is also required. While as Pinch (1989), Ackroyd, Hughes and Soothill (1989), Bagguley, Lawson, Shapiro, Urry, Walby and Warde (1990) point out, there is a dearth of studies on the re-organisation and reform of public services, particularly so for those under the authority of local government, it appears this is an issue of such singular importance to the development of property management in local authorities, it is one which cannot be put aside.

Summary

The aforementioned has gone some way to review some of the more contentious issues in the development of local authority property management and set out a number of research questions requiring further attention. It is not meant to provide an exhaustive list or a blueprint for research, but rather an agenda that reflects the issues which have surfaced from the post-AC studies of LAPM and merit further investigation.

References

Ackroyd, S., Hughes, J. and Soothill, K. (1989), 'Public sector services and their management', *Journal of Management Studies*, vol 26: 603-20.

Altfield, R. and Dell, K. (1996), *Values, Conflict and The Environment*, Ashgate, Aldershot.

Bagguley, P., Lawson, J., Shapiro, D., Urry, J., Walby, S. and Warde, A. (1990), *Restructuring: Place, Class and Gender*, Sage, London.

Britton, W., Connellan, O. and Crofts, M. (1989), *The Economic, Efficient and Effective Management of Public Sector Landed Estates*, Kingston University, Surrey County Council, Kingston-upon-Thames.

Britton, W. Connellan, O. and Crofts, M. (1991), *The Cost Approach to Valuation,* RICS, London.

Baum, A. and Mackmin, D. (1989), *The Income Approach to Property Valuation*, Routledge, London.

Cloakley, J. (1994), 'The integration of property and financial markets', *Environment and Planning A*, vol 26: 697-713.

Deakin, M. (1996), 'Discounting, obsolescence, depreciation and their effects on the environment of cities', *Journal of Financial Management for Property and Construction*, vol 1 (2): 39-55.

Deakin, M. (1997a), 'The development of computer-based information systems for local authority property management: the underlying issues', *Journal of Financial Management for Property and Construction*, vol 2 (1):59-83.

Deakin, M. (1997b), 'The development of computer-based information systems for local authority property management: the application', *Journal of Financial Management for Property and Construction*, vol 2 (2):59-85.

Deakin, M. (1997c), 'An economic evaluation and appraisal of the effects land use, building obsolescence and depreciation have on the environment of cities', in Brandon, P., Lombardi, P. and Bentivenga, V. (eds) *Evaluation of the Built Environment for Sustainability*, Chapman and Hall, London.

Dent, P. and Bond, S. (1992), 'Public property holdings: evaluating the assets', *Property Management*, vol 11 (4):314-318.

Gibson, V. (1991), 'Who can manage operational property best: the private or public sector?', *Property Management*, vol . 9 (1).

Gibson, V. (1994), 'Strategic property management: how can local authorities develop a property strategy?', *Property Management*, vol 12 (3): 9-15.

Gibson, V. and Carter, E. (1996), 'Is property on the strategic agenda?', *Chartered Surveyor Monthly*, January: 34-35.

Hambleton, R. (1993), 'Consumerism, decentralisation and local democracy' in Roberts, P., Struthers, T. and Sacks, J. (eds) *Managing the Metropolis*, Avebury Press, Aldershot.

Hambleton, R. (1989a), 'Urban government under Thatcher and Reagan', *Urban Affairs Quarterly*, vol 24 (3): 359-88.

Hambleton, R., Hoggett, P. and Nolan, F. (1989), 'The decentralisation of public services: a research agenda', *Local Government Studies*, January/February: 39-56.

Joroff, M., Lovargand, M., Lambert, S. and Franklin, B. (1993), *Corporate Real Estate*, (Re: 2000 Management Team), Massachusetts Institute of Technology, Cambridge MA.

Pinch, S. (1989), 'The restructuring thesis and the study of public services', *Environment and Planning A*, vol 21: 905-26.

Veale, P. (1990), *Managing Corporate Real Estate Assets*, Massachusetts Institute of Technology, Cambridge MA.

Young, P. (1994), 'Market valuation with no market', *Journal of Property Valuation and Investment*, vol 12 (3): 9-27.

Index